JAMES AGEE

AND THE

LEGEND OF

HIMSELF

JAMES AGEE

AND THE

LEGEND OF

HIMSELF

A CRITICAL STUDY

ALAN SPIEGEL

UNIVERSITY OF MISSOURI PRESS

COLUMBIA AND LONDON

Copyright © 1998 by

The Curators of the University of Missouri

University of Missouri Press, Columbia, Missouri 65201

Printed and bound in the United States of America

5   4   3   2   1   02   01   00   99   98

Library of Congress Cataloging-in-Publication Data

Spiegel, Alan.

    James Agee and the legend of himself : a critical study / Alan
Spiegel.

      p.   cm.

    Includes bibliographical references and index.

    ISBN 0-8262-1182-8 (alk. paper)

    1. Agee, James, 1909–1955—Criticism and interpretation.   2. Self
in literature.   I. Title.

PS3501.G35Z894   1998

818'.5209—dc21   98-21590

                                                CIP

Designer: Stephanie Foley

Typesetter: BookComp, Inc.

Printer and binder: Thomson-Shore, Inc.

Typefaces: Amasis and Minion

FOR ANNE

CONTENTS

ACKNOWLEDGMENTS

PECIAL THANKS to Carl Dennis and Martin Pops, who read every word of the original manuscript and made countless suggestions for improvement and transformation.

Other friends and colleagues offered counsel and support: Carole Adams, Bob and Peggy Boyers, John Brenner, The Chubster Society, Anthony Foti, Craig Frischkorn, Clyde Haupt, Brian Henderson, Govindan Kartha, Amy Kottler, Marc and Larry Lowenthal, Peter Lushing, Margo Penman, and Howard Wolf. I'm indebted to all, but especially to my expert typist Barbara Pajda, whose efficiency and patience were exercised through many revisions in the midst of a busy schedule (hers, not mine). Finally, I want to acknowledge the one person who more than any other urged and suffered this book into being—my wife, Anne Elisabeth Adams. With love and admiration, this one's for her.

JAMES AGEE

AND THE

LEGEND OF

HIMSELF

CHAPTER ONE

INTRODUCTION

Legends

HIS IS A BOOK THAT attempts to study what James Agee wrote as opposed to who he was or what he did when he wasn't writing.

Willful distinctions between a writer and his work are commonly made at the outset of projects of this kind, and I have little doubt that the present instance of such parsing will finally prove no less rash and peremptory than any of the others. Perhaps even more so. Such claims are always easier to legislate than execute in the case of any writer, and in Agee's case better announced as aspiration than accomplishment: not because this writer was more "autobiographical" than most (or so we are told), but because he has become more configurational (or so we have made him). While at the present moment the exact status of each of his works remains highly problematic, the man himself has been fervently, persuasively, and perhaps permanently conflated into a distinct figment of public romance, a legendary shape in the landscape of our literary mythography. "In a very real sense," runs one extreme version of a common refrain among critics, biographers, and assorted memorialists, "Agee's life was his most successful creation": as if all that fiction, criticism, poetry, and reportage were merely the diversionary by-product of his moonlit off-hours, as if on the job his best and busiest energies were always employed in the design and distribution of the self.[1]

Celebrity watching is still one of this culture's most efficient antidotes to the poison of dead time in a leisure economy; our national pastime of converting an artist into a screen star while dragging his art along as a stand-in is the customary price serious work usually pays for permission to leave the cell of the specialist and enter the marketplace. It's a fate common enough for a lot of American artists, but who would have predicted it for James Rufus Agee? Certainly no one during his lifetime.

It was not exactly a long life, and while he lived it, not a particularly famous one. He was born in Knoxville, Tennessee, on November 27, 1909, and died of heart seizure forty-five years later in a New York taxicab on May 16, 1955. What happened in between these dates was, at least on the face of it, nothing very sensational. The major markings in his brief literary career (to stay with that only)—and in their chilliest and least intimate form—proceed as follows:

At the age of six, Agee lost his father, Hugh James Agee, in a car crash on May 18, 1916. Three years later he enrolled in Saint Andrews, an Episcopal boarding school for boys near Sewanee, Tennessee, where his mother, Laura Tyler Agee, had taken him and his younger sister, Emma, to live, and where eight years after her husband's death she married the bursar, Father Erskine Wright. After Saint Andrews, Agee attended in succession Philips Exeter Academy in Exeter, New Hampshire (1925–1928) and then Harvard University (1928–1932). During his stay at these two institutions he cultivated a passionate attachment to books, movies, and music; demonstrated talent in, and won prizes for, the writing of essays, poetry, and fiction; and in general involved himself in the customary activities of the precocious and gifted literary-minded schoolboy and undergraduate youth (e.g., editor of the *Exeter Monthly*, president of the *Harvard Advocate*, etc.). Upon completing his education and for the next eighteen years, he worked primarily, and often exclusively, for the publisher Henry Luce and his chain of popular magazines: as a staff writer on *Fortune* (1932–1938); as a book reviewer at *Time* (1939–1941); as a film reviewer at *Time* (1941–1948); and finally as a writer of special features at *Time* and *Life* (intermittently, 1945–1951). By the time he left full-time reviewing in 1948 in order to write for the movies (e.g., on *The African Queen* in 1950, *The Night of the Hunter,* 1954, etc.), and then television (e.g., the Lincoln series for *Omnibus* in 1952), his life had seven years left to run. By then, however, he had already achieved most of the modest public reputation that was to be, more or less, the only one he would ever know. And this was built largely on the movie reviews he wrote for *Time* as well as the more intensive film criticism he simultaneously wrote for the *Nation* (1942–1948), the only non-Luce publication to require his services for any extended period. A successful film collaboration such as *The African Queen* and the acclaimed Lincoln scripts may have seasoned this renown, adding spice and perhaps some bulk. But beyond a limited circle of friends, reviewers, and very few readers, who knew more and perhaps even better of him, the brunt of his fame was founded upon his work in and for the visual arts.

During his long magazine period and slightly after, he produced the three works that constitute the only books bearing his name and published during his lifetime: a volume of poetry, *Permit Me Voyage* (1934); a study of three tenant families in Alabama (with the photographer Walker Evans), *Let Us Now Praise Famous Men* (1941); and an autobiographical short fiction, *The Morning Watch* (1951). The first and third of these sold poorly; the second hardly at all, a legendary flop.[2] I think it fair to say that these works had relatively little to do in shaping his literary and artistic visibility, such as it was, in the general estimate of the myopic public. If this judgment seems less than fair, it is qualified somewhat by the judgment rendered by Agee's obituary notice in the *New York Times,* a document in itself sufficiently amusing to become one of the more grotesque antiques of Agee evaluation in the history of his evolving reputation. The headline runs "JAMES AGEE, 45/POET AND CRITIC"; the subhead, "EX-FILM REVIEWER FOR TIME/DIES—WROTE SCE-NARIOS/NOVEL AND NARRATIONS." "Novel" was not of course the posthumous novel *A Death in the Family* (1957), which would have to wait another fourteen months before making its famous debut, but the novella *The Morning Watch.* "Narrations" (cited in the article) were those written for the documentary "The Quiet One," which the *Times* movieman Bosley Crowther had found "beautifully simplified and phrased," and the travel film "Green Magic," which had opened just that week.

"Poet" was pushed as hard as "Critic" as the article informs us that "Archibald Macleish, a poet of established reputation, said the young writer had a 'delicate and perceptive ear' [this lifted from the twenty-one-year-old "Foreword" to *Permit Me Voyage*]," and that the *Times Book Review* had admired "the young writer" for, among other things, "his positive faith in enduring values." The obit runs eleven paragraphs, but only the ninth refers to the writing of "a text and picture book [sic] in association with Walker Evans, the well-known photographer," and, while acknowledging the "high praise" from "many critics" received by this "book," quotes only Ralph Thompson's in-house review, which adjudged *Let Us Now Praise Famous Men* to be "arrogant, mannered, precious, gross."[3]

These, then, are most of the external facts and a few of the early estimates of a career that one needn't fuss with at great length: for the facts are, I believe, fairly well known and have been expertly investigated by others; and those early estimates ceased to matter entirely within months of their subject's death.

When James Agee died, two remarkable things happened at once: first, he got rid of his mottled life, and second, he almost instantly began to work his way into stainless myth. And as Agee became myth, every fraction of his troubled works and wrangled days became ripe for hagiographic transformation. In 1955 all of his published writings were either out of print or buried in anthologies. Less than fifteen years later much the best part, and then some, of everything he ever wrote, including all the works previously mentioned—published books, criticism, journalism, film scripts—as well as letters, collegiate fiction, unfinished poems, draft fragments, etc., was between hard or soft covers and selling to a concerned readership. Part of this interest was of course the result of the highly successful publication of the Pulitzer Prize–winning *A Death in the Family*. But an even greater part came—as it continues to come—from an even more potent source. When James Agee died, he left behind not only three wives, four children, and an unpublished manuscript, but also an amazingly loyal, impassioned, articulate, varied, and altogether remarkable host of friends and admirers—all seemingly, as it were, highly confessional—who in the form of many published reminiscences, interviews, and the like, have not ceased to mourn his passing—his company, his companionship, the very aroma of his physical being—from that time to the present.[4]

Nowadays, Agee has become something of a magical and figural presence whose person, appearance, and manner of life preside, as it were, over a body of heightened attitudes and experiences that may or may not have anything at all to do with either himself or his actual accomplishment.

1. AGEE AND THE AGEEANS

But what kind of presence and for whom? Right now our comprehension of Agee's writing is inseparable from our fascination with Agee himself, and before one can even begin to pry one from the other, it might be helpful to examine the depth and quality of this fascination. No one involved with any aspect of Agee, the man or his work, is immune to this fascination. No Agee enthusiast could or would even want to be: if you are touched by the power of the writing, you are also touched by the personal power of a man who seems to spill himself everywhere in his work, and the voices that speak of this personal power also speak of what happens in the writing, even though they seem to speak only of the man. Moreover, the cult that has gathered about Agee, while responsible for a lot of silliness, is also responsible for the lion's share of all continuing interest in every facet of this author, as well as some of the most eloquent and committed testimony to the man *and* his work that no one would want to ignore, or in any way be without (e.g., the brilliant memoir by Robert Fitzgerald, first-rate criticism by Dwight Macdonald and Robert Coles).[5] Most important, one does not want even for a moment to underestimate the power of myth, which is virtually collateral to the birth of strong emotion itself; and even the most violent repudiation of it is more than likely to involve evidence of its most impressive transformations. One does not even hope to replace myth with "data" and "information," for neither can be grasped in cold blood (the opposite of mythologizing being neither "factualizing" nor "historicizing," but cunningness and calculation). Rather, one renovates and enhances myth, refurbishes one version with its sophisticated kin; a simpler with a subtler; a rough with a smooth; or, to shift metaphor, one fabulous skein settling upon another in layers—one hopes—of increasing refinement and delicacy, as well as—one fears and risks—increasing attenuation and self-consciousness. If I'm irritated by the current crop of fabulations perpetuated by the Ageeans, it isn't because these whoppers are necessarily false (myth is truth at its most humanly impassioned), but because I find a lot of them bloated and untuned. And rampant: allowing for the subterranean seepage of myth, it is more than likely that even the most disinterested and pristine of Agee critics, including the present one who can pretend to be neither, has already become an unwilling sharer in one or more of the marginally distinct but permanently entangled Agee cults.

Actually, of course, there is only one cult, but in the interests of clarity and order, I'm going to distinguish at least three interrelated varieties of adoration: herewith, the cults of Poor Jim, Saint Jim, and Plain or Country Jim.

Taking this last faction first: Let's admit that there is an Agee dilettante, for instance, who knows this writer by not that much more than his odd name—first and seventh letters of the alphabet uttered in quickstep— remarkable face, and the muzzy association of these with the croon of beautiful words, the fierce pride of starving farmers, and democratic vistas lowering everywhere like cardboard backdrops on the southern soil. Maybe this admirer is a young undergraduate, maybe a teacher, maybe he or she *has* read most or all of *A Death in the Family* ("beautiful"!), certainly recalls the opening lines of the Prologue, and maybe, too, has browsed through enough of "the other one," the long one, to feel guilty for not having gotten round to reading it through. But this person really means to do so, and really "loves Agee," and, generally speaking, has imbibed just enough of his atmosphere to cherish that parcel of the writer's world that plants him forever and ever in the hills of Tennessee (barefoot?); or perhaps in a sharecropper's cabin during the Depression (Evans is setting up the camera); or on a hose-wet lawn in the Knoxville twilight ("disguised" as a child); or maybe (yes, for sure) within the frame lines of that well-known and undoubtedly ubiquitous Helen Levitt photograph.

Helen Levitt snapped her photogenic friend many times, but for the admirer she needed to get him only once. It's a haunting shot (date unknown), one that fully corroborates all the beautiful sentences, renews contrition for the long book unread, and has probably done more to romanticize the guileless innocence of the Plain Jim image than any fact of biography. The dark, doe-eyed young man stands in the bone-bare white doorway of a shadowed interior, as if recently emerged from the surrounding dimness, and greets the camera with peek-a-boo reluctance, leg and shoulder lagging back behind the door jamb, neither in nor out, nascent, vulnerable, blinking wet in the wake of seeming adolescence just past. The body sags against the jamb like a lazy farm lad melting into the porch post, the arm tucked behind the back like a shy prairie swain. The loose work shirt is bare at the throat and the baggy unpressed trousers rumple about the seemingly frangible body with the virtuous inelegance of homespun; the thick, gauche, turned-out shoe freezes with anvil-like discomfort on the polished wood. The setting is not "rustic" (it's Bleecker Street), but the Spartan line, uncluttered space, and simple symmetrical cropping are strictly in the American Puritan plain style; face and figure pose themselves as enemies of sham, vaunt, and artifice; the glance gathers a harvest of youth and dream, enough to shame any number of blackboards, reading rooms, book clubs, Houghton Mifflins, and Henry Luces—if it knew even faintly of their existence.

This version of the American writer as young sapling is of course a staple of the native egalitarian romance that also enshrines the cracker-barrel philosopher, the log-cabin president, the Abstract Expressionist in cowboy boots, and the twelve-tone symphonist who sells insurance to the locals. In this romance libraries and universities are replaced by a genius of landscape, the dream of the republic as a paradisal garden, and a mystique of its citizenry as children of the Learning Tree. Here a writer might write a book without ever having read one, a witling grow wise just by playing hooky, a president rule a nation and be "above politics," for these acts and expressions are conceived magically as the moral inflections of rural American folk energies and inspirational forces emanating from a sanctified and unspoiled geography. People who subscribe to the myth of Country Jim are happy to avoid awareness (or simply never knew) of the hillbilly hero enrolled in Yankee institutions; or of his "life" with sharecroppers as something less than a seven-week sojourn on assignment for a businessman's magazine; or of the fact that from the age of sixteen to the end of his life, for good or ill, whether by instinct or design, this native son spent most of his days and nights not in deep southern loam, but in and around Exeter, Cambridge, Brooklyn, Greenwich Village, the Chrysler Building, Frenchtown, N.J., and Hillsdale, N.Y.

Still, for the cultist, this Northern City Jim can be consigned to the merely "circumstantial"; his heart must have been in the right place (i.e., down yonder), even while the rest of him made application for Guggenheim money and filed copy with the editors of *Fortune*. For whatever cosmopolitan flaws may be detracted from his regional purity, the utter and essential decency of the man himself can never really be in dispute. And when it comes to contemplating (and promulgating) the hero's moral and spiritual character, as opposed to his regional and indigenous mystique, the cult of Country Jim must give over to that of Saint Jim. If you think of Agee as just a backwoods poet and a good ole boy, you certainly cannot know anything about him and probably haven't read much of his writing either. The followers of Saint Jim, on the other hand, know all there is to know, and (one presumes) have read all there is to read, and consist largely of Agee's personal friends and acquaintances—critics, editors, poets, novelists, filmmakers, professors, wives, ministers—all fervent adherents of a man whose vitality, loyalty, and compassion amounted to something like a genius for fellowship, including the ability to inspire such qualities in others. The tales of Agee's charm and generosity are numerous and unstinting, from the impulsive, tear-filled child of eight who on the spot offered his shoes and socks to impoverished farm boys to the mature author and critic whom even the least sentimental of judges found "impossible to dislike."[6]

Here, excerpts from a well-published eulogy (circa 1967) by the late film director John Huston (with whom Agee collaborated on the screenplay for *The African Queen*) provide a somewhat egregious specimen of what for many has long since become cult gospel:

> It's all to the good that so many of you now know James Agee's writing—his novels, his criticism, his poetry. (In a sense it was all poetry.) I wish that you also could have known Jim himself.
> Let me begin by describing him physically. He was about six-two

and heavy but neither muscular nor fat—a mountaineer's body. His hair was dark brown, his eyes blue and his skin pale. His hands were big and slab-like in their thickness. He was very strong, and except for one occasion, which I only heard about, when he stove a *Time* editor against the wall, he was always gentle towards his fellow humans with a kind of gentleness usually reserved for plants and animals.

His clothes were dark and shiny. I can't imagine him in a new suit. Black shoes scuffed grey, wrinkled collar, a button off his shirt and a ravelled tie—he wore clothes to be warm and decent. Jim's elegance was inward. I doubt whether he had any idea what he looked like, or whether he ever looked into a mirror except to shave. Vanity wasn't in him . . .

His regard for other people's feelings was unique in my experience. I don't believe it was because he was afraid of hurting them, and certainly it had nothing to do with gaining anyone's estimation. It was simply that his soul rejoiced when he could say yes and mean it to something someone else believed in . . .

He is smiling. It stops raining all over the world. A great discovery has been made. He and another are in complete agreement. We who beheld that smile will never forget it.[7]

Granted, this is a bit much even for the Ageeans, but then a lot of the published material in this Memories-of-Agee category melts down to essentially more restrained and analytic versions of Huston's hype. Granted, too, that its author had spent virtually a lifetime working within an industry and a social milieu where slush and high hokum comprise a kind of communal idiom, where even commentary on the weather could become an occasion for hyperbole. Granted this—still: has any modern American writer of Agee's stature provided the occasion for, and been subjected to, so much undiluted moonshine? Certainly none has been the subject of so much adoring reminiscence and reverential pleading, and almost as certainly none has had his writing so lovingly but firmly placed in a position ancillary to the writer himself. In the popular imagination, even the burly myth of Papa Hemingway includes the middlebrow enshrinement of best-sellers such as *For Whom the Bell Tolls* and *The Old Man and the Sea,* and even Fitzgerald's glittering starship entails the entry of "Gatsby" into the vernacular. But in introducing Agee to *his* general public, an admirer such as John Huston can conceivably pass over

everything he ever wrote with one off-handed and patronizing sweep—
"In a sense, it was all poetry"—before focusing his subject proper: "I wish
you could have known Jim himself." And who exactly is "Jim himself"?
He is Huston's Young Mr. Jim, an amalgam of the Ageean rural and
seraphic mystiques—a real Jimjam here—compounded with details and
code words redolent of assorted types and sizes from folk legend: there
is the ghost of Lincoln the Railsplitter and Jim Bridger the Hillsman
in the "mountaineer's body" and the "slab-like hands"; a hint of Saint
Francis in the allusions of commiseration with flora and fauna, and the
"Vanity wasn't in him," etc.; and more than a bit of Nature Boy out
of Tiny Tim in the smile that makes you happy as it reroutes the rain.
The occasion for these remarks was the writing of a "Foreword" to a
collection of Agee's film scripts, but as to the subject's capacities, or lack
thereof, as a writer for the movies, Huston has nothing to say (though he
more than anyone would be in a position to know).[8] Rather, as is often
the case in the effusions of the Saint Jimmers, aesthetic considerations
dissolve in the light of moral ones, and the hero's being in the world,
and his reverence for it, takes precedence over his achievement in it, as
if the very form of this being and reverence were replete with its own
aesthetic intensiveness, as if the achievement itself were one among the
many flowerings of sympathy and decency habitual to a man whose spirit
and personal expressiveness far exceeded, and eventually subsumed, the
gross particularities of any actual makings and doings.

But even the most fervent admirers of Saint Jim will readily admit
that this vibrancy of being, however charismatic, was neither serene
nor unblemished; few are unaware of the harsh streaking in their hero's
make-up that, within the perimeters of legend, render him both martyr
and tragic figure: martyr in the harm that was inflicted upon him by
external promptings beyond his control, tragic in the harm that was
self-inflicted. Poor Jim! Here then is another major faction of the Agee
personality cult composed of some of the usual personal friends and
admirers, as well as members of a post-Ageean generation of scholars
and biographers who, while by no means repudiating the saintly master
image, certainly manage to limn the celestial nimbus in dark gray, seeking
to present a more balanced portrait by supplanting mere eulogy with
heavy supplements of Freudian strip-mining and social-historical savvy.

Actually, these Ageeans subdivide into two properly respectful but equally grim-visaged camps: the first gathering under the wing of the Dark Angel, the second before the altar of the Sacrificial Lamb.

The first approaches its subject as a figure of "high genius and self doom,"[9] whose allegedly eccentric and disjunctive literary production was synchronous with, and largely generated by, the churnings of a self-destructive psychology. In this camp we find the careful enumeration of Agee's excesses and indulgences: women, alcohol, personal hygiene, bad work habits, etc.; as well as the tales of the miserably tormented youth who stoned to death a nest of fledglings, and promptly threw up; of the Christ-obsessed altar boy who carefully calculated and fantasized his own crucifixion; of the strange college student who gained access to the Boston City morgue and spent a lot of time peeping and poking about; of the incorrigible but promptly penitent adulterer given to pounding the wall with his forehead and pummeling his body with his fists; of Henry Luce's most brilliant, but near suicidal, staffer, who, on one notorious occasion, was spied dangling from the ledge of a window in the Chrysler Building fifty stories above the street.

With all the foregoing in mind, it is instructive to note how one publisher attempted to puff the eloquent but rather cautious and eminently unsensational letters to Father James Flye—a teacher at St. Andrews, and Agee's friend and lifelong spiritual confidante—into a full-blown American gothic. (The same blurb slightly amended was also used for this publisher's edition of *A Death in the Family*):

> James Agee, author of the Pulitzer prize winning *A Death in the Family* was the most prodigiously talented writer of his generation and one of the most tragic figures of our time. He had three wives and four children. He drank too much. He drove himself beyond the endurance of any human being. He was torn by guilt and self-doubt. He was haunted by the idea of suicide and obsessed with achieving greatness. His death at age forty-five was probably the greatest blow to American literature since the passing of Thomas Wolfe. This is his most intimate book, a starkly revealing account of the internal and external life of a tortured twentieth-century genius.[10]

In a manner similar to John Huston's press agentry, Bantam's tabloid-style conflation takes us to that level of raw fantasy where more guarded and intellectually respectable treatments would not. Still, even more sober and psychologically adroit accounts of the Agee "tragedy" share something of the moral and emotional temperature of this publisher's purple tear: a familiar Philistine stew of vicarious attraction, rabbitlike recoil, and bogus dismay. The passage seems equally enthusiastic about the size of Agee's indulgence (booze, self-doubt, death wish, etc.) and the size of the "blow" supposedly inflicted upon American literature by his death, as if the second situation were directly dependent upon, indeed were fully beholden to, the first; that is, the scale of Agee's "genius" is to be accounted for not by his actual art, but by the open-shirted romanticism and turbulent decadence of his manner of living. In the time-honored cost accounting of middlebrow morality Poor Jim pays for the dash, effrontery, and sheer oddity of being "the most prodigiously talented writer of his generation" by going to pieces as a man.

The second faction in this group also acknowledges the hero's defeat, but views it less as a tragic instance than a representative one. Here Agee's particular brand of swashbuckling masochism can be summarily and euphemistically filed under what Dwight Macdonald once described as "the worst set of work habits in Greenwich village,"[11] and his true problem perceived as a fascinating but characteristic species of the artist's career failure in mercantile America. Here Agee's history becomes another version of the poet-aristocrat among the helots, a nineteenth-century, romantic, secularized, and quasi-Marxian updating of the Sacrificial Lamb in which, starting out in the Depression, miserably pledged to a national ethic of success and security, the poet flings the body of his genius on the altar of commercial America, sells his talent to Henry Luce, fritters away his best writing years as a slavey on *Fortune*, *Time*, and finally at the end as a second-level functionary in a second-class industrial art known as "the movies." In a footnote, these admirers will often bemoan Agee as a Renaissance or at least ambidextrous artist in an age of specialization, a vast and turbulent ocean syphoned off through a garden hose; not just a novelist manqué but also a frustrated filmmaker resigned to remake in the imagination the bad movies he reviewed in his columns, doomed to false starts and unfocused ambitions; a genius of the half-baked, of unrealized and unrealizable projects, of Napoleonic art campaigns permanently outflanked by cultural circumstance; the hapless dreamer of an encyclopedia of labor trilogy that never pushed past its first installment, of his only full-length novel that never got a final draft, of the Byronic epic poem that died in mid-canto.

But whether one rides with Lamb or Angel, both parties of the Poor Jim contingent join forces under the banner of a morbid and finally unseemly paradox: the hero's figural power brightens and battens as his personal biography darkens and worsens. This cultists' faith seems to fuel itself on the instinctive belief that Agee's triumph was his tragedy, and the peculiar hardihood of his reputation blossoms on the spoiled soil of psychic torment, squelched ambitions, and botched books. But what if Poor Jim had lived longer and written more, or finished more of what he had already written, or simply proved better fulfilled in his personal fortunes? It's hard to resist the impression that such a Lucky or Luckier Jim would nowadays severely challenge the devotion of any number of his loyal mourners, consoling tongue-cluckers, and commiserating head-shakers.

2. AGEE IN THE CLASSROOM

Plain, pious, and poor: Sacrificial Lamb, Tragic Sufferer, Selfless Saint, Frontier Bard. A complex and fascinating figure to be sure, but then the magnetism of this man has never been in question. The point rather is that such a figure is beside the point, and probably should have been all along. How did we ever let him loom so large? If Agee's writing matters, certainly Agee matters too: but if Agee has come to matter more than his writing, then either something is lacking in the writing or in the way we persist in thinking about it. Of the ten full-length books on or about, or at least significantly associated with, Agee, only four represent sustained critical treatment of what he wrote, and the last of these appeared almost nineteen years ago (more on these books later). Of the remaining six, two are critical biographies, two compendiums of reminiscence, one an estranged son's memoir (of his early years with brief but evocative reference to his famous father), and one a psychological portrait of the artist's personality (based on primary materials, books, letters, interviews, etc.).[12] All six are in their different ways and degrees absorbing, even useful, works; absorbing because the subject itself is absorbing, and useful because even the least of them cannot help but cast some light on the writing produced by the subject even if the primary focus is elsewhere. In the main, however, while these books help demonstrate and solidify the position of Agee the man as a figure of mesmerizing resonance, they do relatively little to help establish or clarify the position of Agee the artist, the literary artist, the writer whose presence or lack of it in literary culture must finally be understood and judged primarily on the nature and quality of what he wrote. For many, this Agee remains a highly equivocal figure; for some, a muzzy and peripheral one; for a few, he simply isn't there at all and never has been.

(But here I want to pause, and specify what I mean by "many," "some," and "a few" in reference to Agee's literary standing. I speak in the main of professors, critics, and students of English and American literature, members largely of an academic community by and through whom the writings and reputations of English and American writers are usually, for better or worse, recognized or ignored, advanced or demoted, sustained or derailed. I also speak here and in what follows as a teacher, a member of this community, drawing conclusions based in part on personal experience of students and other teachers. I make no comment, however, on the acumen and legitimacy of this body of readers in determining our culture's fate [i.e., what does or doesn't get read], subjects beyond the scope of the present one. The power of this body, as everyone knows, is a function of the cultural politics of the present period, and an investigation of its findings represents a simple inquiry, not an endorsement.)

Check out any of those huge compendia of Modern American literature compiled mostly by English professors, and disseminated among other English professors and their students throughout the college community for the purpose of conveniently surveying (and also preserving) samples of the work of the most significant American writers of our century (e.g., see recent or even older editions of such popular anthologies published by Norton, Macmillan, St. Martins, Little Brown, etc.). Now one doesn't wish to overestimate the value of the college textbook as either indicator or arbiter of taste and judgment; many instructors of course program their own classes without recourse to such prepackaged conglomerates. But if you want to know one major and demonstrable way a canon begins to get canonized, the literary anthology represents a reasonable place to start finding some answers. In the present instance, you will discover that along with the anticipated and obligatory "Modern Masters" (Faulkner, Fitzgerald, Hemingway, Eliot, O'Neill, etc.), there is room for many important but less exalted figures, including those prose writers whose major work was more or less contemporary with some of Agee's, such as Steinbeck, Wolfe, Dos Passos, West, even on occasion Wright, Farrell, Odets, and Caldwell. There may even be room in some of the trendier grab bags for such semi-pop figures as Raymond Chandler and Dashiell Hammett. But amid all those thousands upon thousands of translucent onionskins, few samples of Agee's work, either whole or in part, are likely to appear.[13] Now do all those anthology professors really judge Agee's writing to have less "intrinsic value" than that of Steinbeck or Wolfe, "The Chrysanthemums" and "Only the Dead Know Brooklyn" to be better representations of the art that emerged during the Depression than any section of *Famous Men?* Apparently so. But hasn't all that fuss from the Ageeans, some of whom are or have been themselves distinguished and influential professors, had any effect at all? (It has been happening now for more than thirty years.) My distinct impression is that a lot of concerned teachers of English neither accept nor reject Agee but simply don't know what to do with him. My guess is that those anthology professors, along with a lot of other literary academics, are either not familiar with the full range of Agee's best works, or, knowing this range, find it too fragmentary and discontinuous to get a handle on it: it's easier just to leave him out as a sport, an unclassifiable. Perhaps the only other American writer of Agee's stature with a comparable position in the academy is Henry Miller, who is also the object of a cult, also without a pigeonhole, also generally unrepresented in literary anthologies, also making space, as it were, for his inferiors.

The truth is that Agee's best books seem so different from one another that an admiration for one won't necessarily send you rushing to another. The English professor who finds the literary performance in *Famous Men* to be extraordinary isn't likely to experience the equally extraordinary performance in the criticism because its subject (movies of the forties) doesn't interest him professionally or otherwise. The result is that Agee is likely to be remembered by one book or another, or sometimes even more than one, without the artist himself being recognized as the formidable creator of a rich and cohesive oeuvre. Agee is read, and often with the greatest admiration, but only in bits and pieces. No one audience reads him whole, save for the Ageeans, who, as we've seen, have other priorities.

I would also suggest that different and relatively segregated audiences read different and seemingly segregated parts of him, rarely banding together, sharing tastes, or pooling interests and findings. Of all Agee's books, perhaps only the warmly accessible *A Death in the Family,* in its different editions and twenty-three-plus printings, commands what might loosely be called a general readership outside the university, though this same readership does not embrace a long and difficult work such as *Famous Men,* or a "specialist's" work such as *Agee on Film.* In the academic community, however, the modulated and deeply "modest" qualities of Agee's novel are likely to be passed over in favor of more dramatically aggressive and high-profile American fiction.[14] It is rather *Let Us Now Praise Famous Men,* than which profiles come no higher though it isn't fiction proper, that is at least nominally read in the classroom—and perhaps only there—but then again, not necessarily in literature classes (the Houghton Mifflin 1980 paperback lists it as "Sociology"), and not necessarily as a whole. When that formidable Ageean Dwight Macdonald taught it at S.U.N.Y. Buffalo, he did so by excerpts, as do most of my colleagues. Since material in the classroom is by definition class-ified, material as notoriously "unclassifiable" as the unexcerpted *Famous Men* doesn't necessarily appear there as often as its reputation would indicate. Still: whatever class (sociology, literature, history, folklore, etc.) reads *Famous Men,* it won't be the same class that reads the film criticism. *Agee on Film* is generally read only by those with special interests in its subject, mostly and unsurprisingly by students and teachers of film who are also likely to seek out the film scripts but not much else by this author. Unlike the literary criticism of Poe, James, and Eliot, for instance, the movie criticism of Agee is rarely read or taught anywhere in the academy as literature. As for *The Morning Watch,* that little book, in or out of the university, doesn't seem to be much savored by anyone these days except the Ageeans; and finally, even those worthies have ceased trying to make a case for Agee's poetry, pace Macleish and the *New York Times*.

The upshot of this taffy-pull is that while Agee immediately became, and has long been, the object of a cult, he has yet to become the object of an informed and serious literary consensus. Though widely known, he has neither been placed, nor rated, nor perhaps even fully understood, by those people professionally and allegedly engaged in such matters. You cannot even say of him, "The jury's still out on Agee," not when those jurors are all attending different trials.

Does any of this really matter? Only if Agee as a literary artist matters. This study grows out of the unstartling proposition that he does; and in the light of the foregoing, I'd like to talk at length about the four books by this author that I think matter most. Not that these books are all of equal value, to be sure, but they are his four most significant and substantial creations, the ones upon which—most would agree, I think—any just and reasonable estimate of his work should be based: *Let Us Now Praise Famous Men, Agee on Film, The Morning Watch,* and *A Death in the Family*. Some might want to add the short fable "A Mother's Tale," or perhaps his most remarkable film script, "The Blue Hotel," but none I imagine would want to leave out any of these four.[15]

Naturally I'd like to apply for a certain amount of leeway in approaching these very suggestive books, room to move around in a number of different directions—cultural, formal, psychological, etc.—but amid all this seeming eclecticism, I do have a pronounced and recurrent bias.[16] Given the current standing of Agee and his work, as well as the kind of criticism both have garnered thus far, I'm going to stress two broad and complementary themes above the others. First, I want to focus on Agee not as a poet, a critic, a novelist, a screenwriter, a journalist, a "parajournalist," a "nonfiction novelist," a moralist, or (least of all) a personality—all of which, to some degree or at one time or another, he was—but primarily as an *imaginative* writer, that is, a creator, which he was to the greatest degree and all the time, and in everything he ever wrote. This means that I'm going to explore as fully as possible a quality that from the very start has been neglected in our thinking about this author: the made-up, artificial, or, if you will, transformative quality—or what current critical discourse might call the quality of "literariness"—

in all his writing (not just in the fiction proper, but in the criticism and documentary work as well). This richly formal trait takes us, I feel, to the very heart of Agee's artistic enterprise, yet previous criticism has remained resolutely obtuse in recognizing, let alone examining, it. And with good reason: Agee often presented himself as an enemy of the artificial or strictly formal, a proponent of "life" over "art," of "fact" as against "fiction," of "the holiness of human reality" as opposed to the artist and his books. And Agee's critics have tended to take him at his word and thus have seriously confused his expressed aspirations with his actual practice and accomplishment.[17] I want to show that what Agee actually did was a lot more original and evocative than what he hoped to do.

And second, because Agee was an imaginative writer in everything that he wrote, we'll find the same level of consciousness—pressures applied, effects created—uniformly present throughout his work: the same themes and patterns, the same images and obsessions—indeed, virtually the same story, an auto-mythology, a developed figure of self-realization (see part 2)—evolving in continuity from book to book, in spite of the ostensible changes in subject matter. In this manner I see Agee as not only a consistently imaginative writer but also a consistently *unified* one. Here too I find previous critics to have been remiss, tending to compartmentalize Agee's creations, and perpetuating the truism that this author worked in widely different forms and genres and did unique but unconnectable work in all of them. Like most truisms, this one isn't true enough: Agee did indeed produce original work in different forms and genres, but he always ended up sounding like Agee, talking Agee-talk, parcelling out different chapters of the continuing legend of himself. This unity is apparent not only in the works concerned in this study but also in those not included here—the poetry, the film scripts, and the assorted prose. I will quote from and allude to some of these materials whenever I find that they help us understand the book or the issue under discussion, but on the whole these works don't represent Agee at his best, and I'm not going to explore them at any length. I find the scripts interesting, but minor (see chapter 5 for more on this); the assorted prose interesting, but marginal; and the poetry interesting, but not very good. And while it's probably fit and proper—and ecumenical too—that one should find something interesting in *all* the writing of a writer one admires, even when some of it is less than first-rate, I don't see why these interests must be, so to speak, aired in public, particularly when one hopes not simply to share an enthusiasm, but to create one where it doesn't necessarily exist. Agee's major achievement is sufficiently extraordinary to make and win his case; with the lesser work, the discussion can only devolve into tedious sessions of plea-bargaining.

Besides: I find a certain amount of bad faith in picking one's way through work one doesn't enjoy, or fully respect, simply because one finds it "interesting." Usually what one means by such tepid and pasteurized "interest" is that something is part of an interesting subject, not that it is interesting in and of itself. The "disinterested" (i.e., academic) mind often professes such "interest" in virtually everything. The critic, however (and alas), rides only the nag of his preference; leaves "disinterested" interests to the technocrats; takes real interest only in something, not everything.

My own interest in Agee begins with a simple and unqualified love for his language—the sprung diction, the magical combinations, the powerful, devious, and altogether unprecedented musculature of the Agee sentence, progenitor of a distinct sound, a new voice—that represents what I take to be his most singular, if not most important, contribution to American letters. Having come to criticism about Agee only long after having come to Agee himself, I was naturally surprised and discomforted to learn that the priority of interests of many of his admirers was sufficiently different from my own to make me sometimes think we were reading different writers. But this simply could not, and cannot, be true; many might have begun with interests similar to my own, and then developed these interests into others. I suppose my relation to the current critical situation is a little like that of a man who enters a much loved and beautiful house—much loved because beautiful—in order to study the architecture, only to discover that the house has long since been converted into a shrine; and while he only meant to study structure, shape, stresses, and relationships, he cannot do so without removing his hat or even from time to time dropping to his knee. He hadn't planned on this, reverence being neither his intention nor much in his line. But still, he's more than willing to catch himself in an occasional reflex of worship, for he knows well enough that much of the original impulse that sent him up the steps and through the door was also a kind of worship; and that much of what he once loved (and still loves) about the house is part of everything that helped turn it into a shrine. And while nowadays parishioners flock to this dwelling for reasons of their own, he doesn't mind that either: for behind the rising clouds of incense, he can still make out the soaring shapes of the vaults and archways, the dazzling design—and still he finds it stirring. And so he feels, at some level beneath conscious awareness, do they. And so they might all be, more or less, members together. Only some time ago, some of them, some of *us,* stopped looking. I want to look again.

CHAPTER TWO

TALES OF THE SELF

OW THERE ARE OTHER MYTHS about Agee: not the ones we have made and imposed upon him, but others of greater importance that strictly speaking represent the legitimate business of criticism. These are the myths made by Agee of and about himself, necessary and essential myths that virtually any writer needs to give aesthetic identity to his creation. I'm talking now about Agee's construction of a projected or configurative self, a persona that in many instances may seem to coincide with what we know, or think we know, about the "real Agee"; in other instances, not at all; in still others, the exact relation between the imagined and the actual may be impossible to determine. In any event, when discussing an artist's heightened imagination of himself, it is probably best to withdraw all major claims to biographical fastidiousness or amplitude of external detail. What follows is an analysis that, while generally based on the agreed-upon facts of the Agee biography, attempts to stake out a map of the interior life cobbled together from the different but continuous versions of the Agee persona as they appear in his books. One version is called "Rufus" (*A Death in the Family*), another "Richard" (*The Morning Watch*), another "James Agee" (*Famous Men*), still another simply "I" (*Agee on Film*). If I downplay Agee the man, it is because the man was fact, not legend, and it is the legend that spreads across and infiltrates the terrain of his created fantasy, the figures, settings, structures, issues, tics, and obsessions as they emerge in his writing. If true to all of this, then true enough; the rest can fend for itself.

The tedium of the clock, the decay of the flesh, the killing sameness of routine existence, the vagaries and limitations of the daily self— any or all of these may be sufficient reason for the artist to plunge within in search of a second self. Another may simply be the practical need to find solutions to problems on the job, the underground tunnel that leads from point A to point B in creation, and so get the work done. Whatever the reason, the making of an auto-mythology is the artist's passport to transfiguration: "I is another," runs Rimbaud's famous formula for converting an ordinary man into a seer. And American artists in particular have made themselves into specialists of such outsized projections of the waking dream. Whitman, for instance, arm akimbo, hat slouching over one eye, became the star of his own pirate movie: "Walt Whitman, a kosmos, of Manhattan the son, turbulent, fleshy, sensual, eating, drinking and breeding." Henry Adams cast himself as the bewildered tuba player for a delegation of duffers stranded on the platform of history watching the Twentieth Century Unlimited flash past the station: "Henry was a helpless victim, and like all the rest, he could only wait for he knew not what, to send him he knew not where." Hemingway gave us the stoic's version of life in Marlboro Country, a solitary wrangler rolling his own (Krebs's mother, for instance, says, "There can be no idle hands in His Kingdom." And Krebs says, "I'm not in His Kingdom.")[1] And still others would never rest until they could descend upon us like the veritable Voice out of the whirlwind: "I wrote and directed. My name is Orson Welles." (This roaring modesty, Your Humble Servant performed by Jehovah, from the voice-over end credits of *The Magnificent Ambersons*, 1942.)

And Jim Agee? As romantically insistent as any of his countrymen, his tale, on the face of it, was that of the eternal son—sometimes a doomed Icarus, sometimes a Promethean firebrand, sometimes a Prodigal repentant—but always the deracinated offspring, the wandering "orphan" (as the six-year-old Rufus defines himself in *A Death in the Family*)[2] in search of the original home and family, first lost, then found and lost over and over in a series of temporary substitutions (good, but somehow never good enough) and transitional reenactments (close, but never the thing itself), stop-gap displacements ferreted out in natural landscape, in the agrarian poor, in a mystique of ancestors and "famous" founders, in a tradition of artist-liberators, in a theater of silent images, in dreams of childhood renegotiated—all these: figures and metaphors of *origination,* touchstones of a life made legend.

The tale, of course, is a familiar one, a classic: the sad-eyed stranger steps from the shadow and reveals himself as the lost child come home; to the quilt on the lawn; to the family car; to the neighborhood movie; to the mother and the father, the temple and the fount. *"And those receive me,"* says the voice of childhood revisited in Agee's last novel, *"who quietly treat me, as one familiar and well-beloved in that home."* But then, there's a twist: *"But will not, oh, will not, not now, not ever,"* the voice continues, *"but will not ever tell me who I am"* (8). The purity of the traditional romantic quest pattern of exile and return, paradise lost and regained— as ancient as Joseph and his brothers, as classic as *Great Expectations,* as contemporary as *Wild Strawberries,* as gold leaf perennial as *Ben Hur, The Good Earth,* and *The Wizard of Oz*—is fretted over from start to finish by the hero's self-consciousness, the "universal" archetype worried, fussed, and all but shredded as the expression of a precious, eccentric, and very private sensibility. The ancient search for a home becomes complicated by a modern crisis of identity, and the Prodigal Son lap dissolves into another filial prototype, Hamlet.

The myth of Agee, then, entails a metamyth, a voice that agonizes, anatomizes, and finally fuses with the self-created dream; the hero thinks he finds what he thinks he's looking for, then balks; wavers and double-thinks; takes the measure of his stance, his ambit, ruminating first on one side, then the other, then back and again. The home, say, may be too soiled, or too perfect, for habitation; the hero, say, unwilling, or unworthy, to inhabit the home. He steps forward, back, shuttles in place. The figure in motion becomes a figure in oscillation; the pattern of lost and found becomes a pattern of hesitation; the hero searches for his severed roots, but often in opposite directions at once.

Agee's pitiless self-consciousness keeps pecking away at the clear and generalized line of emotion in myth. And this tendency makes him a difficult and sometimes frustrating writer, but at the same time a writer hip and alert, undeniably one of us, a recognizable contemporary.

Without his critical deportment, his complications and hesitations, his (sometimes maddening) squirming this way and that, the Ageean profile can easily be confused with that of any other American rustic yearning homeward in the immemorial manner, a more sophisticated version of, for example, his (falsely) reputed look-alike Thomas Wolfe, another spawn of Emersonian idealism, another image of the wet-eyed man-child and nostalgic native son. As a self-reflexive artist, however, Agee becomes a Janus-faced modern (like Joyce, like Faulkner), both traditional and innovative at once, conflating indigenous national fantasy (i.e., "orphan" heroes, lost families, everlasting roots, etc.) with the blessed mystery of his own mental turmoil, his intellectual honesty, his orneriness, confusion, and perversity: in short, his full humanness. Agee interrogates his own heightened passion, dissects and dismantles his legend even as he creates it.

1. KING AND QUEEN

But we rush ahead of ourselves: recoils of doubt and deliberation are already the ravaging of legend. The legend itself comes first, and at the root of Agee's romance of himself resides the romance of his parents; that is, one son's fantasy of his mother and father, making of them the eternal figures of terror and adoration, of love, knowledge, and power, that forged the rudder of his imaginative being: "My king and my queen" (82), Rufus defines them. Agee's reading of their drama became the terms of his drama, the perimeters of his moral and emotional vision springing from the transformation of the impress of each upon his early years, and forever after. It is striking how many facets of Agee's allegedly anomalous literary activity bear a congenial likeness—if not an exact replication—of this or that component of his early childhood saga; or how much of what he tirelessly described and ultimately defined as the real or "actual" world around him often synchronized precisely with the terms first predicated by his family coding.

Everything Agee would ever know or conceive of the unitary existence, of integrity and the apple unfallen, could be signified forever in one indelible tableau (again, from *A Death in the Family*) of a man, a woman, and a child lying on a quilt on a lawn on a soft, southern evening; the man and the woman harmonize spirituals, but in deeply different registers; the child (Rufus) lies between them, looking up at one, the other, at both, watching, listening. The conflicted love of this man and this woman and of this child for each, for both as a union, generates a nucleus of tension that radiates outward in time and permeates everything (in greater or lesser degree) that Agee would ever write. I say "conflicted love" because the discord in this prelapsarian harmony (the apple uncertain) is as real as the love itself, one fully coextensive with the other, and flowering from the same forked root: that is, an alliance of differences, the loving contrariness of the man and the woman, the alluring yet fractious otherness of each to each. Both the concord and the strife are passed on to the child and internalized by him.

When the man dies, however, the early harmony and the moment of paradisal union die with him. In the mind of the surviving "orphan," the love—its object now lost and irreparable yet vivid and unforgotten, absent and present both, permanently enchanted in a mist of paradox and supernal mystery—this love idealizes itself, and locks into a permanent adoration tinged with mourning. And as the love intensifies, so too does the strife, its correlated twin; the differences between the dead man and the living woman are now more exacerbated than ever, and particularly so since the woman seems so very different (to the child) in her apartness from the man, her qualities no longer modified by merger. As the man becomes an object of worship, the woman becomes an object of ambivalence, adored for her role in a once perfect union, and for whatever vestige of that role lives on in her, and despised for her defection, however involuntary, from that role and that union. This intensified strife—the conflict between past and present, man deceased and woman alive, categories allied and yet increasingly different (and even so from the beginning)—arranges itself in the child's vision as a polar opposition between which he shuttles in ceaseless debate, aligning himself now with the "man," now the "woman," clashing yet collusive guardians of an identity forming and reforming itself in a condition of perpetual ferment.[3] It is the attempted reconciliation of these oppositions in a child made restless and turbulent by their conflict, as well as the retrieval of a lost unity within the child and the world perceived by him, that becomes the major emotional and thematic preoccupation of Agee's subsequent work (and perhaps life too).[4]

But who are this man and this woman? What are the oppositions between them? It was perhaps the only love story Agee ever knew, at least the only one he could make persuasive to others, perhaps because it was the only one he could believe in himself. It is also one indication of his passionate commitment to the imagination of childhood that he could never make, or even seem to want to make, the story of any of his marriages or grown-up love affairs available to others: rather, the story he told many times, and in many different forms, was the fantasy of the two founding figures that patrolled the borders of his imagination, prime movers of the predominant Ageean images of adult male and female, paternal and maternal principles respectively.

Here, then, a quick composite: the Ageean man is generally earthy, outgoing, sensual, tolerant, easy, and spontaneous; a paragon of natural energy, fiercely independent and antiauthoritarian, irreligious in the orthodox sense and usually devoid of formal culture and education; sometimes reckless, sometimes selfish and brutal, his breeding is entirely rural and demotic, with ancestral roots plunging deep into the American primeval and embracing colonials, pioneers, Indians, and wild animals. By contrast the figure of the woman is prim, proper, genteel, shy, loving, deeply devout, and highly principled; a "queen" of order and discipline, well-meaning but sometimes starchy, priggish, self-righteous, and sternly dictatorial; sometimes adored, sometimes deplored, her backgrounds are strictly urban, bourgeois, orthodox, and institutionalized with serious entrenchments in literature and the arts, the classroom and the church, the office and the home.

In its external markings and strictly as a love affair, the alliance of these two echoes a virtually ageless cultural romance, a staple of almost every species of narrative, from folk ballad (e.g., Robin and Marian), to pop novel (Tarzan and Jane), to grand opera (the nocturnal mix-up between Figaro and his Contessa). One version might tell of the courtship of the shepherd in the valley and the princess on the hill, another that of the gamekeeper and lady of the manor, still another that of the saddle tramp out of Cheyenne and the schoolmarm from Boston. The tale in any or all of its specific instances is among the primal pairings of the West because its components embody an allegory bridging (seemingly) cultural intractables; it is an idealized harmony (social, psychic, and/or aesthetic), however straitened or temporary, effected between immemorial forms of human dissension: peasant and aristocrat, forest and town, seascape and citadel, instinct and intellect, feeling and form, nature's hurly and culture's hierarchy—the formal variants as limitless as the basic prototypes are constant.

Like most specimens of the public mythos, most of the instances and issues cited above, shorn forever of their specific moorings in historical time and individual authorship, have all become, more or less, the property of whole peoples. And need I point out that nothing as raw, hyperbolic, or primordial as, for instance, "Tarzan and Jane" appears anywhere in Agee? While potent with legendary overtones, the dyad imagined by this author—image clusters charged with intimate energies, private fields of force—still belong to no one but himself, flowering forth in whorls of literary expression as intricate, subtilized, and personally identifying as grain on the thumb.

Specifically, then, he presents his odd-couple fantasy in either one of two ways: concretely, as developed characters who exist in linked but contrasting relation to each other; and abstractly, in the form of symbolic oppositions that a projected self must then choose between (see following sections). I think we'll find the figures and procedures in both forms of presentation worth comment and exploration. I'm assuming, however, that even casual readers of this writer are relatively familiar (through films and theater) with most of the treatments in the first group. Here we find, for instance, the marriage of Jay and Mary Follet (*A Death in the Family*), the most loving, idealized, fully dramatized, and overtly autobiographical version of the original fantasy (and perhaps the only official literary rendering of the marriage of Hugh and Laura Agee). But then very busy and colorful ghosts of the same contrasted pairing reemerge, this time as the basis for a romantic adventure farce, in the knockabout love boat of Allnut and Rosie *(The African Queen)*, the former gross, grizzled, and gastric, the latter rigid with astonished gentility, bridling with ladylike miff. And, then again, as the focus of a comedy of manners and culture conflict in the honeymoon journey of frontier Sheriff Potter and his city-bred bride (film script, *The Bride Comes to Yellow Sky*). In the script for *Noa Noa,* by contrast, the basic prototypes have been thoroughly cauterized, the genders homogenized and faintly homoeroticized, in a fictional account of the mismarriage between a hard, cynical Gauguin and a soft, saintly Van Gogh. And in *The Night of the Hunter,* a black fairy tale for adults (a hellish version of the Three Little Pigs), the figures have split and become enemies outright, locked in a deadly "custody" battle over orphans (!): still, every vestige, however demonized, of the primary contraries remains intact, as the wild, wandering, lady-killing (in both senses), false preacher Harry Powell prowls and howls about the house of tart, tight little Miss Rachel, fairy godmother with Bible and switch stick, protector of homeless children and defender of the true faith.

It seems to me fairly irrelevant that most of these examples have been culled from commissioned screenplays based on material written by others. Agee was offered numerous projects, but it is reasonable to suppose that the ones he chose to work on were the ones that had some personal interest for him; that is to say, they were the ones chosen for him, as it were, by his formative influences, by everything that made him in bias, focus, and absorption the kind of man he had become. And such principles of psychic economy can also be applied to his nonfiction projects: in *Famous Men,* say, for all the facts he could have told us about the personalities of George Gudger (simple, open, the man in the field with a short lifeline) and Annie Mae Gudger (pinched, worried, designer of the interior)—both of whom seemed to him "not other than my own parents"—he selected those details that allied themselves most comfortably with the half-remembered, half-dreamt stipulations of personal memory and desire. Indeed, at times, reading him whole and thinking about the innumerable elisions and delicate transformations in his art, one could almost imagine of him what Stephen Dedalus once imagined of Shakespeare (as one can also imagine it of both Dedalus and his creator), that he too had "found in the world without as actual what was in his world within as possible." Occasionally, one could even think this of the movie reviews: for instance, the only time Agee elects to examine the parental influences on a film director is the one time he decides, or, perhaps more accurately, divines (and perhaps too precociously in this instance) that what was "possible" in shaping Preston

Sturges's imagination—a Europhilic, art-loving mother and a down-home, undercultured father—had long since been felt as "actual" in shaping his own.[5]

2. RADIANCE

The parental alliance was important for Agee not just in and of itself, but also in shaping the terms by which he invented himself; that is, each figure in the union was important in helping to mold a third figure: the questing orphan that was Agee's self-projection for purposes of creation in art. And in making this figure come clear, it will be necessary to try to understand Agee's special relation to each parent figure separately, and not just as a specific human entity, but as a symbolic extension of the human, as part of the powers, artifacts, and observed phenomena, that envelop and distinguish the young hero in relation to his surroundings.

It's no secret that Agee's feelings about his own father were reverential, unswerving, certainly inspirational, and, in the end, perhaps overwhelming—but in a special and curiously tonic sense (as we shall see). Hugh Agee was both father and more than father to his son. Biographers tell us that arrangements in the Agee household often reversed the traditional roles of mother and father, and it was Laura Agee who generally embodied the conventional "male" passion for obedience and legislation, while her husband took on the more tender, permissive, nurturing part, providing his young son with the customary "maternal" emotional and physical securities and comforts.[6] As a child in the crib, for example, and frightened of the dark, Agee would cry for his father, and it was Hugh Agee who soothed his brow and sang him to rest. In time, the boy came not only to cherish the father's rough and abrasive (to him) masculinity—the strength, the irreverent laughter, the gusto, and the "vulgarity" (as his mother might have called it)—but also to forever associate these "hard" qualities with sensitivity and compassion, decency, and, occasionally, an almost maidenly innocence. Later the crusty gentle, coarsely caring, rudely sweet, "motherly" earth father becomes something of an Agee specialty, vestiges of which appear not only in Jay Follet, Potter, Gudger, or Allnut in love, but also in the portraits of Bud Woods ("a sort of father to us," *Famous Men*) and Lincoln (to whom Jay Follet is specifically compared by a neighbor). This commingling of paternal qualities and functions continues to appear in the creation of specific characters, and, more broadly, in both Agee's choice and treatment of the subjects central to his art—childhood, farmers, and movies—subjects seemingly disparate, but actually all evolving from, and forever revolving about, the domain of a single, parental determinant. It is obvious, for instance, how Agee's intense idealization and semi-identification with the impoverished southern farmer ("half my blood," *Famous Men*, 415) begins with his own lifelong obsession with his—that is, his father's—ancestry in the backcountry farmlands north of Knoxville (for example, his grandfather's farm, where Hugh Agee was born and raised, figures prominently in *Famous Men*); or how his celebration of film, particularly of the "silent" period, and indeed of the entire populist and warmly "vulgar" cast of the art, starts with and in some sense never departs from the ecstatic pleasure he derived from accompanying his father to the local moviehouse and sharing in Hugh Agee's favorite form of relaxation.

For the most part these instances are so directly and patently connected with the by now well-known details of the Agee family record that they hardly bear further rehearsal. More revealing, however—certainly more pervasive—is the way in which the image of the father, the very aura of his world and being, are transformed by the author into a phenomenology and, finally, a mystique. It's hard to fully appreciate the transcendental or religious impulse and texture of so much of Agee's writing without equal appreciation of his romantic transformation of the paternal figure into a kind of divinity with the attributes of power, beauty, radiance, and fecundity. By a "kind of divinity," I mean precisely the kind to which we may ascribe the term demiurge, the primogenitor, the source and founder of the line. Contact with this sacred fount is at the heart of Agee's obsession with the salvific powers of contact with the past, one's childhood and origins in earth, lost time, and an ancestral heritage forgotten and forsaken by all save the magical restitutions of memory and imagination. Something of this divinity surges in the Lear-like figure of the "old wild king," the maimed but untamable spirit of the soil, that epigraphically introduces *Let Us Now Praise Famous Men* and, of course, in the "famous men" themselves, "the Fathers that begat us," the "righteous" overseers of the old South; in the "princely" snake of *The Morning Watch,* "royally dangerous and to be adored and to be feared"; and in the kind of artists and artistry that Agee prized above all others, "the great and primitive artists" (*Agee on Film,* 314) and their seemingly effortless creation.[7] Of D. W. Griffith, the source and founder of the line of earliest masters of film, Agee wrote, "to watch his [Griffith's] work is like being witness to the beginning of melody, or the first conscious use of the lever or the wheel; the emergence, coordination, and first eloquence of language, the birth of an art: and to realize that this is all the work of one man" (313).

The vision of the paternal source figure, the magnus pater, creator of life and art-in-life (or what Agee once described as "the aesthetic reality within the actual world")[8] and of all the associations that accrue to this figure, its signs and markings, ultimately gathers upon its eminence the might and authority of a collective. The mother and her "orphan" son may be singular, but the image of the father is both unitary and legion. One of Agee's earliest reveries of Knoxville ("Knoxville: Summer 1915," *A Death in the Family*) is not of Jay Follet per se, but of a row of young fathers (of whom we presume Jay is one) holding their hoses, adjusting their streams in the most exquisite, consummate, and unself-conscious forms of art and craft, and feeding their lawns. They are festooned in images both sanctified and doomed (Jay will be gone within the year), *"tasting the mean goodness of their living like the last of their suppers in their mouths* (5)"; images both elemental and generative, *"these sweet pale streamings in the light . . . the urination of huge children stood loosely military against an invisible wall"* (5). These watering fathers are the symbolic wet nurses and procreators of childhood, common-man heroes of parthenogenesis ejaculating a world, one lavishly given and then swiftly taken: Agee's world.

With the prologue as a numinous ground base, we can follow Jay Follet's evolution from an extraordinary man, husband, and father into a divinity local to the Follet home, and from there to a much greater home as a fluttering yet emphatic presence in nature. For Rufus, abandoned and crying in the night, his father is the ultimate rescue figure, a paragon of luminance, heeding his screams and shattering the encroaching darkness with a room *"full of gold"* (87). He is also to the little child a body of vast, enveloping strength (*"His hands were so big he could cover him from the chin to his bath-thing,"* 101), and to others, one of strength combined with great physical beauty: "He had the most magnificent physique I've ever seen in a human being" (174), says Rufus's Uncle Andrew after viewing Jay's corpse on the night of his death. And it is also Andrew who at this time is made aware of "a prodigious kind of energy in the air" (197) about the body, the same "noiseless and invisible energy" (263) that Rufus perceives in the air outside his house on the morning after the fatal crash. It is the same energy that on the previous night has already coalesced into the form of Jay's putative ghost, a moving presence that enters the Follet home and eventually the room where Rufus sleeps with his sister Catherine; and it is here that Mary Follet also feels this invisible power, "as if she had opened a furnace door: the presence of his strength, of virility, of helplessness, and of pure calm" (190). Rufus learns of Jay's final transfiguration on the day of his burial when Andrew tells him of "a giant butterfly" that alights upon the lowering coffin, and in a thoroughly characteristic surge toward radiance, springs "straight up into the sky" from the darkness of the grave, the colored wings catching "fire in the sunshine" (335). And Rufus thinks: "Miraculous. Magnificent" (335).

The dissemination of the parental source into the natural setting (grave, butterfly, sunshine, etc.) officially sanctifies the natural elements, landscape, foundations in primitivity, and buried time zones (crib nights, nickelodeon days, the historical South, forbearers as old as totems), as well as those people and places—their dwellings and artifacts (costumes, furnishings, and implements)—that live in close proximity to the holy cradle in earth. The powers of the father both fuse with and activate the powers in nature, and the surviving orphan now goes forward in life by traveling, as it were, backward in time, seeking out the "miraculous" and "magnificent" traces and afterimages of vanished glory: the repossession of a lost world. Qualities and effects once tagged indelibly to a child's experience of a masterful parent are now fetishized in different times and spaces, still resonant with memories lost and found. There is the quality of energy, for instance: in *The Morning Watch,* when Richard and his two cronies seek their liberation in the woods surrounding Our Lady Chapel, "such a wave of energy swept upwards through their bare feet and their three bodies into the sky that they were shaken as if a ghost had touched them" (92). Or even more typically, there is the quality of luminance. *Famous Men* hypostatizes and finally overvaluates virtually every grade and source of solar effluence from the crepuscular to the paralyzing; venerates the camera as one of the "central instrument[s] of our time" (11); challenges the exertions of perception itself with a "cruel radiance" (11); eulogizes the coal-oil lamp above Agee's writing table in the Gudger home; and perhaps most memorably dramatizes Agee's confrontation with the "Signal," "a long bright rod of light" that enters the "dark and shuttered" front bedroom during his secret search through Gudger's spaces, transforming a phial of glass into "a sober grail, or divinity local to his home" (187); in this manner, twenty years after, rekindles Rufus's moment of rescue from a cavern of night by a godhead *"full of gold."* Of course, one may readily conjure Agee the critic recycling this very scenario on several hundred occasions, each time he achieved his consummation in light at the movies (the darkened theater, the projector's beam, etc.).

Now when you read some of his critics, you may get the distinct impression that Agee found the "holiness of human reality" just about everywhere he went. And sometimes reading Agee himself may also leave you with a similar impression; for instance, an entire section of *Famous Men* composed of nothing but transpositions from the dicta of William Blake, "Everything that is is holy," and the like. But to really believe this of Agee is inadvertently to shanghai his dedicated heart into the service of his loose lip. Agee's practice often runs counter to his professed principles, so much so that this form of counterpoint itself becomes the most binding and veracious of his unprofessed principles. And while he may actually have believed in, and sincerely meant to discover, the "holiness" in "everything that is," his actual celebration never strayed very far from those forms of making, doing, and being that he could instinctively connect with the functions and attributes of the paternal source figure. This means that, as a matter of practical and *felt* literary itinerary, his active visionary line runs from the wilderness to the farms to the suburbs, and then without flagging begins to bend sinister, turning to scorn, sarcasm, and outrage as it approaches the courts of sophistication (i.e., away from the source figure), the characteristic ways, means, and practitioners of metropolitan living. As a poet of particular moments in landscape, or the follies and self-deceits of the urban middlebrow, Agee scores so many apocalyptic bull's-eyes that you might think he broke bread with the prophets every day of his life: but as a cosmic commiserator, however well intentioned, he's something of a Wet Willie. His palest and least persuasive literary gestures—such as "A Mother's Tale"—drip glycerine tears for the entire race, while some of his most rigorous expression—as in *Famous Men* and the film criticism—is also his most pointed and excoriating, finding scant divinity in city slickers, social reformers, landlords, movie moguls, the actor's ego, committees, civic organizations, political parties and programs, all forms of authority, genteelism, and orthodoxy.

Naturally—Agee being Agee—his most particularized scorn is often reserved for intellectuals like himself (he once remarked to F. W. Dupee that "Men of letters are death, just death"),[9] just as his most authentic and turbulent reservoirs of faith are reserved for those acute gestures of raw innocence and boisterous spontaneity at the furthest remove from his own highly calibrated critical and analytic faculties, the advanced weaponry of his professional identity. The most knowing and knowledgeable parts of him all but collapse in veneration before the unknown and unknowable, those harsh, mysterious, and unreasoning powers, that "cruel radiance" that nominally flows through "all" creation but actually, allowing for the paternal bias, takes an emphatic detour through those fetishized parts of creation characterized by their freedom from the overt and effortful ministrations of intellect (from, that is, complexity, self-consciousness, the capable imagination). In this manner, Agee pitches his personal altar before the enigmas of "senseless" natural process (birth, death, generational ties); the confusions and helplessness of children and "plain people"; the savage, disruptive, and even "murderous" energies in uncoopted folk, popular, and all manner of anti-art (e.g., letters, postcards, home snapshots, the documents of the semiliterate); the unarguable articulacy of the animal body and the exercise of the brute senses; the unmediated thing as against the language that would attempt to target and colonize it; the actual as against the artifactual; the finality and stasis of pure being as against the gallop of an open-ended becoming.

All these he venerates, but mostly in opposition to himself. Everything he reveres, and to which he aspires, constitutes an internalized other, or not-self, against which he marshals the awkward and dead-weight inadequacy of what he takes himself to be. But where he worships is precisely where he (often knowingly, willingly) falters; it is also where his otherwise somewhat familiar, but utterly genuine, romanticism goes bizarre, singular, and completely contemporary. To merge with and embody the powers of creation are the ostensible goals of his quest, yet to accomplish these goals is also to become one with creation itself, to penetrate and assimilate the circle of its sacred secrets, and thereby become one's self a power in creation; that is, a creator, another originator, another source and founder of the line. This means that the promotion of the self to the seat of origination will challenge the primacy of the paternal ideal in dream as one's actual father has already been nullified in death.

It isn't surprising, then, that Agee's regular form of veneration waffles just this side of incarnation: the reverie of union can only be effected in a desecration, and Agee's art can neither envisage such a desecration, nor condone a sense of self as desecrator. The closer he comes to his ideal of purity and perfection, the more he is consumed in awareness of the violence and corruption of his needs; the greed in his yearning; the rapacity in his hunger; the urge to devour camouflaged by the urge to merge. So like Moses gasping his last in Pisgah, just short of the Promised Land, Agee glimpses the portals of his paradise, extols the splendor and ripeness of it all, and then (purposefully) stumbles just short of entry. It is here, somewhere between the perfection of the not-self and an inferno of self-disgust, that Agee develops his well-known (notorious?) stammer-and-stall technique, his aesthetics of equivocation, or, as it may be more widely recognized, his rhetoric of "failure." Call it what you will, this strategy remains for me the most extraordinary spiritual gridlock of his generation; and so rhythmic and deliberate is its appearance that "strategy"—an artistic device rather than a cry from the heart—is what I take it to be: an almost lifelong jitterbug of affirmation and denial, of penetration and withdrawal, of celebration and abuse, in the face of divine mystery.[10]

Readers long familiar with Agee are also doubtless familiar with the outward signs of his ritual crisis; that is, precisely, whenever Agee finds himself faced with the realization of his most cherished aspiration, some ineffable perfection or quixotic ideal—say, for instance, the essence of Gudger's character, or the artistic and spiritual grandeur of films such as *Shoeshine* or *Monsieur Verdoux,* or the teleology of death (as in *A Death in the Family*), or what he once described to Father Flye as the "whole problem and nature of existence" (the "problem" of *Famous Men*)—he characteristically professes one form or another of paralysis or inarticulacy.[11] He might, for example, bemoan his lack of talent or his inability to do full justice to the job at hand; or beg for an adjournment (for example, if it's a film review, postpone his critique for the next column); or abruptly break off one means of approach and start over again with another (in *Famous Men,* interrupt a prophetic voice and manner in midsentence and take up a more limited stance); or simply dunk his object altogether and swim into a verbal swamp of highfalutin density and semi-incoherence.

Now these seemingly "masochistic" rites of self-debasement are not to be understood too quickly nor, least of all, taken at face value: for the results of this rhetoric of "failure" represent the very opposite of failure. Agee's professions of incompetence and confusion, however sincerely motivated, actually function as a kind of talismanic formula for release, a magical abracadabra whereby he can placate his gods (i.e., the paternal "radiance"), preserve the inviolability of his aspirations, and at the same time effect a transition in seeking his own creative level: in other words, his "failure" to realize the ideal allows him the freedom to realize himself; to shift focus from object to beholder, from the quality of the aspiration to the condition of the aspirant, from his earthly paradise to the many shapes of his "profane," "fallen," quite wonderful, and thoroughly human self. True: the essence of Gudger's character may never appear in the pages of *Famous Men* (a moot matter), but the essence of the young Agee's character, the reporter who lives with and studies Gudger, emphatically does. True too: the final answer to the ultimate purpose of human suffering may never be forthcoming in *A Death in the Family* (how could it be?), yet the artistic and spiritual integrity of Rufus, the child who never ceases to ask the right questions, is unforgettably present. And true enough: the film criticism may not unlock all the secrets of the imagined worlds of admired directors such as DeSica and Chaplin (it may not even be right about them either); still, Agee's reviews as *personal* performance—as vision and literature as opposed to film exegesis—rank among the most invigorating and ennobling in the whole history of the craft.

Needless to say, Agee never became the kind of superhuman creator with whom he sought and feared union, nor did he ever make the kind of art that seemed to grow as spontaneously as the grass on those lawns tended by the Knoxville fathers of his childhood. If the true creator was "radiance," Agee became the kind of creator who worshiped "radiance" but from a position, as it were, of darkness (in his crib crying for his father; at night on Gudger's porch, writing his book; at the movies ["Night was his time," wrote Walker Evans of his friend (*Famous Men,* xi)]). If true creation was effortless and unself-conscious, Agee became the premier celebrant of those qualities, but only in creation of his own that was effortful, deliberate, difficult, and self-aware. If the best people were simple and innocent, they could only be fully known as such in the laser beam of a complex, agonized, and unremitting consciousness, in the tragic heroism of an intellect at war with itself. If an age of giants and fecund emanation passes with one's childhood, one could mourn that passing only in an era of weak knees and withered dreams, the demilitarized zone of the present tense ("a time," he said, "of artistic cowardice, cynicism and despair" [*Agee on Film,* 145]). And if Agee never became the kind of creator he wanted to be, what kind of creator did he in fact become? Let us say that in the absence of heaven, he had no recourse but to make of himself a special type of the modern artist, a type of which, we must add, he was the best example—and perhaps the only one.

3. "SONNYBUNCH"

So far we've been describing the fact and some of the functions of Agee's reflex of self-castigation, but as yet have said little of its source. As implied, his sense of personal unworthiness seems to increase virtually in direct proportion to the excitement of his approach to the signature of his origins. Why so?

We tend to think of Agee's deepest family emotions as funneled solely through his father, and this of course is a mistake, ignoring as it does the powerful impact of Laura Agee and her relatively sophisticated family backgrounds (i.e., the Tyler line) on the emerging mind and imagination of her young son. I think one could fairly say that Agee's search for and celebration of his father were ultimately conducted under the banner of his mother—however, it was a standard borne with considerable reluctance. Put bluntly, I would also suggest that for all his love and need of her, Agee never forgave his mother for being herself and not his father; never forgave himself for whatever remnant of her regime he found in his nature (apparently a great deal); and perhaps, at the deepest level, never quite forgave either of them for being alive together in the present with the best parts of all their possible worlds (and themselves) lost in the mists of early childhood. Not even as a young boy did he ever fully come to accept the shrillness and anxiety of his mother's governance as opposed to the relaxed authority of his father's; the full repertory of her inflexible pieties and genteelisms, particularly her deepening immersion in and obedience to the dictates of Anglo-Catholicism; and the chilly distance all this put between herself and his immediate need of her.[12] Nor in all likelihood could he have admired the fact that eight years after his father's death, she achieved the symbolic capstone of her severance from the past and surrender to her present dispensation by marrying Father Erskine Wright, a man of the cloth in every way the living opposite of her dead and theologically indifferent husband.

But mostly I would say that Agee's complicated blend of devotion to and ill-concealed rage against the maternal figure grew out of his hunger for self-definition; out of the fear that in his love for and dependency upon his mother, he could not become the kind of person he wanted to be; that he might actually become (indeed, might already be) more abidingly his mama's boy than his father's son, and thus unworthy to fashion himself in the "radiance" of the paternal memory. Recall: that "radiance" is "cruel" and that one obviously needs grit to stand in its glare; for instance, in *Famous Men*, Agee suggests that if his writing were ever good enough to attain the force of true revelation, the reader "would hardly bear to live" (13). As judged by some of his statements, his recurrent fear is not only that he isn't simply "good" enough, but, more aptly, not hard enough. He once described Rufus as a "soft and precocious child" and so "doomed to religion and the middle classes" (i.e., his mother's world). In the novel, Rufus also worries that he disappoints his father because he may not

TALES OF THE SELF

be bold enough, and that Jay praises his intelligence to others because he cannot honestly praise his bravery.[13] Again, at twenty-seven, Agee's ultimate self-condemnation in *Famous Men* is that he had become too "softened and sophisticated" (415) to fully embrace his agrarian heritage as represented by the brambled existence of the tenant farmers. It is also during this period that we find him specifically deriding the psychic yield of his education under the maternal yoke in the following ditty:

> Mummy you were so genteel
> That you made your son a heel.
> Sonnybunch must now reclaim
> From the sewerpipe of his shame
> Any little coin he can
> To reassure him he's a man.[14]

The cloistered youth can only counter a "genteel" upbringing by rediscovering his virility in a "sewerpipe." Even as a boy, Agee tries to defy his mother's influence by resorting to a disruptive pattern of behavior, a kind of grotesque imitation, almost parodic, of his eccentric imagination of his lost father. He becomes a "problem child," a brawler in the streets, a cussing rowdy, a tormentor of small animals.[15] And throughout his adult life abrupt resurgences of this domesticated delinquency reappear in the migrant hoboism of his summer vacation from college; in the bohemianism of his Greenwich Village days; in the later years of the gap-toothed smile, the unpressed clothes, the unwashed body; in the marathon tippling and hangdog promiscuity. But these rebellions are generally soft-boiled and frequently end in shame and remorse. They are fudged from the start, evolving as they have from a camouflaged need for love and recognition beneath the maternal thumb, a belligerent and backhanded offering of the self that means to woo the mother but only on the father's terms, that pleads for feminine favors but only in the abrasive manner pleasing to a "soft" son's fantasy of a hard master.

Still, as the "Sonnybunch" rhyme indicates, Agee knows his true fate: he may try to toughen himself in the mire but only *because* his mark is mother's milk. His gift for language, his passion for literature and self-expression, his aesthetic and critical standards and moral scrupulousness, the whole interiorized cast of his intellectual and ethical conscience, can properly be considered his mother's, not his father's, legacy to him. It is at the studio of his mother's brother that he studies painting, from her sister that he learns the piano, thus initiating a lifelong passion for music and composition. Even his first official entry into the literary life, however much a detour it proves to be, is as a poet following the example first set by Laura Agee's own poetic ambitions; the title, *Permit Me Voyage,* picking up on the journey metaphor of his mother's publication *Songs of the Way,* a little volume of twelve religious poems. And one does not exactly have to jump inside this writer's skin to figure out which of his two widely disparate inheritances—staff or distaff?—consorts most readily with his innate temperament (if we may be egregious enough to presume what that is): the exercise of the pen or harvesting with bindle stiffs? the gestures of consciousness, rumination and analysis, imaginative concentration and transformation, or pestering birds, drawing blood from his enemies, or, yes, even living with farmers in Alabama?

Actually, the answers to these stacked questions aren't necessarily as obvious or obligatory as I may have made them appear. The explosive persona most of us recognize as Agee's is, in fact, inconceivable without complete ratification of *both* sides of his divided nature; he can only gravitate so far toward one extremity before feeling the tug of the other and reversing course. In most instances, the conflicting claims of his full parental legacy account for the many contradictions and irregularities that constantly seem to characterize his personal history and accomplishment: the "hillbilly" who went to Harvard; the scholarship student who dutifully returned from his midsemester hitchhiking and rail-riding to three-piece suits and an editorship at the *Advocate;* the flaming radical who earned his keep from the pockets of the arch-capitalist, Henry Luce; the film reviewer who wrote for both the conservative *Time* and the leftist *Nation;* the devoted friend who became the unswerving adherent of both the left-wing Dwight Macdonald and the right-wing Whittaker Chambers; the artist who perpetuated the romantic myth of the provincial South, but elected to live mostly in the cosmopolitan North (as did his Michigan-born mother after her second marriage); the aesthete who cherished the untutored, unwilled, natural beauties in found folk objects, but largely did so according to the official benchmarks and rankings already sanctified by high culture (e.g., the symmetry of Gudger's house evokes the contrapuntal structures of a Bach fugue; the hue of his faded overalls finds validation in "the blues of Cézanne," *Famous Men,* 267, etc.); the one-of-a-kind critical stylist who devoted his concentrated energies to scrutinizing the (then) most popular and commercial of all mass art forms, but in the classiest, most discriminating and demanding style ever to engage the subject on a regular basis.

Sometimes these anomalies seem to collide like boxcars (for example, his dual residency in both high northern and deep southern cultures); sometimes they seem to bear startling but delicious fruit (his film critical style). No writer of his generation seemed to live out so many paradoxes and inconsistencies as passionately and strenuously as he did; no such writer seemed to center his art about them with such compulsive and stunning relentlessness. No exception to the rule, the young orphan hero is born of the oppositional forces that constitute his fosterage: an alienated mother and a paternal memory. He is invariably "young" because at whatever age we find him, six or thirty-six, he is engaged in the process of learning new things about himself and his environment. The four major Agee texts are all concerned with the acquisition of identity in which the young hero tries to discover who he is and what he believes on the basis of the experienced contraries within and about him. He is also invariably an "orphan"—not by birth, but by experience—because he finds himself increasingly isolated in the present as a result of his enforced severance from parental or ancestral origins in the recent or remote past.[16]

Every sundering of the family chain also indicates a major glitch in temporal and cultural continuities, a breach in the natural alliance and exchange between historical generations, as well as between past and present. Every sundering, however, further inspires the possibility of rescue: an attempt to restore continuity and alleviate pain that usually arises when an isolated and emotionally ailing orphan figure in the present tries to link up with some remnant of his repressed or forgotten past. For example, a self-destructive journalist is saved from himself by contact with avatars of his lost patrimony (*Famous Men*); a constricted and disenchanted altar boy finds release and renewed vitality in convergence with his long-buried and darkly primitive self (*The Morning Watch*); a restless and lonely young father takes unexpected satisfaction in a solitary night journey back to the hill country of his childhood and the bedside of his ailing father (*A Death in the Family*); a dissatisfied film critic, who adjudges the sound film to be so "sick" that movies seem to have forgotten how to be movies, reaffirms the grandeur and purity of image in the all-but-ignored "parent" generation of silent filmmakers (*Agee on Film*).

Of course one would do well never to overestimate the remedial nature of any of these "rescue" sequences. The achieved solutions of the young quest hero may legitimately strike any reader as every bit as racked and perplexing as his original problems; in some cases, the new cure is as dire as the old ailment (Jay Follet's return to his childhood home eventuates in his death). A writer as self-conscious as Agee only travels down new roads fueled by the negative energy of his spurned alternatives, the satisfaction of his hungers often bought by eating himself alive. If we associate the lost past with the world of the lost father and the present crisis with that of the living mother, we must ask ourselves whether the young hero can ever feel fully at home in either realm. The domain of the paternal source is properly that of the immortal creator spreading his lavish seed in the last glow of the Edenic garden, the domain of the maternal guardian that of the mortal artist laboring amid the orthodoxies of the cultural moment: and the former, for all his adoration of it, fills the hero with shame and self-doubt; the latter, for all his need of it, fills him with open scorn and muzzled rebellion. Still, out of the thrust and counter-thrust of each world emerges perhaps the only face in the mirror one can legitimately claim as one's own. I would describe the paternal memory as constituting a version of the ideal or romantic self, the thrust of the hero's deepest aspirations and dream of pure being; the maternal present as representing, for good or ill, a version of the "real" or existential self, the daily facts of his continuous becoming (practically speaking, who he is as opposed to what he wants). Obviously, in order to live with a measure of harmony, it becomes necessary for this figure to effect some kind of union or reconciliation between his two worlds. And while, as indicated, this was the ostensible goal of Agee's quest in art, can we actually conclude that such harmony was in fact ever fully achieved? Another matter moot, to be sure, but I have my doubts: any attempt to unify these deeply personal oppositions in his work, however brilliant or "successful," could only result in a *symbolic* synthesis, a created effect in and of art, and thus a "mere" imitation and mockery of the "radiance" of the original union that for Agee was not art at all, but actuality (or more precisely, another "aesthetic reality within the actual world"). That original union was the function of divinity, while Agee's synthesis would be at most the happy and effective solution of a mortal artist, and at the least the effete effusion of "a softened and sophisticated" self: and either way would be a profanation of the sacred, unacceptable to him. No, given the impossible nature of his adoration, the only logical way to realize and embody his childhood glory would be to break his pen and join the paternal ghost: one way—perhaps the grimmest—of interpreting the incomplete status of his final novel.

As long as Agee finds himself yearning for a supernal but ever-receding harmony in life while condemned to the consolation prize of his art, the orphan hero will never be successful as a synthesist nor entirely at peace with himself. Rather, he is more successful—and certainly more successfully understood—as an equilibrist juggling the antinomies, tensions bristling and unresolved, intact, but, as it were, in tow. While his assumed goal may be transcendence through union, his actual goal becomes acceptance and sufficiency through containment, struggle, and endurance to the end. In this manner, he becomes himself the battleground of his paradoxes, a threshold figure between "parents" treading the interface between linked but rivalrous realms. He is the watcher who strikes (*The Morning Watch*), a "spy" but for both sides (*Famous Men*), an "orphan" but with a family (*A Death in the Family*), an "amateur" teaching professionals (*Agee on Film*). His "failure" to resolve himself and his struggle becomes the matter, the singularity, and finally the triumph of his art: the embroidering of self-reflexive forms out of the confessional of his "defeat," the poise of his hesitancy, the speed of his oscillations, the burnished texture of his "galloping melancholia,"[17] the deep thickets of his rummage, and the high hopelessness of his radiant quest.

CHAPTER THREE

A FANTASIA OF
THE ACTUAL

*Let Us Now Praise
Famous Men*

When I was in my father's house, I was in a better place.
—RUDYARD KIPLING

ET US NOW PRAISE FAMOUS MEN was Agee's second publication, the first and greatest of his major accomplishments. Nothing he ever did before or after could match it for ambition, power, and audacity, for—as he might have had it—those "nascent oxygen" qualities of freedom and insolence. Certainly he lived to produce other significant, even extraordinary, works; writing more disciplined and decorous than *Famous Men*, also more forthright and accessible, without doubt more ingratiating and companionable. But in no other book is one exposed so rudely to the astonishing breadth and sheer nerviness of his genius. In no other does one find so many of his bright and dark angels operating at full flame: the extravagance and resource of his language, the almost magical apprehension and reproduction of the density and intricacy of the physical world, the furnace blast of his moral consciousness, the muscle and vigor of his youthful aestheticism. And along with these and deeply engrafted to them, other qualities less fetching: the straining and the gaucherie, the preening poeticisms and the tortured obscurities, the leaky faucet of his self-indulgence. Never again would this writer seem to give so much of himself—of both the marvelous and the addled—to a book, never again would he seem to have so much in him to give. An older, more practiced Agee would doubtless have written a "better" book, but doubtless a lesser one. Nowadays the follies of *Famous Men* seem virtually organic to it and strictly of the Blakean variety: a noble dementia persisted in to the point of wisdom, and all-of-a-piece with the inclusiveness of its epical aspirations.

The book may well be the preeminent literary work of its period; that is, the most important achievement in American prose, in or out of fiction, to appear between the publication of Faulkner's first great novels starting in 1929 and the emergence of the early writing of Bellow, Ellison, and Mailer in the late forties and early fifties. And more than this: strictly as a work of nonfiction, Agee's creation may also be one of the very few American works of the modern era to come within even hailing distance of our nineteenth- and early-twentieth-century classics of personal confession and rumination, observed experience, poetic fact, and homecooked philosophy: *Walden* (1854), *Life on the Mississippi* (1883), and *The Education of Henry Adams* (1907).

An important book, then, a unique and imposing book, but one, I must add, with few takers. Highly respected and duly acclaimed—from Lionel Trilling in 1942 ("a great book"), to Alfred Kazin in 1986 ("a truly American classic")—*Famous Men* remains to this very hour, like its author, something of a cult item, a specialty act.[1] For many readers, both common and uncommon, this great anomaly invariably takes its place on the shelf alongside those other bulky, esteemed, often assayed, earnestly perused but largely unread native American and émigré unicorns and gargoyles, such as *Pierre, The Golden Bowl, A Fable, Ada, Gravity's Rainbow,* and *Ancient Evenings:* a truly *American* classic.

After all, how many of even its most ardent admirers have ever so much as intimated that *Famous Men* is anyone's idea of a good time? Is the casual impression of the casual reader of this unwieldy and perplexing work that far off the mark? Here is a book that purports to be a faithful record of the life of a tenant farmer during the Depression (summer,

1936), but spends most of its pages examining not people, but furniture, clothing, woodwork, weather, and landscape—all manner of atmosphere and inanimate objects. And here is a "nonfiction" that makes fun of made-up ("imagined") works of art and professes alternatives to such artifice, and then proceeds to fill its own aggressively made-up pages with poetry, interior monologues, theatrical set-pieces, unwitnessed happenings, stylized sermonettes, lyrical mystical cadenzas, and the like. And here is an authorial presence, a chinese box of blues, *ecstasis,* and self-pity, that hangs the melancholy of its dejected self-absorption about the neck of the reader like an albatross, that incessantly prates absolute love for and fidelity to its subject but cannot stop examining itself long enough to tell us what a farmer really sounds like.

However exaggerated, Philistine, or simply wrong-headed these impressions may be, the truth about this book is that it remains more than a little off-putting even to people who have long since succumbed to its raging grandeurs. While the achievement of the text may be vastly greater than any of its real or imagined stumbling blocks, few, if any, of the major works of modern American prose, outside of select examples from high modernist and postmodernist fiction (e.g., Faulkner, Nabokov, Pynchon, etc.), seem to work so hard to resist access and familiarity, to snub even those hardy residues of toleration and goodwill that any serious reader might shore up against the intractabilities of a famous and famously difficult book. The fact that the work begins, for instance, with the Walker Evans photographs, surely one of the premiere examples of lucid and direct visual discourse in the annals of camera art, only makes the text which follows seem that much more convoluted and tendentious, bewildering with its forests of literary apparatuses—epigraphs, verses, preambles, prayers, notes, footnotes, appendices, divisions and subdivisions, etc.—eccentric proportions, and treacherous chronological displacements. Book 1, for example, is five pages; book 2, almost five hundred. The formal or official conclusion appears a full thirty pages before the actual conclusion, this actual conclusion following rather than preceding a long section of "notes and appendices." The reader is formally introduced to the farmers only in one of the final sections ("Inductions") just as he is exposed to their innermost thoughts and dreams ("A Country Letter") almost from the start, long before he even knows who they are. Abruptly and willfully, from section to section, the author regularly disrupts form and continuity by juxtaposing one kind of treatment against another and very different kind: straight journalism, intimate confession, metaphysical speculation, questionnaire, ethnographic field report, verse forms, inventories and catalogs, newspaper clips and trims, polemics, invectives, and eidolons. Agee has made a creature that can neither be held nor handled, let alone tagged or muzzled. Put baldly, what often seems to bother most readers, old and new, pro and con, about *Famous Men* is that it is impossible to determine what it is; and few things are more unsettling to the orderly and imperious parts of the mind than objects that cannot be named.

Now I think it is essential to realize at the outset that the difficulty of this book is deeply bound up with its unclassifiability, and that both the difficulty and the unclassifiability are deliberate and necessary to its form and central to its meaning; that Agee not only hasn't got the slightest interest (of course) in writing a "beloved" book, a cushiony classic in brown veal (as if one could actually will such a creature) but that the book he *must* write is an impossible, unutterable, and unrealizable book; and that some of the characteristic problems of the reader in entering and taking possession of *Famous Men* are also some, and perhaps the most telling, indications that such a solitary, refractory, and incommodious project is indeed being undertaken.

The intellectual drama of *Famous Men* begins with the fact that Agee is attempting to write a book that in a very exact and literal sense cannot be written, or at least one, as he informs us many times, that he is incapable of writing. The form that he gives to his work after three years of intense and undeviating labor is the form appropriate to this fact. Both the "Preface" and the "Preamble" insist that the kind of book Agee hopes to write is nothing less than an "exhaustive " (xv) record and analysis of "unimagined existence" (xiv) of actuality as it exists outside of works of the imagination. His goal, then, is to perceive "the immediate world . . . as it stands," but for him, this also means as it stands resonant with spiritual force, "so that the aspect of a street in sunlight can roar in the heart of itself as a symphony," so that one is made aware of "the cruel radiance of what is" (11). In other words, "to recognize the stature of a portion of unimagined existence" (xiv) is to recognize the opposite of the flat, the prosaic, the gross *materia* of the positivist; it is to recognize that "unimagined existence" as it is immediately aligns itself with "certain normal predicaments of human divinity" (xiv). To perceive the actual "as it stands," then, is also to be made aware of the infiltration of it by such "divinity." And to embody such perception in a book is to make a kind of book of homely divination, a backyard gospel full of the power of the sacred as it is revealed in those "certain normal predicaments."

As far as the author is concerned, that book never gets written; that book remains the incorporated but unfulfilled dream of this book; this book is a mere shadow of that book: "Of this ultimate intention [an "exhaustive" record and analysis "of unimagined existence"] the present volume is merely portent and fragment, experiment; dissonant prologue" (xv). He also refers to his book as "a swindle, an insult, a corrective," but asks the reader to keep his "ultimate intention . . . steadily in mind" (xv). That "ultimate intention" as intention (only) becomes a major theme of this book, and much of the heroism and stir of *Famous Men* reside in Agee's bootless yet insistent struggle to epiphanize the Unnameable and the Ineffable.

So then: while his professed and original intention may be a rendering of "unimagined existence," his actual accomplishment—or as near as brevity may be allowed to traduce it—is a successful and one-of-a-kind dramatization of his failed efforts to render this condition. The absolute and infinite nature of the Actual (i.e., reality in the Ageean sense: "unimagined existence" imbued with sacred intimation) makes its presence felt and known precisely through a dazzling and exhaustive record and analysis of the traces and signals attesting to its absence; that is, precisely, its all-but-thereness.[2] This extraordinary record and analysis of traces and signals constitutes a large part of what this book is about.

But I think we misconstrue his work greatly if we mistake Agee's original aspiration for his achievement, or try to explain or defend his achievement solely in terms of this original aspiration. And we make a more important error if we imagine that Agee himself also mistook what he aspired to do for what he actually did. The last words of the "Preamble" are these:

'Beethoven said a thing as rash and noble as the best of his work. By my memory, he said: "He who understands my music can never know unhappiness again." I believe it. And I would be a liar and a coward and one of your safe world if I should fear to say the same words of my best perception, and of my best intention.

Performance, in which the whole fate and terror rests, is another matter. (16)

Famous Men is born of the drama in the space between these two paragraphs. This complex imbroglio of slated intentions and mottled motives, of effortful flights of idealism teetering against calculated arias of impotence, makes this book perhaps the most uninhibited and self-reflexive of modern American epics: at once a tragic-heroic saga of the sanctity of agrarian life, as well as a new-fangled, "postmodernist" rumination on the personal and philosophical impossibility of ever realizing such a project.

In the discussion that follows I'd like to explore both Agee's "best intention" and his actual "performance." The first two sections ("With Failure Foreseen" and "Two Reveries") will stress the former and discuss different shades of Agee's dream and its frustration, the kind of book he wanted to write and some of the reasons why he could not write it. Sections 3 and 4 will focus on "performance" and examine the book that Agee actually wrote, the story, such as it is, emerging from a ruin of ideals and the human triumphs, such as they are, salvaged from the jaws of a paralyzing defeat; and particularly how all this affects the two central subjects of his work: Agee himself (section 3, "The True Tastes of Home"), and the farmers (section 4, "Gods in Ruins").

1. WITH FAILURE FORESEEN

There was little doubt, even before he undertook his journey south, that Agee regarded the Alabama project as one of the momentous events of his life. Just getting the assignment from the editors of *Fortune* was enough to produce in him that admixture of joy, veneration, obligation, and holy terror that would be sustained throughout the next several years as part of both the creation and the expressive content of *Famous Men*. "Well,

I think he knew in his bones that this was going to be something big for him," said his friend Robert Fitzgerald, who was with Agee when he received his new commission. "He knew that given a month or two in the Deep South, looking into the lives of the impoverished was going to electrify a great deal of his nature that had not yet been given an opportunity for full expression or for full employment, that this was going to test him and all that he had much more than anything that had ever come up before. So he was scared. Scared clean through of facing this thing." "The best break I ever had on *Fortune*," Agee wrote to Father Flye (June 18, 1936). "Feel terrific personal responsibility toward story, considerable doubts of my ability to bring it off, considerable more doubts of *Fortune's* ultimate willingness to use it."[3]

We also know that the experience itself in every way lived up to his anticipation of it. Every page of his book attests to the overwhelming impressiveness and singularity of an occasion that had resulted in what Agee now believed to be a truth, a human "actuality"; and few writers of his generation ever used these badly bruised, mocked, and contested terms with greater authority than he did. Unlike many of our contemporaries, this writer usually placed unhesitating faith in the findings of his own "unassisted and weaponless consciousness" (11), in general seemed undaunted by the swindles of cognition, and rarely felt impelled to enter into the labyrinths of the illusion/reality game. Rather, Agee returned from Hale County, Alabama, with vision and purpose, consumed by the validity of what had happened to him.

But if his initial convictions were ratified, so too were his initial hesitancies: *Fortune* did not use the article that eventually became the book that had been anticipated from the start; and indeed his sense of doubt as to bringing "it off" permeates the finished text as a kind of counterclaim to the authenticity and unequivocal certainty of the event itself. These doubts reduce themselves essentially to the uncertainty of making what was actual for him just as actual for others. *He* had experienced the radiance of what is, and this "radiance" had made him, as it were, a convert to its powers. His anxiety resided in his ability to find forms of expression adequate to this experience and by these means reproduce it in its exact, pristine, and inviolate condition. His problems then were essentially problems of communication (not cognition), and in this respect, his worry spread in three directions: toward the sender, the receiver, and the means of conveyance between them; in other words, he had doubts about (1) himself, (2) his reader, and (3) his language, about the competency of the first, the receptivity of the second, and the truthfulness of the third.

WRITER, READER

As author of the project, Agee never seems to run out of eloquent ways to remind us of just how badly he has betrayed the majesty of his ideals. Nothing is more characteristic of the writer in this his greatest work, nor helps to establish the rise-and-plunge, surge-and-halt rhythm of this book more definitively than his ceaseless refrain that he cannot do justice to his project. "To come devotedly into the depth of your subject," he tells us in a typical instance, "your respect for it increasing in every step and your whole heart weakening apart with shame upon yourself in your dealing with it: To know at length better and better and at length into the bottom of your soul your unworthiness of it: Let me hope in any case that it is something to have begun to learn" (319). To be sure, there was grim satisfaction in all this. There were few more effective ways of stressing the unutterable nature of perfection than by contrast with his own personal and curiously articulate sense of inadequacy. But even beyond this (that is, even when perfection or "holiness" is not at issue): between the intention and the act incessantly falls the author's characteristic form of negative self-assertion, the stance of an artist certain of his uncertainty, fecund and resourceful with the energies of self-doubt, resolute with the inventions of recession. Agee's admissions of failure become less important as honest blurts of failure than as fascinating forms of admission: his dashed efforts to realize the dream keeps him talking about the dreamer. Before long, a definitive character emerges (more of this later).

So the problem of the author's personal "unworthiness" may be only partly real, partly rhetorical. The problem of the audience, however, is more palpable and less ambiguous. Agee in his anguish and awareness is free to struggle against what he takes to be the limitations of his value and skill, but the limitation of the audience is that of a deeply entrenched complacency, and it is in the nature of complacency not to conceive of itself as a problem (hence the problem). Even if Agee were not certain of his uncertainty and fully capable of writing the book he thinks he cannot write, he knows very well that such an audience would not be capable of receiving it. In the presence of the truly sacred, such an audience "would not go near it at all" (13). And even here in the serious and seriously compromised work ("a swindle") he believes he has written, the cunning of such an audience lies not in ignoring his words (he might rejoice in such clearly drawn battle lines), or even in rejecting them outright (perhaps the surest sign that he has achieved something near the pinnacle of his goals), but in agreeing with them all too readily and thus deflecting both the shock and the hurt of the spiritual renovation they offer through what he calls the "emasculation of acceptance" (13); that is, the rationalization and dilution of radical revelation into preconceived and socially acceptable categories, such as "art" or conventional wisdom (for example, an editorial in the Sunday Supplement). What was meant to challenge and transform one's life now merely entrances, entertains, or tickles the curiosity as a version of make-believe and a cud for chewing. "Official acceptance is the one unmistakable symptom that salvation is beaten again," he tells us in the "Preamble," "and is the one surest sign of fatal misunderstanding, and is the kiss of Judas" (15).

But who is this audience, and how does one subvert the dodge of its deceptive acquiescence? Certainly the audience to whom Agee writes is not the same audience of whom and for whom his book is written, that is, his dedicatee, the impoverished farmer. At different times and in different places, *Famous Men* actually addresses two very different kinds of reader, but each by essentially the same means, the intimacy of the second person. Only sometimes (as in "Inductions") "you" will refer to one or more of his cherished Alabamians, while at other times (particularly throughout the "Preface" and "Preamble") "you" will refer to members of this other audience, this vast, self-satisfied gaggle of book-buyers composed of the secure and the franchised: the liberal, socially concerned, culture-ready bourgeoisie, sensible and agnostic, materially avid but spiritually slack, possessed of kindly but thoroughly vitiated intentions. To be sure, a cool and cautious customer, decent and well disposed, but secretly pledged to Safety First and Touch

Me Not; above all, lacking in valor: much understood, little respected, obsessively appealed to, and in the end generally distrusted, by this author.

Still, it was this audience, and not the farmer, that formed the majority of his presumed readership, the fate of his struggles on behalf of the aggrieved having to wait upon the attentiveness of the craven. It was here where the work had to be done, priorities reshuffled, awarenesses expanded, a sense of "what is" installed. In these efforts, Agee aligned himself with a venerable tradition of American mentorship—a tradition including artists and prophets, specialists and technicians, as well as drummers, grifters, and kooks of every shade and suasion—dedicated to the cause of redressing the perceived yearnings and deficiencies in its fellow countryman: vulgarity, materialism, mendacity, self-absorption, along with all forms of daily incompetence, dysfunction, and the general inability to make do. Confident of diagnosing the aches and needs of his neighbors, the customized author as service unit classically elects to secure attention via the claims of neither art nor beauty, nor even entertainment nor escape, but rather those of a vigorous pragmatism. These include operationals for living and the possibility of a more expeditious life—everything from how-to, Mr. Fix-It, and do-it-yourself manuals (original Yankee inventions) to the protocols of the dinner table and the campfire (Emily Post, the Scouts' handbook) to apocalyptic ready-mades for moral transcendence (Emerson's *Essays*). The kind of book you will find more of in America than anywhere else is a book that professes to tell you how to live better than you do, be better than you are, and in every case get it done and keep it flying; that is, no matter how lofty the enterprise, such a book will pitch some quotient of its delivery and appeal on the honorable level that competes with the utility value of two-by-fours and jumper cables.[4] Agee's instructional, for instance, in self-reclamation is thoroughly in the native remedial manner, as nearly methodical and anatomized as a page from Betty Crocker, a work schedule by Poor Richard, a blueprint from *Popular Mechanics,* or the receipt for tools and supplies printed in *Walden:*

> Get a radio or a phonograph capable of the most extreme loud-
> ness possible, and sit down to listen to a performance of Beethoven's

Seventh Symphony or Schubert's C-Major Symphony. But I don't mean just sit down and listen. I mean this: turn it on as loud as you can get it. Then get down on the floor and jam your ear as close to the loudspeaker as you can get it and stay there, breathing as lightly as possible, and not moving, and neither eating nor smoking nor drinking. Concentrate everything you can into your hearing and into your body. You won't hear it nicely. If it hurts you, be glad of it. As near as you will ever get you are inside the music: not only inside it, you are it. Your body is no longer your shape and substance, it is the shape and substance of the music. (15–16)

In these opening pages, it's hard to say whether Agee has actually come to instruct his reader or to admonish him ("But I don't mean just sit down and listen . . ."), or perhaps more aptly, to instruct him by means of admonishment ("I mean this . . ."). We only know that he is all over him, all but throttling him in an exasperated, near lethal, embrace. And why not? For good and ill, this liberal middle-class fence-sitter is both Agee's mortal enemy and his fraternal twin. By occupation, habitation, education, upbringing, and a perhaps unauthorized set of class affiliations (including immediate family backgrounds), Agee probably has more in common with the comfortable and well-fed members of his readership than he can perhaps either tolerate or fully admit in cold print. On the other hand, this reader is also the principle abettor and beneficiary of an economy responsible for the farmer's misery, and in his defense systems, a virtual octopus of tepid tolerations, fully capable of defusing the utility value of any idea simply by welcoming its existence as thought while ignoring its potential for enacted experience. Agee's uneasy remedy for cooption by appeasement is to write for his audience by writing against it, to invigorate his mentorship with insult and assault, sarcasm and abuse, to adopt the negative remedials of a latter-day Jeremiah and rage in the hope of not being agreed with too quickly. Bypassing the customary attacks on the Capitalist enterprise—its dog-eat-doggedness, the lopsided apportionments of its wealth, the very quiet and legalized ruthlessness of its power set-ups—he forages instead for the mental and moral roots of the dilemma: bourgeois placidity and limitations of consciousness; the hideousness of "good intentions" and spineless sympathies; conveniences of mind that manage to filter out both the visionary artist's radical stance and the uncharted excitements and dangers of a true liberty.

But through it all, he fumes without hope, as if in complete certainty that his timorous congregation will always be more stubborn and powerful in its passivity than he can ever be in his aggression. As in most of his battles, Agee assumes defeat here before he even enters the lists: "Wiser and more capable men than I shall ever be have put their findings before you, findings so rich and so full of anger, serenity, murder, healing, truth, and love that it seems incredible the world were not destroyed and fulfilled in the instant, but you are too much for them: the weak in courage are strong in cunning; and one by one, you have absorbed and captured and dishonored and distilled of your deliverers the most ruinous of all your poisons" (14).

The didactic or hortatory impulse in American letters typically legislates an open work that completes itself in usage; ideally, an inspired reader, not the final page, finishes the book. Either the design of such a work continues to unfold itself in the cluttered momentum of daily living, or you might just as well, *faux de mieux*, call it "art." But Agee can envisage no such audience activation for his (or perhaps for any) book. His flock may lend an ear, permit itself to be entertained, and, yes, enlightened too, may even proffer the enthusiasm of its applause and cold-comfort charity of its guilt and goodwill, but this author knows that no effort or resource of literary genius can ever enforce a single member of his slippery readership to put his life on the line in response to something, anything, he may have read in a book.

THE WORDS

And this brings us to the third side of Agee's triangulated despair, perhaps the thorniest and most conflicted of his problems: the ineffectuality of the words themselves. Even if the writer were more capable than he is and the audience more courageous than it could ever be, the medium itself must be what it always has been: a bumbling stranger in the land of "unimagined existence." Of all his creative travails, it is the failure of language that inspires Agee to his most complicated and concentrated chain of speculation (in mainly the middle sections of "On the Porch: 2").[5]

Now at any point in his varied professional life, this writer was fully capable of writing as both sovereign prince and loyal minister of his Anglo-American parlance (even though he did not always do so), as one who could at any time readily aver, and demonstrate, as he does in *Famous Men*, that "words could, I believe, be made to do or tell anything within human conceit. That is more than can be said about the instruments of any other art" (236). But in *Famous Men*—such is the special nature of his project—Agee has no wish to deal in "human conceit." In principle and intent the Alabama farmer, George Gudger, is no "human conceit" but, Agee insists, an actual human being breathing not in the imagined world of "conceit," but in the actual world of other human beings. In this work as in no other, Agee dedicates himself to try to render this being, not as imaginative concept, but on its own terms as unmediated Actuality: and for *this* sort of Sisyphean labor words may not be just inept and inapt, but wildly beside the point. And in an act unprecedented for its time and place, Agee pushes to the center of his project an unstinting awareness of how the tools of his trade betray the student of Actuality: "they [words] are the most inevitably inaccurate of mediums of record and communication, and . . . they come at many of the things which they alone can do by such a Rube Goldberg articulation of frauds, compromises, artful dodges, and tenth removes as would fatten any other art into apoplexy if the art were not first shamed out of existence" (236). As examples, he cites (passingly) two notorious snags in the ontology of language: first, words falsify "through inaccuracy of meaning as well as inaccuracy of emotion" (236–37) the things to which they refer; and second, words "cannot communicate simultaneity with any immediacy" (237). The problem of "inaccuracy" refers to the immemorial lack of identity between word and thing, the utter misappropriation of any designation; the problem of "immediacy" notes the signal failure of words to keep pace with, or even halfway adequately represent, the lightning temporality of things in concert.

As we are repeatedly (and perhaps numbingly) informed nowadays, words can never be integral or consubstantial with the things they mean to represent. They may signify or symbolize things, but never embody them; they may point, but never grasp. The squirt of noise that prints out as "chair" has less to do with the nature of the object upon which one sits than the most picayune and gratuitous of the chair's material properties, say, the mulled or softened tip at the base of its left leg, or the shattered veil of dust salting the barrel of the rear stretcher, etc.: the quiddity of the chair—the thickness, wired immediacy, and bulging thereness of it—are qualities and categories of chair-experience forever lost to language.

With similar ineptitude, words can only present themselves consecutively (Indian file) while things occur synchronously (in pow-wow). There is simply no way for print or utterance to catch up the continuous and spreading present tense of things, with, that is, the way all parts of a thing and its relationships present themselves as a contrapuntal happening (i.e., all parts present to each other at the same time and at each moment of their being). The moment of a chair, say, is indistinguishable and properly inextricable from its network of ambient extensions; the direction, shape, and quality of the changing light that strikes its surfaces; the density and volatility of the air that envelops it; the innumerable objects present to and angled about it; the purely human presences and activities occurring on or near it; the parts of the space that contain it; the space itself; that space in relation to others, and so on: a virtual cosmos of relationship, all part of the chair as the chair is part of it, and integral to the chair within the instant. Given such a packed and cantilevered instant, words can only hope to represent it slowly—the instant long gone, the moment as history—and laboriously, an interminable caravan of verbal camel plop supplanting a winged and effortless *SHAZAM*!

Small wonder, then, that as antidote to all the epistemological boondoggling inherent in literary "truth," Agee plumps for the advances upon the actual made by the instruments of science and the mechanical-visual arts: before all else, extolling the camera, both still and cinematized, for its obvious illusion of a mirrorlike doubling of physical surfaces, and its seeming affinity for the synchronous sprawl of a living moment (here, obliquely, also urging the necessity for the presence and contribution of a photographer as his coauthor). In comparison with photographs and motion pictures, the most veristic of literary arts, reared as it must be upon a sonic coding both presumptive and whimsical, cannot help but undermine its fidelity to the phenomenal world even in the act of making its pledge. In this vein, Agee even takes time to cite and condemn the defections of those modes, media, and authorial assumptions one would imagine most congenial to his own interests and practices—at the very least, those friends and near relatives of the book he professes to be trying to write: specifically, the promiscuous latitudes of journalism ("a successful form of lying," 235); the gross and straitened methodologies of literary realism and naturalism, which fatally heap both "time and weightiness" (235), material flab and glue, upon the object depicted; and most pernicious of all, the "killing insult" of the willing suspension of disbelief, for Agee an admission that reduces even the most veracious of the arts to make-believe and withholds from its reader "the simple but total honor of believing it [art] in the terms in which he accepts and honors breathing, lovemaking, the look of a newspaper, the street he walks through" (240).

Here and throughout these literary overhauls, Agee's discourse is both spirited and prescient, his dialectical poise, as usual, knotty yet familiar. Still, I doubt very much if many contemporaries will be properly bowled over by the novelty of any of his arguments, accusations, or discriminations per se. Nowadays, our toniest writers and trendiest professors routinely engage in such radical exposures and "unmasking" of the literary medium *vis-a-vis* an objective reality, hardly even pausing to champ at the bit, let alone curse the situation, as did Agee. Nowadays, an impressive segment of the literary community is all for advertising, even celebrating, the utter and complete segregation between the actual and its literary representation; the "autonomy" of the word; the advent of the "writerly" text; the witty and exuberant roundelay of signifiers forever estranged from a dowdy and thoroughly patronized signified. What our wordly wise and linguistically unillusioned generation defines as a source of creative, and (for some) even political, possibility and play, Agee viewed mostly as a source of pining and frustration, a desert isle of lingual quarantine where reality's castaways burned in vain for a lost but never-to-be-forgotten Eden of being, truth, and "radiance": a position that perhaps oddly but everlastingly marked him as the definitive wallflower at the postmodernist party to which he was doubtless invited, and may in part have even hosted, before anyone else.

For let us be perfectly evenhanded on behalf of this author, and point out that he was perhaps the first important American writer to explore these metafictional matters in any sustained, exacting, and impassioned manner; the first to incorporate these awarenesses as part of the, so to speak, dramatis personae of a book; that he was meditating upon such aesthetic surgeries (i.e., the severing of word and thing, life and text, etc.) at least three decades or more before it became fashionable, and finally standardized, to do so; and that what must, after all, only come off as standard operating procedure to the meta- or sur-fictionalists of the 1990s must have appeared striking and even original to those few hundred concerned readers who bothered to find out in 1941. Recall: for an entire pre-Ageean literary generation, the regnant mode of policy and practice in serious fiction had to be that of social realism, accurate and "truthful" depictions of class customs, division, and divisiveness, in particular of a depressed and betrayed proletariat, by writers such as Steinbeck, Dos Passos, Farrell, Caldwell, et al. And here for the first time in Agee, readers (then and now, for that matter) could recognize the characteristic voice of the protest endeavor—the outrage, the despair, the dark wit—newly transposed to a level of theoretical and aesthetic dispute. Here for the first time readers could also learn that the problem and the anguish of the socially committed writer need not, and did not, derive solely from an acute response to the diseases in the body polity, or the struggle of poor against privileged, or even to the corruption of pilgrim dreams, Jeffersonian ideals, and all the failed false promises of the New World. They could learn that this problem and anguish could and in fact did begin with the defections in the infrastructure of communication by which these desperate facts (diseases, corruptions, etc.) were to be transmitted and finally known, understood, and perhaps acted upon; that the very system of rhetoric and expression that would enlist aid for the betrayed could be itself a source of betrayal.

But even this was not all. At the same time those early readers could learn this, they must also have found it puzzling to perceive further— perhaps even a contemporary will find it striking—that Agee by no means leaves matters where he seems to, or doubtless where *our* literary vanguard might think he should. What must be obvious to any reader at any time is that *Famous Men* itself is replete with precisely the categorically "wrong" sort of descriptive materials and procedures; that is, cataracts of literalist representation, naming, list making, exhaustive descriptions of objects in the immediacy of their living moments, etc.—in brief, a dazzling display of those very effects in which, as the author insists many times over, words are fated to fail.

How, then, does one account for *this?* If Agee represents a bitter demurral to the leaders of his own generation, he also provides (we shall now discover) a firm disclaimer to the language purists of ours. Coming upon the heels of his theoretical despair, his enthusiastic assaults upon the physical reality may seem deeply paradoxical only because the necessary failure of language, and the chastisement of its corrupt usage, represent but one side of his double-edged grasp of the full ontology of the word. The gist of his complex stance may best be epitomized in the following crammed, richly evocative, yet thoroughly representative orchestration of discursiveness, analogy, and metaphor:

> . . . words like all else are limited by certain laws. To call their achievement crippled in relation to what they have tried to convey may be all very well: but to call them crippled in their completely healthful obedience to their own nature is again a mistake: the same mistake as the accusation of a cow for her unhorsiness. And if you here say: 'But the cow words are trying to be a horse,' the answer is: 'That attempt is one of the strongest laws of language, just as it is no law at all as far as cows are concerned.' In obeying this law words are not, then, at all necessarily accusable, any more than in disobeying it. The cleansing and rectification of language, the breakdown of the identification of word and object is very important, and very possibly more important things will come of it than have ever come of the lingual desire of the cow for the horse: but it is nevertheless another matter whenever words start functioning in the command of the ancient cow-horse law. Human beings may be more and more aware of being awake, but they are still incapable of not dreaming; and a fish forswears water for air at his own peril. (237)

Actually, two cardinal "laws" of language and procedure emerge from these compacted flourishes; and throughout *Famous Men,* in one form or another, Agee strains his faithful best to serve both of them. First: *words must fail;* they are in fact obliged to do so, and in this manner realize one legitimate way of remaining true to themselves. When words cannot do what they set out to do—that is, embody the objects to which they refer—they fail only in relation to those objects, but not in relation to themselves. In failing, rather, they continue to reaffirm a "completely healthful obedience" to their own linguistic purity and integrity. Second: *words must continue to yearn toward their object.* Words may indeed fail to embody their objects (that is "all very well"), but it need not follow from this that words must then abandon the effort to reach out beyond their own sonic purity; that effort, rather, "is one of the strongest laws of language," it is—he names it—"the ancient cow-horse law," the striving of the word to embrace a thing independent of itself. Unlike a cow that becomes grotesquely untrue to its nature the moment it tries to approximate the nature of a horse (that approximation "is no law at all as far as cows are concerned"), the stretching of the (cow-) word toward its (horse-) object is another way words have of legitimating themselves.

Now, he suggests, one may obey or disobey this second law. If one disobeys it, then in effect one automatically rejects the impurity implied by such lingual (cow/horse) yearning, accepts the chasm that yawns between word and thing, that is, accepts "failure" (accepts the first law of language and that only); and as one logical consequence, devotes oneself to the "cleansing and rectification of the word," by implication an essentially homeostatic enterprise pledged to the self-perfection of a world of words sequestered from a world of things. Agee has fond hopes for such an enterprise (it has become, of course, something very like *our* enterprise), and offers "that possibly more important things may come of it than have ever come of the lingual desire of the cow for the horse" (if only he knew!). But the metaphors (i.e., those of "human beings" and "fish") that follow these characteristic encouragements clearly suggest the grim consequences attendant upon such deliberate dedications to purity and rectitude: cryptic hints, for instance, of fatal reconditioning, like the "fish" that "forswears water for air"; of unnatural attentions and attenuations, like the "human beings" who hypothetically try to forestall their dreams with increasing increments of consciousness; of moral depletion and disarray, as when (in a footnote two paragraphs forward) linguistic "failure" is described as not only an "obligation" but also as "the deadliest trap of an exhausted conscience" (238).[6] For Agee, the ancient lingual law, that of the cow-word and its doomed yen for its horse-object, is one before which even "cleansing and rectification" must finally yield.

But on what grounds? By way of explanation, let me extrapolate from within the outer reaches of Agee's two ripely suggestive figures of speech: like those "human beings" inescapably bound to their dream—in spite of all efforts to oblige the imperial acquisitions of a wide "awake" consciousness—the hankering for the Actual represents the whole emotive, unconscious, subrational, and visionary life of the word; that which determines the entire striving, fluxing power, however hopeless and benighted, of a partly personal and aural construct conceived to arrow across the void separating the writer in his isolation and the world in its plentitude. To be understood not as an embodiment, but rather as a *dream of the Actual,* the flexion of the word, like the spiraling ascension of the dream phenomonology itself, is that which generates both the aspiration of the word as well as its directionality: beyond the haze of sound and phantom, beyond, that is, the threshold of dream and verbality itself, and outward toward the implacable gravity and supernal stasis of all things that simply are, the myriad inhabitants of a world without end. Also (still extrapolating): like "water" to the "fish," Agee further implies that this world of things may also represent the originating context of the word, the elemental breath and magma of its livingness, conditions not to be forsaken without dire risk.[7]

Now upon percolating both of these poetic figures, I want to suggest how deftly Agee has managed to nudge his whole notion of lingual man (and fish), his passions and perils, along a track parallel to that of the mythic motifs of his own spiritual biography. His worry over words, language crisis, etc., seems to emerge not at all from any formal concern with linguistics, deconstructionist philosophy, or even from some specialized critical interest in the historical evolution of literary forms and techniques, but rather from a highly intimate set of private compulsions and priorities, stemming from what we have been describing as the ongoing legend of himself. Thus: the dream of words, like the employer of words, may also align itself with a quest for abandoned origins, a primal and irretrievable nook in the domain of the actual; so, too, the state and status of words, like their author, may also be viewed as orphaned, paupered, inadequate, cut off and cut out, yet inconsolable in their exile, pushing beyond themselves toward the portals of home in "radiance," a sacred space forever sealed off from any form of occupation.

Just as failure, then, is built into language, so, too, for Agee, is an idealist potential, a quixotic urgency to forswear failure in pursuit of a lost kinship and solidarity with an object. Let us call this pursuit the homing and attempted completion of the word.[8]

THE INEVITABLE ARTIST

We have then two seemingly paradoxical and self-imposed rules of language, and Agee, as indicated, has his reasons to insist upon the ratification of both: his way with words indeed becomes to yearn *and* fail, fail and yearn, over and over; dying and regenerating amid agonies of brinkmanship this side of embodiment. It is his adherence to the first lingual law that compels him to write the strange and unprecedented manner of book we have before us. It is his adherence to the second that compels him to write period. It is his adherence to *both* laws, however, that equally necessitate and underwrite at least three complementary formal operations that continue to define his creation as one of the quirky and unsettling, yet thoroughly unique and still formidable, rhetorical achievements in American modernism:

(1) *Jamming*, or what nowadays we might want to call metacommentary (or even in some quarters "metafiction"). No one can doubt that Agee is upon the instant both ready and willing (if only he were able) to scotch every bit of insight he has ever gleaned into the limitations of the literary artist and the faithlessness of his words if he could but make a single particle of Gudger and his world, "unchanged and undecorated" (233), live and breathe on its own terms within the confines of his book. But this utterly genuine goal is forever scored by the nagging awareness that the task to which he dedicates himself—than which there "is no worthier and many worse subjects"—is also "essentially and finally a hopeless one" (233). The fate of the Actualist in literature is unequivocal: language abhors an unmediated Gudger, and the committed but scrupulous writer hastens to jerry-rig some kind of truce between his subject and his medium. Agee then does not hesitate to present Gudger and his world, but does so in the spirit of what he calls "failure foreseen" (238); that is, an attitude of purpose that only allows the discourse to proceed through the invocation of a quasi-ritualistic pattern of disbelief (thus,

outflanking the customary suspension of disbelief). In other words, Agee will not merely "present" Gudger and his world, but continually interrupt such presentation "to talk about what you present and how you try to present it" (238), to comment upon the whole range of problems of both the artist and the tools of his craft (most prominently in the second and third "On the Porch" sections, "Preface," and "Preamble," but intermittently throughout). This metapresentation becomes this writer's way of italicizing, explaining, and even partly mitigating, the distortions in the original presentation, distortions that come as no surprise but rather are, as implied, anticipated from the outset by foreknowledge of one's limitations, as well as those of one's audience and medium.

Such foreknowledge becomes finally the basis for a kind of literary morality: here is a book that will righteously strip bare whatever "illusion of embodiment" (238) the author's dubious talent for enchantment, and audience's dubious penchant for escape through enchantment, might conspire to create; that will openly chant as often as necessary that the Actuality of "Gudger" has escaped once again: that one has merely botched and traduced him as before; that a botched and traduced "Gudger" may be better than no "Gudger" (that is "all very well"), but in attempting to do what could never be done (first linguistic law), even though it should and must be done (second linguistic law), the author and his instruments have once more committed an inevitable (and perhaps understandable) species of literary perjury. In such circumstances, the guilty author's chief anxiety, and only recourse to attain even partial remission, is "to make clear that a sin is a sin" (238). Hence, jamming.

Jamming is the author's way of confessing and absolving himself and his instruments, of situating both on the right side of his complex linguistic regulations. Jamming also implies that if Agee cannot give us an unmediated Gudger, he can at least attempt to give us an unmediated Agee's doomed struggle to realize an unmediated Gudger. Jamming then inculcates habits of self-referral, shifting the balance of emphasis in literary transmission away from one ostensible subject toward another; here, from an objective story, to the author and the story of his authorship (thus, foreshadowing another literary tendency that contemporary practice has managed to fetishize to an extremity). In this declension, the "absolute, dry truth" (234) of a cinematized Gudger gives way to the "relative truth" of Agee's literary impressions of Gudger ("this truth emerges *only if* I am as faithful to Gudger as I know him . . . But of course it will only be a relative truth" [239, italics Agee's]).

But even here, the first law of language proves a jealous god, the logic of its commandment remorseless and implacable: if words *must fail*, then an unmediated Agee is no more possible than an unmediated "Gudger." Agee himself, "unchanged and undecorated," thus must also give way to another "Agee," the author impressed into patterns of verbal insistency, the words perforce mandating a transformed persona and vocalized self: in other words, the Jammer jammed. Agee of course never really investigated this logic to its bitter end, never seemed to dispute the necessity for some kind and degree of authorial charade, the problem of an unmediated "Gudger" obviously being anguish enough for one book. Nevertheless, his tough-minded approach to language, as well as his natural instincts as an artist, recurrently posed similar problems of aesthetics and literary epistemology that could hardly be ignored. In general, his quest for some bedrock of unassailable reality beyond language, yet glimpsed in and through language, kept running aground amid the subterfuges, metamorphoses, and self-sufficiencies of the words themselves; that is, wherever he turned he could not avoid the entanglements of the literary art, as well as that which went hand-in-glove with linguistic "autonomy": the inadvertent chicaneries of the literary artist.

Frequently, Agee seems harried to the point where all he can offer his reader is little more than the beached heroism of his good intentions set against the obvious "faking and artifacting" (245) of literary practices from which—in spite of all his much-heralded "antagonism to art" (245)—he could not refrain: "Though I may frequently try to make use of art devices and may, at other times, being at least in part an 'artist,' [he calls the other part 'scientist' although there was never less likely a candidate for this role than he] be incapable of avoiding their use, I am in this piece of work illimitably more interested in life than art" (242). After such direct and considerable admission in the subordinate, the well-known credo of the main clause—with its hallow inflation ("illimitably more"), pale pronominal ("interested in") and bromidic opposition ("life" against "art")—can only strike one as stillborn and anticlimactic. In any event, there was more than a modicum of bad faith in Agee's Actualist aesthetics, and he knew it: the problem wasn't simply a matter of outfoxing the ontology of language; there was also the ontology of the artist to consider. There was Agee himself and his much-resisted, highly fraught, but inalienable identity as a creator. Once again Agee found himself in a position where the most prominent and available candidate for excoriation resided in whatever proclivities he deemed most natural to his own conflicted sense of who he was. Try as he might, he could not prevent his high-minded interests and "life"-affirming ideals from smashing up against the wailing wall of an art everything in him could not help but make. This glaring discrepancy between intention and act, vision and construct, etc., leads to:

(2) *The argument forsworn;* or the most prevalent form of jamming in Agee's arsenal of self-referral. Since the artist and his language, in spite of every effort to the contrary, cannot help but secrete art and not "life," the conscientious Actualist learns to conceive of his efforts as creation by default, as "only" art, as art-for-the-want-of-something-better, as a battlefield of stopgap measures, tentative sketches, imperfect presentations, false starts, abrupt reversals, and disparaged attempts—gestures signaling the frustrated measures taken to achieve a perfection beyond mediation. In the light of such measures, Agee becomes a specialist in the rhetoric of the pulled punch and double-deal; of narration by disclaimer and apology; of art that denigrates its own auspices; of De Kooning–like preservations of slashings and erasures, discards and dry runs.

To these ends, we may consign all of those notorious and prodigious prefatory embarrassments, those very Ageean fawnings and scrapings, treadmillings of remorseful conscience, before whatever he deems to be "the way it was" (241). Here for instance, before beginning a rather brilliant description and analysis of cotton picking, he confesses the secondhand nature of his materials, his woeful lack of knowledge and understanding, and whatever use (a deep blush here) he may be forced to make of the creative faculty (just in case you thought that he thought he might be getting away with something).

> Of cotton farming I know almost nothing with my own eyes; the
> rest I have of Bud Woods. I asked enough of other people to realize

> that every tenant differs a little in his methods, so nothing of this
> can be set down as 'standard' or 'correct'; but the dissonances are of
> small detail rather than of the frame and series in the year. I respect
> dialects too deeply, when they are used by those who have a right
> to them, not to be hesitant in using them, but I have decided to use
> some of Woods' language here. I have decided, too, to try to use my
> imagination a little, as carefully as I can. I must warn you that the
> result is sure to be somewhat inaccurate: but it is accurate anyhow
> to my ignorance, which I would not wish to disguise. (328)

In brief, everything that should not be present in unmediated depiction—unexperienced experience, information by proxy, shameful surgings of the artist's afflatus—is present. Presumably, the way it really "was" can only be deduced, or better divined, from pedantic cross-checking to what is palpably not there. It hardly seems to matter at all that what follows proves to be a long, lyrical, hieratic, fairly magnificent evocation of the works and days of hands, of flora, soil, and human labor, using not just a "little" of the "imagination," but obviously a great deal. Recurrently, it is the "imagination" itself that seems to play the knave, forever running off with renderings that result in virtually the opposite of what is wanted, negative tracings of an incomparable positive; for example, the following introduction to a descriptive portrait of three tenants sitting on a porch: "They were of a kind not safely to be described in an account claiming to be unimaginative or trustworthy, for they had too much and too outlandish beauty not to be legendary. Since, however, they existed quite irrelevant to myth, it will be necessary to tell a little of them" (33). He then proceeds to tell of them in a dazzling, very metaphorical, highly "legendary," but also imaginative and therefore apparently not "trustworthy" manner, for the next four and a half pages. (Note too that a "beauty" which is "outlandish" and "legendary" somehow manages to affix itself to persons who are themselves "irrelevant to myth.")

Sometimes the dismissal arrives during the presentation itself, wrenching off the narrative with abrupt confessions of failed and failing powers, a receding object, a draining emotion, and an alienated tongue (the following in the midst of describing one of Gudger's rooms):

> But from where I say, 'The shutters are opened,' I must give this
> up and speak in some other way, for I am no longer able to speak

as I was doing, or rather no longer able to bear to. Things which
were then at least immediate in my senses, I now know only at some
great and untouchable distance; distinctly, yet coldly as through
reversed field-glasses, and with no warmth or traction or faith in
words: so that at best I can hope only to 'describe' what I would like
to 'describe,' as at a second remove, and even that poorly: . . . (403)

Occasionally, in an excess of weariness or self-disgust or both, he
hauls himself back from the entire goulash of fading aims and aesthetic
compromises and boils everything down to one humble and very trite
pie: "nothing that follows can pretend to be anything more advanced than
a series of careful but tentative, rudely experimental, and fragmentary
renderings of some of the salient aspects of a real experience seen and
remembered in its own terms" (245–46). At other times, in a similar
mood, he simply elects to sup at the plate of his own soured grapes: "all
I want to do is tell this as exactly and clearly as I can and get the damned
thing done with" (243).

I think that at least part of Agee's blanket-funk may have grown
out of the awareness not only that he could not do what he wanted
to do, but that what he was doing might also be appallingly similar to
what already had been done; that in breaking free of the "faking and
artifacting" of social realist fiction, he could only discover, in effect,
the "faking and artifacting" of social realist nonfiction. By the light of
his own incessant and vexed findings, no matter how "unimaginative or
trustworthy" his renderings, few if any could avoid the tantalizing stigma
of "legendary" or "imaginative" achievement, or even at their very best,
a vagrant temptation—so alluring, so pernicious—that perfect "illusion
of an embodiment"; that is, as far as he was concerned, the "poet's"
perfections of art camouflaging themselves as "nature's" perfections
of life.[9] And these two perfections were not only of a different kind
and order of excellence, but, for this writer, of radically different value
too: specifically, they underscored the unbridgeable difference between
the easy and spontaneous blossoms of a natural divinity or demiurgic
force, as against the premeditated constructs of a mortal and laboring
consciousness; in effect, the Ageean difference between the miraculous
and the made, epiphany and art, God and himself.

Was this then, in fact, the situation? If so, no one told him he had to like it. A prickly and unremitting sense of art's demoted status, generating in turn hostility and resistance to the burdens of artistic inevitability, result in:

(3) *Implosions of art;* or art agonized from within, and the argument mangled somewhere short of outright distortion. This is perhaps the most controversial of Agee's representative effects—surely the most extreme—in which we find deliberate spasms of outrageous or dis-combobulating writing, or, bluntly, what some might want to insist upon as "bad" writing. I say "deliberate" for the peculiar strain of such writing not only does not appear in Agee's other literary productions—as overwrought as some of this material can sometimes become (e.g., parts of *The Morning Watch*)—but also, more significantly, follows naturally from the reiterated stipulations of an uncodified but firmly articulated stance on language and reality. Actualism itself produces an aesthetic base to support calibrated cadenzas of self-indulgence, frenzied flights, and periodic bouts of overkill. Thus: in the name of the Ineffable, we sometimes watch Agee crank his American language beyond its own natural propensity for luxury, density, suppleness, and precision; be-yond that point where luxury declines into extravagance; where density congeals in glut; where suppleness ramifies in a crow's nest of blurrings and diffusions; where precision intensifies and peaks in vainglorious assumptions of the deracinated sublime, a uniquely Ageean and uncondi-tional overreaching—a suicide run to elucidate the Unutterable—which simultaneously seems to topple over upon itself and down the visionary chute into nebulous dither and cloudy vastation. Here, for instance, he describes the way in which the natural sounds of night dwarf the silences of the sleeping farmers:

> In their prodigious realm, their field, bashfully at first, less timorous, later, rashly, all calmly boldly now, like the tingling and standing up of plants, leaves, planted crops out of the earth into the yearly approach of the sun, the noises and natures of the dark had with ceremonial gestures of music and of erosion lifted forth the thousand several forms of their entrancement, and had so resonantly taken over the world that this domestic, this human silence obtained, prevailed, only locally, shallowly, and with the

childlike and frugal dignity of a coal-oil lamp stood out on a wide
night meadow and of a star sustained, unraveling in one rivery sigh
its irremediable vitality, on the alien size of space. (20)

One may of course grumble at some length over such a passage. I think
grumbling, however, in this instance—as in similar instances throughout
this book—to be somewhat beside the point: that is, I don't think it
a matter of *primary* significance (which is not to say that it doesn't
matter at all) to ask, for example, what exactly are those "noises and
natures of the dark" doing when they lift "forth the thousand several
forms of their entrancement"? (And why "entrancement" anyway?) Or
to wonder whether a phrase like "unraveling in one rivery sigh its
irremediable vitality" doesn't exist more for its alliterative roll than
its intelligible substance? (Is it not, after all, something like the sound
emitted by someone tossing in his sleep?) Or whether the fastidious ear
might not want to reject that "irremediable vitality" after all as so much
prefabricated building material? Or whether the whole passage, with its
mule-drawn overload of flummery, gout, and supersubtility, is not way
in excess of what is being stated? (But of course nothing is being "stated":
rather a nocturnal experience is evoked, a contrast between cosmic and
human postures.)

As you can readily see, I'm of two (or more) minds on this issue. "Bad"
writing? Maybe: but also maybe on a more exalted level of concept and
nuance than most conventional "good" writing. "Bad" writing? Perhaps:
but also principled, the logical outgrowth of the laws of language upon
which the author has reared the entire aesthetic framework of his book.
While such implosions of the semichoate may be greeted with vestigial
befuddlement or even distant disapproval, they are more accurately
perceived as this artist's most desperate efforts to break free of himself
in a seizure of words, to scuttle his art, his artist's identity, the coils
of language itself, and dissolve into the quick of his home in things,
his blazing enclave in "life." Of course, trying to use language to flee
language is a little like trying to execute a jailbreak by enumerating the
bars of one's cage. In both cases, the effort itself becomes the means
by which the topography of constraint only emerges into sharper, more
savage, relief. And Agee's moments of wrenched transcendence often

function best (i.e., most practically), in spite of their liberational intent, as instances of neither traditional art nor most certainly "life," but rather as relatively successful aural approximations of that raw indeterminacy from which both art and "life" may be said to evolve. In any event, they are not to be rejected out of hand, or, for that matter, at all: rather, they are to be experienced and felt in context as the dissonant climaxes of a histrionic point-counterpoint, an intellectual agon, that compelled their author from one end of his book to the other.

Jamming, foreswearing, imploding: strange gods. Perhaps we are wisest finally to think about this work apart from the more conventional categories of "fiction" and "nonfiction" altogether; to understand that in shunning the "novel" and assaying the "documentary," Agee arrived at his own original vanguardist form significantly related to both yet demonstrably different from either. This is the form evolved out of art's struggle against itself, out of modern form's impulse to ravage its own processes even as it advances and acquiesces to their inexorability. We would also do well to think about this work as not only the most finished expression of a whole decade of American social realist achievement— which it most certainly is—but also as the most penetrating critique of this effort ever made, a virtual anatomy of its serious hobblements and evasions. Let us at least put aside that wheezy and by now knee-jerk notion (partly promoted by the author himself) that finds the freshness and originality of this book to reside in its fidelity to, and evocation of, "real people," "real life," "the way it was," "the holiness of human reality," and what not. Such a book is neither fresh nor original, and of course Agee did not exactly write such a book.

Such a book—the book of "life," of anti-art, the book which denies all books—is really an ancient and venerable American song first heard at least as far back as Whitman's *Leaves of Grass* (not a "poem," we are told, but "the origin of all poems"), and ringing just as clear, if somewhat more boisterously, as recently as Henry Miller's singspiel, *Tropic of Cancer* (also, "not a book," but "a prolonged insult, a gob of spit, a kick in the pants," etc.); and perhaps even more recently, and darkly, in William Burrough's *Naked Lunch* (no book either, but "Revelation and Prophecy of what I can pick up without F.M. on my 1920 crystal set with antennae of jissom").[10] Past or present, these are some of the proclamations that have become part of the American writer's declaration of independence, not only from the confines of the book he is writing, but more importantly from the confines of that Old World historical matrix of all books and book-making out of which his book perforce must emerge; from all the genteelisms, artifices, and constrictions of what more than two thousand years of a moribund Indo-European art and literature have produced, the culture of palsied kings and dying continents. This is the American artist's unwanted heritage, permanently supplanted by a shining new dispensation: habitation in a precultural Garden of Eden, the reign of innocence reborn, and the god-intoxicated fire of bards, prophets, and oracles forever replacing the secular ministrations of scribblers, rhymers, and book-makers.

Agee, too, writes out of many of the premises of such a robust and sanctified tradition; and in *Famous Men,* even carries along with these premises much the same formal-technical baggage of his predecessors and successors. This includes all those "neo-primitive" devices to signify in print archaic levels of preliterate consciousness, a sophisticate's calcu-lated assumption of the unsophisticated (i.e., the faux-naif): specifically, inventories, catalogues, prayers, chants (cf., *Leaves of Grass*); torrents of raw fact and unprocessed data, of non- or extraliterary materials, such as photos and newspaper clippings (cf., the invoices and cost-accounting in *Walden,* the maps, charts, and drawings in *Moby Dick*); quantities of the vulgar and the obscene, the squirmingly intimate, of the confessional, the prophetic, and the apocalyptic (cf., *Tropic of Cancer, Naked Lunch*); ritual raillery against art and tradition, protestation that one isn't merely writing a novel, a poem, or a work of art, but is writing what invariably gets left out of such work; that one finally isn't writing at all. "If I could do it," says Agee in his "Preface," "I'd do no writing at all here. It would be photographs; the rest would be fragments of cloth, bits of cotton, lumps of earth, records of speech, pieces of wood and iron, phials of odors, plates of food and of excrement" (13).

At any point in *Famous Men,* Agee is perfectly capable of sounding like all our other classic American warblers. But with one enormous and definitive difference: his *unhappy recognition that he cannot write such a nonbook book,* that no one can legitimately write such a book, and further, that everyone of his anti-art, "life"-embracing gestures has

been permanently short-circuited by this recognition: by his dramatized despair, doubt, and confusion; by his reiterated disapprobation of
himself, his medium, and his audience; by, above all, his towering self-
consciousness of all of this, the vigilant heart of his contemporaneity
that forbade him entry into the visionary fellowship of his confident and
optimistic predecessors (such as Whitman and Thoreau), and even those
headlong moderns (such as Miller) who were conspicuously without this
self-consciousness.

It was this same self-consciousness that insisted upon a continual
reexamination and redefinition of the kind of book he was attempting to
make. On page 15, for example, we find him shouldering the traditional
American standard: "Above all else: in God's name don't think of it
as art." By page 245, however, he has already learned to view such
experimentation in quieter tones of desperation, "call it art if you must."
On page 319, the end in view, he utters what may be the soberest
assessment of what he has tried to do, and precisely what he has actually
done: "Let this all stand however it may: *since I cannot make it the image
it should be, let it stand as the image it is;* I am speaking of my verbal
part of this book as a whole" (italics mine). And what, in conclusion,
is "the image it is"? *Let Us Now Praise Famous Men* is a creation of
modernist art, critical and self-referential; a dreamlike meditation upon
a failed embodiment; a rhapsody of chastened and penitential mimesis
that strives toward, and fails, as Actuality (or, for that matter, actuality),
just as it abjures, yet succeeds, as art and artifact.

2. TWO REVERIES

"This is a *book* only by necessity" (xvi), the author initially cries in a
characteristic excess of aspirational energy. In the end, however, the truth
proves otherwise: by necessity this is only a *book.*

But to consider *Famous Men* as a species of literary art in no way
enjoins anyone on this side of the page to enroll in the current critical
fashion that finds it necessary to attribute the term "fiction," or for that
matter "novel," to everything from a memoir to a laundry list, thus adding
further slack to categories that were already drifting promiscuously in

their infancy. To focus a palpable vein of fiction in a work of seeming fact doesn't automatically brand it "fiction"; and if "novel" means anything distinct and exact at all, it should never affix itself to construction as anomalous in treatment and material as Agee's maverick achievement.

Famous Men obviously recoils from the consecutive dramatized action and continuous figural presence of traditional fiction, or perhaps fiction of any kind. On the other hand, as an imaginative creation based on actual occurrence, it does present a consistent heightening of character and event, an elevation of fact to level of rapture and intensity, an angry, feverish, metaphorical, and metaphysical habit of, and sense of, being— in short, an entrenching of its subject in a visionary way that should indeed put one in mind of great romantic poetry, and great visionary novels too. So while it is a mistake to speak of this book as a member of that famous family of Depression yarning that would include, say, *U.S.A.* (1936) and *The Grapes of Wrath* (1939), I find it equally fruitless to lump it with those roughly contemporaneous "nonfictions"—sociology cum craft, sensibility, and nicety of scruple—where the kinship is at least superficially more overt: works such as George Orwell's *The Road to Wigan Pier* (1937), Caldwell and Bourke-White's *You Have Seen Their Faces* (1937), or the George Rouquier film *Farrebique* (1941, much admired by Agee).

Neither novel, polemic, nor documentary (though readily mistaken for the latter two), *Famous Men,* fifty years after its inception, continues to affirm its earned and honorable status as a modern American wild card, a flowering of eccentric, hybridic, and all but nongeneric art, perhaps best savored as a compote of literary categories—part epic, confession, and anatomy, but none of these exclusively. Still, to reiterate it: most unambiguously *art.* This means, foremost, that Agee has found formal shape for his feeling, a pattern of expression for his findings and observations; that he has, quite simply, a tale to tell, not just an occasion for reportage or a cause, but a story with a structure, a beginning, a middle, and an end. As in many stories, this structure embodies character and theme, and these unfold and resolve themselves as the structure unfolds and resolves itself. Again, as in many stories (particularly those of a fictional nature), this process of unfolding and resolving entails conflict, growth, and transformation. The structure, however, is roomy, lax, and porous; beginning, middle, and end do not necessarily occur in that order; character reduces itself finally to one fully developed figure, the line of whose adventure threads hesitantly amid the author's many preoccupations; theme glows bright and dim, flickering in a desultory manner throughout the storm of the book's waywardness. But to speak of this work as an artistic entity is finally, and only, "to make clear," as Agee himself reminds us, "some essential coherence in [this book] which I know is there, balanced of its chaos" (319).

Of what does this "coherence" consist? What is the nature of Agee's story? Up to now we have been talking in the main about the artist and his book; now I want to turn to the man and his quest. Actually, inflecting the terms of the discussion does little to change the gist of the subject itself: in either case—whether we talk of aesthetics or autobiography, language or psychology, word or wish—we still confront an image of embattled Platonism, of riven motive and precarious ideals, the narrative that emerges out of the tension between dream and flesh, what this author wants or can imagine as against what he must learn to accept.

Why then has Agee really come to Alabama? Why was this project, as Fitzgerald put it, "going to electrify a part of his nature that had not yet been given an opportunity for full expression or full employment"? I think it will become clear that his ostensible quest, the initially stated "business," of the "Preface"—that is, "to prepare, for a New York magazine, an article on cotton tenantry in the United States" (xiii)—is somewhat different from his actual quest, his true "business" down all these country roads.

The real aspiration of *Famous Men* surfaces in "Inductions"—one of the final sections, and arguably the most powerful, moving, and intimate of all the straight narrative sequences—and not only appears to have little to do with "cotton tenantry," but even seems partly remote from the somewhat canned and derivative effluvia of Agee's "human divinity" (xiv) proclamations; that is, these aspirations are in every way more personal, specific, and fugitive, though no less apocalyptic, than the originally stated goals of the "Preface." They take the form of two dreams that present themselves to the author as he nears the climax of his long solo car journey from Birmingham to Gudger in what turns out to be his first night under the roof of the house that will form the emotional and symbolic center of the entire Alabama experience, as well as the structural center of the book emerging from it.

The journey itself has been for the most part hellish, with Agee half-mad with heat, lust, and loneliness, and half-suicidal with memories of his "poor . . . bitched family" (384). (His father's motor accident seems to be the obvious point of referral for the episode, its unsummoned but presiding ghost.) But his spirits begin to lift as he gets closer to his destination, and here the transition from doom and despair to hope and possibility is skillfully managed in a quasi-symbolic sequence where Agee first loses his bearings, then finds them again as he comes upon another family of farmers, Fred Ricketts and children, who greet him warmly and show him the correct way to Gudger.

Full of these new encouragements, and with Fred Ricketts beside him in the car, Agee now reflects back upon "all this city-business," his "alien" life in the metropolis (i.e., the passage seems to merge Birmingham with New York City), and particularly upon the difficulties he's had in writing "the piece of work you would give all your blood to do"; and how this work has brought him nothing except a "terrible frustration" (389). But now this "frustration" has "drawn me along these roads and to this place scarce knowing why I came, to the heart and heart's blood of my business and my need" (389). The two reveries follow immediately, and obviously represent not just the concrete embodiments of what has been desired by "heart" and "blood," the fulfillment of his "business" and his "need," but the answer to his "terrible frustration," his solution to the problems raised by "the piece of work you would give all your blood to do," as if "some inconceivable thirst and blaze of aridity . . . had been satisfied twice over, twice differently, with the first not in the least detracting from the second; two 'dreams,' come true" (390).

The first vision begins in shared fantasy as Agee and a dream lover, an adolescent sweetheart, extrapolate from the images inspired by the lyric "tramp, tramp, tramp, the boys are marching, cheer up comrades they will come" (390). The lover imagines soldiers in the First World War, "imprisoned" far from home, listening to the tune as played by a marching band. Agee himself, aided by memories of photographs of the Andersonville prison, launches into a long, perfervid, D. W. Griffithian rescue fantasy of the "last war in which there was much nobility, the Civil

War" (390); of "our grandparents" (390); of the "men of the south" (391); of the "captives" and "guards" in the Andersonville prison, Georgia; and of the arrival of a small party of soldiers, a "brave string" cutting through the opposing armies and advancing "to the rescue" of the prisoners:

> earnest and gallant, bugles blithing, the bravery of whose feet is known advancing, a hundred, a thousand miles, oh, kind, brave, resolute, oh, some day, some time, dangers braved, all armies cut through, past, to the rescue: cheer up; comrades: they will come: and beneath the starry flag we shall see our homes again, *and* the loved ones we left so far away: so far away: whom also I know, my soldiers, and their homes, those delicate frames, white in the white light snow . . ." (391)

As he identifies his own interests with the words of the song, Agee returns all captives to their families and imagines wives, sweethearts, and children all awaiting the return of the soldiers, and even Lincoln, that "mistaken Christ," welcoming them home "as if they had never been away" (391).[11]

Agee then specifically relates this "apparent digression" to the tenant families: "you of whom I write are added to the meaning of this song, and its meaning to yours" (391); thus not only integrating his Civil War reverie with the present moment but finally beyond it, to an apocalyptic future and a new day, as he envisions each of the farmers "encamped, imprisoned" in his "little unowned ship of home" patiently awaiting his deliverance in the "marching and resonance of rescuing feet" that will finally bring "freedom, joy, health, knowledge like an enduring sunlight" (392). He expands the band of farmers to include all the victims of the Depression ("ten million") and conflates even this to embrace "us all, those lovable and those hateful all alike" (392): brothers in bondage everywhere, hungry for release. He assures them "all" that rescue will come "at length," though he does not know how or from where, because of—and here he speaks specifically to the tenant families—that "regard of love we bear one another: for there it was proved me in the meeting of the extremes of the race" (392).

The second vision satisfies the "same thirst" as the first, but manages to be "quite different . . . so silent, and so secret, as the other was wild" (392). Agee imagines himself deep in the woods "beside a spring," leaning toward the surface of the water "as upon a woman, to take her mouth," and peering into the depths

> I see, submerged, stones, the baroque roots of a tree, fine dust of leaves, gray leaves, so delicate, laid and laid among this dust a quilt, the feathering of a bird, whose plumage I cherish nor shall in my drinking disturb: and standing from the heart, a twindling, slender, upward spine (it is a column of gnats at evening, the column of the stars of all universes), that little stream of sand upon whose stalk this clean wide flower has spread herself . . . (393)

He then allows himself to be transported from woodland "spring" to his grandfather's "springhouse," where he appears

> straddling a capacious spring, a place such as that which was at my grandfather's farm, with the odor of shut darkness, cold, wet wood, the delighting smell of butter; and standing in this spring, the crocks, brimmed with unsalted butter and with cream and milk; the place is shut behind me, but slit through with daylight, but the lighting comes as from a submerged lamp, that is, from the floor of the spring of which half is beyond shelter of the house: and here on this floor, too, I see these leaves, drifted and deep like snow, and driven, even beneath the house: and between two sweating stones, sitting there, watching me, shining with wet in the dark, with broad affronted eyes, the face and shoulders and great dim belly of a black and jade and golden bullfrog, big as a catcher's mitt, his silver larynx twitching constantly with scarcely controllable outrage. (393)

It is, he tells us, a vision of a "joy" that is "human" (393).

One can readily see from the foregoing that what began as one kind of study, that of the farmer and his plight, has become another, that of the farmer and his pivotal "meeting" with a seeming stranger from a far-off place who insists he is no stranger at all, but actually an eccentric version of a native son, an exile returned seeking the parental nest.[12] And this is simply another way of saying that while Agee obviously began by intending to write about the farmer, and perhaps the farmer alone, he ended by writing as much about himself; or more precisely about the nature of his relation, and relatedness, to the farmer; how they came together, the discoveries each made of the other, and the meaning of what happened to them in the brief time they lived together.

Agee has come south to relieve a "terrible frustration" and write the book that he could not write up north; not a book primarily about an "undefended and appallingly damaged group of human beings" (7), but, if we honor the thrust of the reveries, a book about how a troubled artist, arid and thirsty, a former southerner and a blocked writer, went home and found both his subject and his artistic liberation in a search for—in the evocation, exploration, and assessment of—his ancestral roots, the landscape of a lost past. Agee's story, then, revolves about a foraging for personal sources in the widest sense, familial, environmental, ethnographical, historical, mystagogical. The farmer and his world are, as avatars of these sources, the visible embodiments of their presence and continuing vitality, central to this search, central not only for themselves but also as a means of evoking purposes even grander and every bit as tragic as their own immediate and wretchedly pressing conditions. For Agee, the farmer represents the spiritual descendants of a deposed and dispossessed "nobility," the living remnants now in ruins of the old and authentic South, of the men of his grandfather's generation, of all those heroic, family-loving, exiled warriors and those patient, waiting, long-suffering children, wives, and sweethearts. The first reverie specifically relates the situation of the Civil War captives to the situation of the farmer ("its meaning is yours," etc.) just as it also relates this same situation to Agee's situation (the reverie is of "our grandfathers" and "the loved ones we left so far away . . . whom also I know," etc.). Thus in the passionate and willful logic of the dreamer, Agee and the farmer aspire toward spiritual kinship, sharers in a common history, and, by extension, a common grief and cause.

The establishment of kinship is vital to the execution of the author's mission; it is vital to insist that in his "meeting" with the farmer he is not offering himself up to the embrace of strangers, but of family surrogates, that turning the lock on childhood memory depends first on gaining entry—and acceptance—at the door of the family that will welcome him as one of its own. Thus the dream-vision strains toward an assertion of filiation even in the face of numerous prickly and unsettling factual sticking points. It hardly seems to bother Agee that, for instance, the concrete analogies between himself and the farmer will barely tolerate any kind of hard-headed scrutiny; that while, say, the farmer may be considered a "captive" (to his economic situation), he can hardly be considered an "exile" (either from home or family); and that while Agee may properly be considered an "exile" (from his roots), he cannot be considered in any practical sense a "captive" to anyone (save himself). Nor does it give pause to the dreamer to consider that Alabama is not Tennessee; or that Agee himself is not a farmer nor even the son of farmers (technically, he is the son of the son of farmers); or that the modest but comfortable suburbs of Knoxville may be in no way comparable to the impoverished farms of Hale County; or that Agee's family embroilments and disarray may not be at all the proper counterparts of the farmer's fallen estate; or that his loneliness may involve desperations of a very different order from that of physical starvation and financial ruin. All such discrepancies give way in the intense rush of the dreamer's commanding needs: both the farmer and Agee, the vision seems to proclaim, are (in a manner of speaking) "men of the south," and, such is Agee's desire and his faith, these "men" will recognize and signal to each other across seemingly insuperable barriers. How else to explain "the meeting of the extremes of the race," and the flush of affection that springs up between ostensible strangers? For Agee, this single emotional fact, the "regard of love we bear one another," obviously clinches the regional affinities and presumably conciliates all social, historical, and emotional presumptuousness.

The need to consolidate propinquity between himself and the farmer is also sufficiently urgent for Agee to imagine not only that their backgrounds and problems might be similar but also that their hopes and dreams might be congruent as well, that the form of salvation envisioned for himself need not be so different from that proposed for his spiritual kin. Thus, while the first reverie seems to pertain explicitly to the farmer and the second explicitly to himself, and while Agee tells us that one reverie was "quite different" from the other, one can observe that in structure and purport the reveries have much in common, that similar wish-fulfillment motifs weave through each of them. I think this is true in spite of the fact that the historicized and messianic utterance of the Civil War fantasy, and the following apostrophe to the farmer, is indeed palpably dissonant to the particularized sensuousness of the spring vision and that of the grandfather's farm; the first is as vague, musical, panoramically populated, and publicized as the second is exact, pictorial, and privately whimsical. Nevertheless, both reveries brim over with grand archetypal gestures of homing and family bonding; both take place in shadows of ancestral memories, as the generalized temporal setting of the first, the world of "our grandparents," is spatialized and specified in the "grandfather's farm" of the second; both envision freedom and happiness, for either captives or exiles, through contact with forces larger and more potent than the isolated self, as the "rescue" mission of the first is complimented by the regenerative kiss to the "mouth" of the woodland spring of the second; and most significantly, both dreams anticipate completion, satisfaction, and fulfillment through union with an enveloping family protectorate, the farmer with fellow sufferers everywhere (i.e., the "family" of man), Agee with the environment of the parental roost. The prevailing remedy in fact offered by both phases of the dream-vision, for the ills of *all* participants, is in each instance essentially the same: that is, an assertion of solidarity, a fusion, however fleeting, of disparate but inextricably affiliated parties; soldiers with loved ones, farmers with brothers in bondage, racial extremity with racial extremity, native son with native soil, Agee the man with Agee the child.

All well and good: but not quite. Even within its own highly idealized terms, the vision is strafed with what seems to be at least partly intentional confusions, ambiguities, and near distortions (particularly in the first reverie) that in turn may signal hesitancies and uncertainties in the imagination of the dreamer. In other words, the aspirations and commitments entailed by the dream may not be as straightforward and uninflected as they initially appear (or as I have made them out to be), and the story Agee wishes to tell may also be more perplexing and idiosyncratic than initially indicated. A brief examination of the specific details of the dream will help to clarify these issues, and perhaps also help to resolve some of them.

Accordingly, the first reverie is, along with all its heartfelt sincerity, also obscure, hectic, and overly strenuous, bathed in that kind of verbal delirium that Agee's writing frequently attains whenever he strains to yank the dogged despair of the present moment in line with his lofty hopes for the future; and especially wrenched here when he attempts to will redemption for the farmer in the face of every ugly indication to the contrary. Still, the indeterminate atmosphere may at least in this instance fulfill a necessary function, as the ambiguity of detail allows the dreamer room to stretch his personal indecisiveness into the furthest corners of reverie. Consider, for instance, the way in which Agee refuses to specify the political affiliations of the Civil War captives. While the general movement of the sequence seems to imply that these soldiers were on the southern side (e.g., analogies stressed between the captives and the southern farmer, the return of the captives graced by reference to Lincoln's legendary generosity to the defeated Confederates, "we shall treat them as if they had never been away," etc.), Agee must surely know, along with every schoolboy, that the inmates at the Andersonville prison were not "men of the south," but Union men. And Agee's dream captives are also presumably Union men, but I find it curious that he isn't insisting that they are and even insinuates that they may be something else.[13] So too does he become excessively bashful in tagging the allegiances (political, geographical) of the "rescue" party itself, "that brave string" which seems to slip in from the "north" (of Andersonville?), yet strangely also down from "a southern continent of clay" (391); and in the following paragraph, invoking another rescue party (this one for the farmer), fine-tuning a cryptogam to himself, he doubts whether this rescue "shall descend upon us over the steep north crown" (392).

It begins to emerge that Agee has left all northern and southern ties and demarcations, all references to who rescues whom, sufficiently blurry to encourage an atmosphere of entry for his own special doubt, doubleness, and general crisis of identity. It is of course Agee himself who is both a citizen of the "north" by residence, profession, and accusations of conscience (and so labeled, he fears, by many a wary Alabamian), as well as a son of the "south" by birth, breeding, and above all emotional need (i.e., "heart's need"). It is also Agee who is forever torn between a sense of himself as both rescuer and rescued, the text presenting him as sometimes one, sometimes the other, often both. As the Yankee writer who would explain the conditions of the southern farmer to the world, he is, against all guilt, hesitancy, and self-disgust, the officially designated rescuer. But as a spiritual orphan of the "south," bewildered and frustrated, Agee is also a victim of the cities, a man cut off from his emotional roots, the urban writer who cannot do the "piece of work" he would give his "blood" to do—that writer has stumbled down country roads himself in need of "rescue."

Finally and perhaps most revealing, I also find it curious that the first reverie presents a rescue fantasy in which the actual moment of rescue may be the most equivocal event in a passage already rife with equivocation; in fact, such a moment never occurs. We hear of the captive soldiers before and after their liberation, but never during; just as the deliverance of the farmer is prophesized but never realized. Instead, the "rescue" anticipated, but unaccomplished, as an apocalypse in the future is concretely envisioned and enacted in the second dream as a fantasy of times gone by. If the first reverie must be judged a modified botch, the second seems to be an unqualified success—objects bursting free from the cracked casings of their verbal skins—as an equivocal myth of history is replaced by an unequivocal myth of the self; as a nickelodeon melodrama of slippery fact, coy radicalism, and dubious conviction fades away before a personal holograph of unalloyed faith in primitive magic, nature's resourcefulness, and a child's allegiance to the powers of the talismanic sign. The prodigal son returns to his parental sources, linking up first with his maternal origins (i.e., "prostrating" himself upon the edge of the spring "as upon a woman"), then with his paternal ones (i.e., the return to grandfather's farm, the presiding bullfrog, etc.); first rescued, then rescuer, rocked in the arms of both his makers.

Like Antaeus, ancient prototype of all wanderers resuscitated in dirt, the dreamer goes to the forest to renew his energies, virtually kiss the earth, as he leans to the spring and sees in the water a floating image of creation (and by extension, a symbol of creativity itself), a giant flower-form, a new organic synthesis compacted of old droppings, natural sediments and debris (roots, leaves, dust, etc.), a drifting embryo in its amniotic bath rising upon its umbilicus of sand (i.e., "a twindling, slender, upward spine . . . a column"): a figure of rebirth, perhaps even of the dreamer himself and his regeneration in the belly of the mothering earth. It is here too we realize that the only "meetings," mergers, and conversions that finally matter to Agee as creator are the ones, as it were, with some personal blood in them, the ones prompted not by any social or political formulation, but by "heart's need"; not the universal bundlings of oppressed masses, but those emotional couplings rooted in sensual consciousness and possessed of the unreasoning authority of blind, bodily urges: the awakening in the wood, the mouth to the spring, the vision of the embryonic blossomer, and the sensate equivalent of the poet's cry, "Drink and be whole again beyond confusion." (The cry here belongs to another poet, Robert Frost).[14]

As childhood follows upon creation, as there is high magic in low puns,[15] nature's "spring" evolves into grandfather's "springhouse." And here the four basic components of the Civil War fantasy—prison, guards, captives, and rescue party—are tilted and transformed into a private flight of domestic adventure, the sojourner's entry into the paternal home likened to the hero come upon the buried treasure in the pirate's cave. The prison house becomes the springhouse, dark but angled with light, the dramatic chiaroscuro reminiscent of an old N. C. Wyeth illustration in a children's classic (e.g., *Treasure Island*); the captives themselves transformed into the insignia of the family table and the glowing hearth, a luminous hoard of nutrients and natural energy (the crocks brimming with butter, cream, and milk, the whole floor beaming from below as from "a submerged lamp"); the stolid threat of the guards wittily enchanted into the nonthreatening, comical outrage of the opulent, elegant, yet curiously reassuring bullfrog ("as big as a catcher's mitt" and as familiar too, a glove designed not merely to field a ball, but to *secure* it) sitting watch over his luscious trove; and finally confronting the guard in no uncertain terms (i.e. "straddling" the boards), the intruder from the woodland spring, the dreamer himself, empowered by the regenerative kiss, emboldened by the very act of reunion, the rescuer rescued. It is indeed a dream "come true."

The charm and vividness of the second reverie should perhaps also convince us, if nothing else does, that all persuasive "rescue" sequences in Agee's work are retroactive, that finally one only makes advances by going backward. The apostrophe to the farmer in the first reverie is necessarily muzzy and hollow for it sets all the occupants of the dream (Agee, farmer, victims everywhere) marching in a progressive, unidirectional, historical lock-step climaxing in some universal future deliverance that the dreamer obviously desires, but apparently cannot envision. To do so would require a mastery of the self and conviction of faith—in the environment, in history—that the dreamer does not, and perhaps never would, possess. The vision of the spring, then, follows rather than precedes the vision of deliverance—that is, the "past" comes *after* rather than before the "future"—because Agee could not imagine the final answer to any "terrible" form of adult "frustration" as anything other than a return to origins. The moment of liberation and apocalypse that precedes the return to childhood is false and equivocal, for childhood itself is liberation and apocalypse, the end within the beginning that resolves all dialectical furor into rugged harmony. As against the enlightened socialist's rational appeal to the linearity of historical advancement, a vision of origins embraces the primitive's appeal to laws of cyclic patterns, to a fatality of permanent recurrences—of days and weeks, of sun and moon, of soil and weather, of growing things and the round of seasons— to powerful subrational forces in nature, and most important for this author, to a dialectics of the youthful heart, the never-ending emotional storms and to-and-fro oppositions that rule the drumroll of childhood: hunger and satiation, abandonment and reunion, captivity and rescue, exile and return.

The order of movement from the first reverie to the second thus indicates a movement backward in time culminating in the discovery of a glowing treasure buried deep (i.e., under the "boards") in childhood. And this movement, in turn, replicates in miniature the order and sequence of the book's great, overall structure as a time-tale told in reverse, and explains finally why Agee's first night at Gudger's house, among the earliest of the Alabama events, appears almost at the end of the narrative in a position of climactic significance (i.e., "Inductions"): this moment of course is the moment of reunion and rebirth, the point of contact between the prodigal child and his "treasure," his welcome at the home of his surrogate family. It is a moment that redefines all the events preceding it, indeed much the bulk of the entire narrative movement, from the early "Country Letter" (in which we find Agee already living with Gudger for some time) to the penultimate "Inductions" (in which Agee first arrives at Gudger's), as a journey back through time concertized as a journey through space. The main narrative then entails a centrifugal walkabout through a stranger's landscape, yet one resonant with common ancestral memory; another's field of vision, yet crowded with private emotion, thick with the ache of the irretrievable, poignant with legend, epiphanic revelation, sacred echoes of an earlier, better day; another's tarnished holdings in time present treated virtually as the findings in an archaeological dig, the all but discarded relics of an ancient ruin—empty structures, silent rooms, tools, implements, decorations, furnishings in arrestment (i.e., as if discovered in varying conditions of abandonment). All of this achieves its full emergence and final clarification in Agee's first night under Gudger's roof, his entry into a circle of impoverished innocence, hosted at the family table and ushered to bed, the ending of the temporal journey in its beginnings and the first stirrings of specific childhood memories. And shortly after this (and retroactively throughout the entire book): the young poet at night on the "home" porch, as if guardian of, however ambivalent, and heir apparent to, however temporary and anxious, the family "treasure" (i.e., the sleeping family itself), its preciousness and fragility, taking his soundings in the southern dark and making his book: precisely the story of how he came to occupy this position (literally his "home" base), and found his power as a maker, as well as the subject of his making.

Before taking leave of these reveries, there remains only the necessity of reminding the reader that while the aspirations behind the dreams may account for much of what happens in this book, the book itself never manages to realize at any point the full and obvious burden of desire contained in the dreams. It hardly needs to be stressed that the Alabama sojourn does not in any way liberate the farmer from his miserable condition, nor also, contrary to the reveries, is the author restored to his actual home, not to mention, of course, the actual environment of his childhood. Each dream is presented in such a manner—"extravagant" and fantastical—that total realization is never meant to be at issue. It is, however, worth remembering that, here and elsewhere throughout *Famous Men*, the wishes of the artist often take the expressed form of "wild" dreams, miracles, and grand-scale conversions that the actual experience of the artist repudiates; and that Agee will insist upon the full indulgence of both the feverish surge of his soaring ideals, as well as the luxuriant despair of their inevitable unfulfillment.

But as is always the case with this writer, the "extravagance" of his hopes, along with the enormity of his defeats, invariably pave the way for his modest, human-sized, but eminently discernible victories. The reveries experienced on the road to Gudger not only indicate what doesn't and perhaps never could take place, but, as already suggested, what in fact does: contact is made, "extremities" do meet, however briefly. As in the first dream, there is recognition between participants; a sharing of friendship, affection, and understanding; and an exchange of hopes and an offering of prayers for a brighter future. As in the second dream, an isolated figure does return to a family home, not his own but a facsimile sufficient to put him in mind of what was lost in the original. Moreover, this figure does begin to refine and complicate the shape of his creative identity, and, most important of all, emerges from his experience to produce a creation itself. One must recall that the context for both reveries revolves about the "terrible frustration" of a blocked writer, and that the reveries themselves are the immediate responses to this "frustration": that Agee's need to go home and "rescue" the past is fully coextensive with his need to write a book (and in this instance actually coterminous with his writing of it); that the most significant result of Agee's "meeting" with the farmer is that everything that happened between them has been turned into writing, that a book has been written. This book is the primary demonstration of, and testimonial to, the fact that "extremities" have come together; that an emotion was shared; that such emotion puts one in contact with an even more evanescent, yet suasive and enveloping, emotion lost in childhood; that this enveloping emotion both releases and validates the "spring" of creativity, those very "human" joys, the glowing securities, integral passions, and nurturing confidences—the conditions and potencies necessary to creation itself. The resulting book is certainly not the book that Agee wanted to write: that book is also one of unfulfilled ideals of this book, an impossible book, the spontaneous ejaculation of a demiurge, a self-effacing spillage of unmediated objectivity, a book fully congruent with all the dreams, miracles, and conversions that do not take place; that book would doubtless have concerned the farmer alone. But when one allows for the man that he was, it is perhaps the only book Agee could write: a book in default of miracles, the only and ultimate "rescue" available to both the farmer *and* himself.

3. THE TRUE TASTES OF HOME

I have spoken of *Famous Men* as a self-reflexive work, the tale of its own making, the making of self-referential art. Now I want to amplify this point by stressing what has already emerged in our discussion of Agee's reveries: that *Famous Men* is also the tale of its maker, the making of a self-reflexive artist, of how this artist comes into possession of himself. If this is indeed a book with only one fully developed character, then this artist is that character, and the story of his development needs to be delineated in some detail. It is this development that gathers the diverse sections of this work into a relatively coherent whole, and constitutes the major happening in this tale as Agee has written it (some might conceivably argue it is the only happening).

I have also spoken of this work in general as "eccentric" and wayward, but I would now add that this part of it, the tale of its maker, is neither one nor the other. It is, on the contrary, familiar and traditional, in essence, if we trust our authorities, one of the tales central to the annals of literary effort: "This was real life, meaningful experience, the actual goal of all quests, this was what art aimed at—homecoming, return to one's family, to oneself, to true existence."[16] This of course is not James Agee, but Russian poet and novelist Boris Pasternak (in the Hayward and Harari translation of *Dr. Zhivago*). And while his remarks may strike some of us as *too* familiar, too traditional, and perhaps redolent of humanist theatrical greasepaint—that is, overdrawn (*all* "quests"?) and demonstrably hoked-up (surely "art" may have more than one aim, etc.)—we also want to remember that ardent part-truths such as these still have the power to clutch the heart even in the act of offending the intellect, and even to the extent of inspiring such phrases as "clutch the heart"; that they gain their authority not through rational inquiry, but rather through the whole history of the moral bias of the tribe, which has long since inscribed imperatives like these among its articles of faith. Still, whether or not we care to accept the sweeping tenor of each one of Pasternak's assertions, perhaps we can at least agree that they aptly describe the caliber of story that Agee has told here, and provide as well a swift summation of the way in which this book finally coordinates its farraginous interests, technical fireworks, and numerous side-winding maneuvers. At any rate, I trust they help us to appreciate this aspect of *Famous Men*—a book that in other aspects we also justifiably appreciate as perplexing, uncategorizable, and postmodern—to be as equable as warm bedding, as profoundly assimilable as a cradle song.

Agee's story is actually a variation of that well-known adventure and quest tale of the young man or woman from a highly civilized and technologically advanced culture who undertakes a journey to a more primitive culture, that is, one technologically backward but also morally and emotionally forward (i.e., vital and vitalizing), and who undergoes a renovation or conversion of identity based on discoveries made within the new environment. The tale might typically concern habitués of the big cities, enervated by urban manners and mores, or perhaps, like Agee, "softened and sophisticated" by overdeveloped mental postures, in some cases superficially leery of the unfamiliar stimuli present in the alternate culture but also at bottom genuinely receptive to the chain of unconscious recognitions activated by ongoing engagement with primal prompting (a.k.a. "the lure of the primitive" or "the call of the wild"). Sometimes these personality crossovers might be disastrous, terrors and demons from within overwhelming consciousness, character gone to dust in thrall to gods dark and cruel, as in those deeply cautionary responses to "going native" in the fiction of Conrad, Waugh, and William Golding. Often, however, the conversion is a salubrious one, resulting in advances toward moral and physical hardihood, emotional integration, "wise blood," etc. Such tonic encounters with the archaic surfaces in the high-art romanticism of writers as diverse as Melville (*Typee*), Thoreau (*Walden*), Tolstoy (*The Cossacks*), Kipling (*The Jungle Books*), Lawrence (*The Plumed Serpent*), Faulkner (*The Bear*)—to name only a very famous few—and reach a kind of apotheosis in the demimythic adventures of those real-life heroes and heroines of culture shock, Richard Burton, T. E. Lawrence, Dian Fossey, and, particularly resonant for Agee, Paul Gauguin.[17]

I also want to make particular mention of that seemingly ubiquitous subtype of this "neoprimitive" pattern in the frequently humorous exploits of the tenderfoot, "paleface," or pampered city brat who, after much testing and pratfalling, eventually earns his maturity under the tutelage of members of a wilderness community, say, Indians, pirates, fisherman, cowboys, desert chieftains, maternal apes, or wise wolves, etc.

Students of Anglo-American culture will doubtless be familiar with this perennial tale as originating in that extensive body of late-nineteenth and early-twentieth-century writing inspired by the settlement of the American West and the expansionist efforts of the Second British Empire in Africa, India, etc. (from the late reign of Queen Victoria through the early reign of George VI); that period on both sides of the Atlantic which fostered, among many others, the young person's adventure romances of Stevenson (*Treasure Island*) and Kipling (*Captains Courageous,* a definitive brat book), the "dude" narratives of Twain (*Roughing It*), Frank Harris (*Cowboy*), and Owen Wister (*The Virginian*), as well as basic character-filler and plot ploy for what surely appears to be every fourth or fifth Hollywood western ever made; from the primal image of gunslingers in a bar shooting at the dancing heels of a greenhorn in *The Great Train Robbery* (1908) to the "paleface" initiation rites of *A Man called Horse* (1970) and *Little Big Man* (1970).

Like many of these books and films, *Famous Men* in its confessional nature also reflects a drama of modern identity crisis in the midst of cultural change, a search for who one is and what one stands for as defined in terms of where one is and the personal allegiances invested in the requisites of a particular place. Like the traditional protagonist in a "neoprimitive" pilgrimage, Agee begins as one kind of person from a complex and sophisticated environment, and ends up as what appears to be a different kind of person in an altogether simpler environment. Like the traditional tenderfoot, Agee also starts out as a man bewildered and estranged, prone to accidents (his car stranded in the mud), social embarrassment (frightening a young black couple), and humorous, near slapstick, encounters (his first night on Gudger's vermin-ridden mattress) before integrating with the farmers and achieving his position as an admired guest and advocate in one of their homes. Finally, like Pasternak's archetypal family quester, the "new" self he attains represents less a wholesale transformation than a return to a part of the self, a lost or forgotten or buried germ of the self, waiting the exact soil and climate of experience to accomplish its growth.

The Alabamian experience, then, doesn't really change Agee so much as it crystallizes him: in the course of his encounters, we watch him become a purer, richer, finer, more concentrated distillate of the self that in some larval form he already is, or, at the very least, gives every indication of becoming. Still, few would doubt that the Agee who has happily lived with Gudger for some time and speaks to us with relative confidence from, say, the pages of "A Country Letter" or the three sections of "On the Porch . . ." is not exactly the same young man we meet in the early "pre-Gudger" stages of his adventure, in the three opening sections of "July 1936," or even the first half of "Inductions." During and after his first night at Gudger's farm, there is a marked and deliberate refocusing of the central character's attitude and demeanor. For instance, the Agee we meet in the opening pages appears before us amid an astonishing blizzard of self-abuse (astonishing even for Agee). This Misery enters the scene agonized and tongue-tied, entangled in a confusion of loyalties (e.g., commissioned by an organ of big business, yet a Communist "by sympathy and conviction," etc., 249), ferocious for crucifixion, suspended in that peculiar and uniquely Ageean form of self-serving that habitually seems to reside in varieties of reflexive accusation. He describes himself (and Evans) in the "Preamble" as an "angry, futile, bottomless, and botched, and over complicated youthful" intelligence and speaks of the "frightening vanity" of his "would-be purity" (9). And we see some of these qualities as well as others in "July 1936," as we watch him embark upon a desperate and misbegotten hunt for sharecroppers, driving with increasing futility up and down rural byways (getting lost once), conducting a series of tentative, half-hearted interviews with frightened, guarded backcountry blacks and hostile, suspicious poor whites, describing himself quite aptly at the end of one of these sessions as existing in "a perversion of self-torture" (31).

   The three succinct and bristling sections that constitute "July 1936" represent in miniature format three different and negative versions of the book's central project: the protagonist's attempt to establish contact and rapport (i.e., achieve a "meeting") with people he respects and admires above all others. Each one of these attempts ends in failure; each one leaves him feeling hopeless, trapped, misrepresented, and misunderstood, utterly the outsider. Whatever he learns of the lives of the oppressed and depressed, and of their art (music, architecture, etc.), he accomplishes in the enforced and straightened guise of the tourist-intruder, the visiting social worker and liberal do-gooder, the schlemiel-reporter from New York. Accordingly, the views presented to him are properly picturesque, "curious" to seekers of curios, deeply estranged postcard poses that only the dude-folkologist may imagine to be indigenous and spontaneous: "Negro" spirituals, church facade, three sharecroppers frozen on a porch. Nevertheless, through it all, amidst gusts of acknowledged bad faith, Agee manages to go through the motions of what is expected of him: "I played my part through" (31).

The first section, "Late Sunday Morning," presents a "meeting" co-erced and commandeered, an exact and corrosive introduction to the thirties southern caste system in operation as a "middling well-to-do landowner" (whose ancestor "had escaped an insurrection of Negroes in Haiti," 26) arranges an interview between Agee and Evans and some very nervous specimen-blacks, and finally a command performance by a black choir. The music is magnificent, and produces the first of Agee's many brilliant genuflections before the grandeur and sophistication of "primitive" art. But immediately upon the music's conclusion, human relations wilt:

> . . . I had been sick in the knowledge that they [the choir] felt they were here at our demand, mine and Walker's, and that I could communicate nothing otherwise; and now, in a perversion of self-torture, I played my part through. I gave their leader fifty cents, trying at the same time, through my eyes, to communicate much more, and said I was sorry we had held them up and that I hoped they would not be late; and he thanked me for them in a dead voice, not looking me in the eye, and they went away, putting their white hats on their heads as they walked into the sunlight (31).

In the following section, "At the Forks," Agee has lost his way, and when he approaches the home of three poor whites (bitterly referred to as "clients of rehabilitation," 35), he is greeted with suspicion and mistrust. "None of them relieved me for an instant of their eyes; at the intersection of those three tones of force I was transfixed as between spearheads as I talked" (34). After the almost obligatory reference to his awkwardness (". . . I was stupid again . . ." [36, etc.]), he is happy to feel a slight softening on the part of the woman and the husband toward him, and at the end of the interview remarks how "the young woman smiled, sternly beneath her virulent eyes, for the first time" (37). But amidst this trio of generally enraged glances, he finds genuine communication impossible, and not for the last time, comments upon his overall inarticulacy, his simple inability to say what he means to those who matter most to him. "I had not the heart at all to say, Better luck to you, but then if I remember rightly I did say it, and, saying it or not, and unable to communicate to them at all what my feelings were, I walked back the little distance to the car with my shoulders and the back of my neck more scalded-feeling than if the sun were on them" (37).

Perhaps his worst moment occurs in the last episode, "Near a Church," when he tries to obtain information from a young black couple, but only ends up startling and offending them. He and Evans are trying to gain admission to an (aptly) locked church when the couple stroll by. Agee hurries toward them hoping to ask "if they knew where we might find a minister or some other person who might let us in, if it would be all right" (40). To his horror, however, they begin to bolt. As is well known, one of the minor and dubious brilliancies of Agee's art resides in the consummate skill with which he invariably manages to anatomize the minute convolutions of his "scullery chaos of gracelessness,"[18] but here in trying to apologize to this couple, one may well find him a touch too successful, and almost wallowing in his gaucherie:

> . . . I came up to them (not trotting) and stopped a yard short of where they, closely, not touching now, stood, and said, still shaking my head *(No; no; oh, Jesus, no, no, no!)* and looking into their eyes; at the man, who was not knowing what to do, and at the girl, whose eyes were lined with tears, and who was trying so hard to subdue the shaking in her breath, and whose heart I could feel, though not hear, blasting as if it were my whole body, and I trying in some fool way to keep it somehow relatively light, because I could not bear that they should receive from me any added reflection of the shattering of their grace and dignity, and of the nakedness and depth and meaning of their fear, and of my horror and pity and self-hatred; and so, smiling, and so distressed that I wanted only that they should be restored, and should know I was their friend, and that I might melt from existence: 'I'm *very sorry!* I'm *very* sorry if I scared you! I didn't mean to scare you at all. I wouldn't have done any such thing for anything.' (41–42)

The scene is as embarrassing for us as it is for him, but not for precisely the same reasons; we don't like what he has done, and is actually continuing to do, to the couple, and neither does he: but even more we don't like what he is doing to himself, though he obviously does, and this too is a source of our embarrassment. It isn't simply that he has sentimentalized the fragility and tremulousness of the fawnlike couple, but, deeply collateral to this, he seems also to have internalized what he imagines them to be feeling ("whose heart I could feel . . . blasting as if it were my whole body"), and so becomes a menace to himself, and in this manner semtimentalizes his own wretchedness, as well as the contours of his self-disgust:

> The least I could have done was to throw myself flat on my face and embrace and kiss their feet. That impulse took hold of me so powerfully, from my whole body, not by thought, that I caught myself from doing it exactly and as scarcely as you snatch yourself from jumping from a sheer height: here, with the realization that it would have frightened them still worse (to saying nothing of me) and would have been still less explicable; so that I stood and looked into their eyes and loved them, and wished to God I was dead. (42)

The Russians have a word for such contortions of the mind, and one that often attaches itself to the conduct of certain characters in the novels of Dostoyevsky (Father Ferapont in *The Brothers Karamazov* is an obvious case in point). The word is *nadryv,* a form of self-laceration that proceeds not from genuine humility, but rather from a flagellant form of pride, vanity, and high-mindedness, or "the frightening vanity" of a "would-be purity." Here, while the protagonist's misery is genuine enough, it is painfully qualified and complicated by the obvious and unsettling pleasure he takes in itemizing, and finally fetishizing, its volume and degree—a "perversion of self-torture," to be sure (poor Jim!).

"Near a Church" is virtually a mirror reversal of "At the Forks." In the latter he, in effect, was repulsed; here he repulses others. In neither episode does he acquire access to the even nominal information he seeks; in "At the Forks" he takes direction to farm country "where we did not find what we sought" (37); here, after asking the couple "what I had followed them to ask; they said the thing it is usually safest for negroes to say, that they did not know" (42–43). All three sections of "July 1936" contain enough suggestion of beauty and humanity to leave him hungry for more: the intricate power of the music; the "paralyzing classicism" (38) of the church facade; the hint of friendship contained in the grudged sliver of a smile. But the end result of each episode discovers the journalist from the North no closer to his goals than before; all three conclude with either the interviewer or the subject turning his back and walking away.

I hope it has already become clear that these experiences appear at the beginning of the book not because "that was the way it happened" (though this may well have been the case), or because such preliminaries happen to be an effective way of introducing the reader to representative instances in the southern "situation" (though they are that too), but primarily to show us what the central character is like before he appears at Gudger's door. These experiences expose us more fully than any "documentary" is ever likely to do to some of the more remarkable knots in this alleged investigative reporter's moral and emotional makeup, and prepare us for a narrative evolution that eventually will loosen these knots, though not entirely smooth them away. They also specifically reveal in this character a desperate, highly complicated lust for personal contact—a rage of loneliness made frantic by the thwarted proximity of its elusive object—far in excess of any purely journalistic or professional need to gather facts for an article.

The movement from "July 1936" to the following "A Country Letter," that is, from these preliminaries to the main body of "Part One"—a jump forward in time from a point just before the start of the adventure to a point somewhere well past the middle of it—represents one of the two most radical and dramatic temporal shifts in the entire narrative. Even more significant, it represents a radical and dramatic shift in the attitude and circumstance of the central character. Suddenly, with scarcely a scrap of transition (actually, a one-paragraph poetic overview of the southern topography, "All over Alabama the lamps are out . . ." [44–45]), we are surprised to discover at the start of "A Country Letter" that the young man who has had so much difficulty in even finding a tenant family, let alone knowing how to talk to one, has already been living with one such family as guest and friend for an indefinite length of time. The author has structured his tale so that the reader who follows the narrative ordering must wonder how the central character emerged from those fruitless interviews, false starts, and red-herring leads to a position of honorary membership in a tenant's household.

We might also want to know how the young man who previously seemed to have so much trouble in saying exactly what he meant—who "could not communicate . . . at all what my real feelings were"—could now muster the verbal confidence and certainty of rapport to drape himself as he does here (i.e., "A Country Letter") in the mantle of a Whitmanian oracle: "I can tell you anything within realm of God, whatsoever it may be, that I wish to tell you, and that what so ever it may be, you will not be able to help but understand it" (51).

We might consider as well how the awkward reporter, who had been repeatedly greeted by the natives with little better than fear, suspicion, and hollow civility, could now warrant and inspire the following compliment from a member of Gudger's family: "I want you and Mr. Walker to know how much we all like you," says Emma Woods, Annie Mae Gudger's sister, " . . . it's just like you was our own people and had always lived here with us" (64). Consider also the graciousness of Agee's response to her, and remember that this is the same person who, just a short while ago, could not seem to enter into any social situation without excessive fits of self-abasement, who could not even bear to contemplate his conduct without first savaging it into microscopic flinders of shame. And while he isn't completely satisfied with his deportment here either (is he ever?), and would certainly like to respond to Emma Woods, whom he finds desirable, more intimately than he does, he cannot conceal from her, from us, or from himself, the healthy pleasure he takes in her gratitude; indeed, the entire significance of the Alabama experience may hinge on (one would argue) the exact import of what Emma Woods has just said to him, and her words, as well as his very effusive reply—a specimen of the happiest flower of southern gallantry—may well represent the positive fulfillment of a near lifetime of unconscious striving: " . . . I wanted her to know how much I liked them, too, and her herself, and that I certainly felt that they were my own people, and wanted them to be, more than any other kind of people in the world, and that if they felt that of me, and that I belonged with them, and we all felt right and easy with each other and fond of each other, then there wasn't anything in the world I could be happier over, or be more glad to know . . ." (65)

Consider, at last, how the confused and desperate outsider of the opening pages, who had recently described himself as living in a "perversion of self-torture," could only a short time later spend his first night at Gudger's farm in a condition of near ecstacy ("Inductions"), who, while having every right to feel at least physically agonized as he tosses about on the children's lice-infected mattress, greets the evening stars with a combination of barely contained rapture and good-natured self-mockery, blessing every item in his field of vision right down to the bedbugs: "I don't exactly know why anyone should be 'happy' under these circumstances, but there's no use laboring the point: I was" (427).

Now these are a few of the matters that the disjunctive ordering of the narrative line might make a reader want to consider: not only how this young man came to be where he is, but how he came to be the way he is. What exactly has happened to this young man?

IN THE REALM OF THE EXTENDED SENSES

Agee will provide answers to this question, but not for a long while; rather he will hold us in suspense as section by section he works his arduous way toward that remarkable expression of initiation, conversion, and the illuminated condition dramatized in "Inductions," the section in which we finally learn how Gudger helps the central character discover himself. In such a manner, the pattern of this character's personal experience runs from the middle of his encounter all the way home to its beginnings, a movement extending for virtually two-thirds of the text, and one that takes the form of a slow reverse tracking shot (to draw upon the technical resources of the medium the author loved most), an extended series of progressively widening camera frames; beginning in intimate close-up, as the central character enters the dreams and collective night musings of the sleeping farmers ("A Country Letter"); and then slowly, section by section, pulling backward and, as it were, outward—roughly speaking, away from the thing viewed and toward the viewer viewing, that is, the author himself—leaving the farmers per se and taking in increasingly more of their material, aesthetic, and spiritual circumstances, through an extraordinary sequence of long, lyrical, personally inflected, descriptive inquiries into dwelling spaces, furniture, tools, animals, clothing, and education; italicizing in the penultimate stages of this movement a lingering long shot of the farmers laboring in the cotton fields ("Work," perhaps the most distanced and least intimate of the sections); and ending at last with the viewer himself (i.e., as if turning the camera around to view the viewer). The actual turning point occurs in "Intermission," a very significant and inflammatory flash-forward to a glimpse of Agee as artist *after* Alabama, with no overt reference to the farmers at all, and the second of the two most radical and dramatic temporal shifts in the narrative (see "Teachers"). This pivotal interlude is immediately followed by the episode of Agee's first contact with the three tenant families ("Inductions"), the stranger's entry into the domestic circle, and with this entry, the official grant, as it were, of permission to proceed through the private holdings already discovered and explored in the previous three hundred pages. Along the route, there have been a number of pauses or shifts above the "story" line for commentary that is by turns philosophical ("Colon"), economic ("Money"), or metafictional ("On the porch: 2"). But generally speaking, the Alabama adventure has divided into three distinct parts: first, Agee alone and searching ("July 1936"); then, the farmer and his environment ("Country Letter," "Shelter," "Clothing," "Education," "Work"); finally, Agee and the farmer in unison ("Inductions"). Now, to shift metaphor from movies to music, after much contrapuntal development and atonal meandering, the narrative proper concludes in a stable key of hushed homophonics, a coda of assonant chords—specifically, the family and their new friends united in prayers and benedictions ("Shady Grove Alabama"), reading hopeful signs and portents ("Two Images")—the last of which officially intones a full recitation of the passage from Ecclesiasticus that provides the context for the work's title ("Title Statement").

The major revisions, however, in the central character's fortunes, as well as within the character himself, occur in "Inductions," and it is this decisive and climactic section to which we now turn (once again; c.f., "Two Reveries"). Agee separates this very long stretch of material—the entirety of his "Part Three"—into three episodes, the second and third of which are further subdivided into titled sections. The first episode describes how Agee and Evans meet all three tenant families for the first time; the second relates the fateful car journey from Birmingham to Gudger; and the third, Agee's first meal under Gudger's roof and his first night in one of his rooms. Like much of this author's best work, virtually all of the material grounds itself in the finical mundane, a sequence of relatively nondramatic, almost static, moments of ordinary being apprehended in an ecstasy of perception: a car ride, a rain storm, a visit to a farm, a mishap in the mud, a meal, a bedding down for the night. Agee orchestrates these relatively prosaic nuggets as the enactment of a sacred rite, the subdivisions of sections two and three entitled according to parts of the Mass, "Gradual," "Reversion," "Introit," etc. Accordingly, in and through the quotidian specific—the shapeless biscuits and the bedbugs, a car wheel revving in a ditch—the narrative manages to evoke a flotilla of quasi-religious and parabolic motif; there is spiritual death and rebirth, a baptismal feast, a visitation, a wayward spirit lost and then found in the grace of his host; a redemption from despair through recognition of a displaced heritage; the prodigal's entrance into a sanctified and inviolate space, one referred to as "the holy house" (394), "the altar of God" (360), the place where Gudger lives.

The first section ("First Meetings") begins, as the last will virtually end, with an equivocal and quietly agonized "baptism"—here rural innocence at the shrine of urban technology—as the three interrelated tenant families of Gudger, Woods, and Ricketts come to Evans and Agee for the first time to have their pictures taken. These "First Meetings" more or less follow chronologically from, and are in some ways roughly continuous with, those other early and abortive meetings in "July 1936," meetings between northern strangers and southern natives (the farmers view the two visitors as "Government Men," 362); and on a superficial level, this confrontation also seems to end in a kind of stalemate. The farmers are made wretched before Evans and his camera, who in their eyes becomes a voodoo man practicing a black and perverted art, "stooping beneath cloak and cloud of wicked cloth and twisting buttons, a witchcraft preparing: colder than keenest ice, and incalculably cruel" (364). The section keys much of its mood of awkwardness and hesitancy by focusing time and again on the shy, defensive, and disheveled Ricketts family, beginning with the nervous and insecure Fred Ricketts and then turning to Sadie Ricketts, her "eyes wild with fury and shame and fear" (364), and finally ending the sequence with an image of her "unforgiving face" (370). But this is one encounter from which Agee isn't going to back off, and, with full awareness of the intrusion he represents, he speaks directly to Sadie Ricketts when he says, "we shall have to return, even in the face of causing further pain, until that mutual wounding shall have been won and healed, until she shall fear us no further, yet not in forgetfulness but through ultimate trust, through love" (370).

Why in this instance is Agee determined to return to people for whom he and his project seem to represent so much discomfort? He has walked away from other encounters, why not from this one as well? In spite of its many awkward moments, the whole incident is related in a relatively positive light, Agee working in tender tones of nostalgia and intimate address (the farmers are always "you," both individually and collectively), as if he and people who have long since become irrevocable friends could now enjoy looking back with affection, even wistfulness, upon how a relation that turned out so warmly well for everyone involved began so anomalously. Actually, beneath its troubled surface, the encounter resonates with hopeful signs and prodigious undercurrents of recognition. It is significant that these impoverished southerners, unlike those in previous confrontations, emerge as neither specimens of Depression life or Dixie exotica, but rather as members of a united family—above all, as parents with children. Agee's response to the latter is instantaneous—"even then we knew you were wonderful . . ." (363)—and in the case of the ten-year-old Louise Gudger, characteristically extravagant: "I realize . . . that I am probably going to be in love with you" (369). In the light of future events, however, the crucial moment of encouragement comes in response to the frightened "unforgiving" Sadie Ricketts herself. I refer to that remarkable instance when Agee senses (asserts? insists?) that Mrs. Ricketts, in spite of all her fear and mistrust of him, is fully capable of understanding and even ministering to the special provenance of his agony and need, the cage of his isolation, the hurtful power and shame of his restless animal thrashing:

> . . . your eyes softened, lost all their immediate dread, but without smiling; but in a heart-broken and infinite yet timid

reproachfulness, as when, say, you might have petted a little animal in a trap, beyond its thorntoothed fierceness, beyond its fear, to quiet, in which it knows, of your blandishments: you could spring free the jaws of this iron from my wrist; what is this hand, what are these kind eyes; what is this gentling hand on the fur of my forehead: so that I let my face loose of any control and it showed you just what and all I felt for you and of myself: it must have been an ugly and puzzling grimace, God knows no use or comfort to you; and you looked a moment and withdrew your eyes, and gazed patiently into the ground, in nothing but sorrow, your little hand now loosened in your dress (365–66).

Agee's description of himself as a "little animal" directly echoes and links him to his description of the Ricketts children as "young wild animals" (363), thus enlisting himself exactly where he wants to be, that is, somehow within the farmer's family orbit. Mrs. Ricketts's "gentling hand" is of course the equivalent of a maternal caress, and the anticipation of kindness and healing and commiseration in a gesture that would free the "iron from" the "wrist" of the "little animal" is really all the inducement that the central character needs; it becomes, as it were, part of his personal incentive to pursue the relation further.

Formal permission, however, is granted in the next section ("Gradual") by Bud Woods himself, the oldest (fifty-nine), "the shrewdest and the wisest" (370) of the farmers, in many ways the patriarchal center of his clan, the one who officially binds in blood the three families into one tripartite unit, as the older half-brother of Sadie Ricketts and the father of Annie Mae Gudger, and unsurprisingly the one that Agee and Evans relate to as a "sort of father" (371). Significantly it is the elder Woods, and not the younger Gudger, who the two northerners first approach with their plan for paid room-and-board; and it is Woods who helps "arrange" the matter with his son-in-law. Now the Bud Woods interview actually takes place after the crucial first visit to Gudger, but Agee positions it *before* the event in order, I think, to stress the decorous and ritualistic nature of each step of his entry into Gudger's world, and to ensure that his relation with Gudger might proceed as if blessed and preordained by paternal mandate; as if, that is, the ceremonial nature of the visit itself might evolve inexorably from one of the most ancient and respected of ceremonies: that of a father granting permission to an outsider to intervene in the lives of his children, as if in a rite of courtship.

Nor do I think this particular romantic overtone to be at all accidental, as indeed the interview itself also strikes a distinctly erotic tone, one that becomes increasingly important as the process of inductions unfold, granting us the first hint of the way to make at least partial purchase on some of the demons vexing the emotional life of the central character. Bud Woods is the only one of the farmers to be presented in relatively overt sexual terms (even the Evans photograph emphasizes this rakishness), and he has recently married his second wife, Ivy, "a serenely hot and simple nymph" in her mid-twenties, who is present during the interview and whose "eyes go to bed with every man she sees" (372); and of course Woods, as he puts it, "don't want to take no chanstes" (371). In a fine, sly little speech, he points out the full practical value of taking rooms with his son-in-law rather than himself: Gudger after all has the room, and "also because, well, you fellers know, got me this woman, here, not that I don't *trust* yuns ([eyes] glittering merrily) but some way don't look right, couple young fellers, old man like me" (371). The whole potentially uncomfortable, even volatile, situation between Woods, Ivy, Agee, and Evans is handled like an ingratiating mini-comedy of manners with all four participants "smiling back and forth cautiously and respectfully, and yet openly" (372). In this manner, Agee wittily and efficiently manages to evoke a classic Oedipal rigmarole ("couple young fellers, old man like me") only to promptly derail the whole business in one good-natured moment of mutual comprehension and mature civility: "Sure, sure," Agee tells Woods, "we understand that: lot rather have it that way ourselves" (371). The relaxed and offhanded treatment of the scene urges us to feel that whatever manner of sexual tension might arise later, it certainly won't (and shouldn't) have anything at all to do with male rivalry, or antagonism between the generations. As the narrative advances, it becomes increasingly apparent that Agee wants his chosen shelter—which now must be with Gudger and not with Woods—to be understood as a *pre*-Oedipal enclave, a sanctified cradle of childhood reverie and presexual harmony, and not a postadolescent bullpen rife with genital jousting. And the Bud Woods interview simply and humorously tries to dispose of one possible avenue of emotional anxiety in advance of the journey to Gudger.

Still, the erotic note has been sounded, and following the Woods interview, the car ride from Birmingham ("Reversion") expands, intensifies, and subtilizes its implications. It is important to recall that when Agee first takes to his car one blistering Sunday in the city, he is only aware of two different but not necessarily conflicting urges: a need to be off by himself, and a need to fornicate ("I knew I very badly wanted, not to say needed, a piece of tail," 375–76). Beyond this, and a very general plan to leave Birmingham, where he and Evans have just taken a brief respite from fieldwork, and slowly drive his way eighty miles back to farm country, Agee has no sharp or immediate notion of why he is in his car or *specifically* where he is going in it. He makes no mention of Gudger at all until well into the middle of his journey (he's leaving Centerboro by then) when it suddenly seems to well up as a kind of minor epiphany that "the one I wanted to see was Gudger" (385), even though at the time Agee doesn't know where he lives. Actually, of course, the central character's internal radar has been leading him to Gudger all along, and far from being nonsequiturs in the logic of his present need, the farmer and his world represent both the apotheosis and highest fidelity of the same amorous hunger that quite literally drives him out of Birmingham; that is, the car drive traces the heavy and often despairing trajectory of a subtle and complicated sex drive, one that initiates as a coarse and deeply ambivalent desire for a "piece of tail," but ultimately evolves and translates itself into the richer, unequivocal passion for, so to speak, the body of the family, the loving envelopments of hearth and home. The urge toward raw sex proves to be only another misdirection, however meaningful, in the panorama of the central character's early misadventures, another external signal of that psychic confusion, that "perversion of self-torture," that begins to unburden itself virtually the moment he perceives the actual nature and goal of his journey. Lust then becomes the camouflage for a deeper, more generalized, less focused, but, in Agee's case, more telling erotic longing and melancholia; and it is only when the central character begins to grope his way toward the true roots of this complex and polymorphous hunger—i.e., toward the understanding that Gudger indeed was "the one I wanted to see"—

that he is also able to reroute the direction of both his car and his passion.

It must also be stressed that the first half of the journey, as well as the events leading up to it, represent one of the bleakest, most desolating episodes in the whole design of the central character's psychic evolution. He describes the mood preceding the Birmingham interlude as "most nearly insane," as resulting in a "nearly incommunicable weight of paralysis" brought on by a "constant dissimulation and slowing to alien pace" (372). The "day or two in Birmingham" among friends and sympathizers, while intended "as medicine," quickly turns toxic as the "regular hemorrhage of talking" only serves to underscore the "terrific loneliness" of everyone involved (373). In this context, the prowl for sex, while ostensibly an antidote to this mood, actually proves to be an extension of it, another species of "dissimulation" (here self-deception), in which all the sexual encounters that Agee manages to fantasize about at the wheel of his car present themselves as either shameful or entirely dispiriting, suggesting the very reverse of sensual satisfaction. He first entertains, for instance, a visit to a prostitute—seen from the window of his car and brutally referred to as a "piece of head cheese"—only to promptly imagine his own sexual dysfunction; "I was good for nothing" (376). He then contemplates a stopover in Cherokee City to make a call on "a middle class young woman" (xxii) named "Estelle," only also to envision her "unappeasable eyes" and decide that this too is "not worth the sacrifice of this solitude" (376). Cruising slowly through Centerboro in the midst of an annihilating hot spell that grips like "a white and silent nightmare" (378), he casts back at last to a sense of his physical body "in the loose milky flesh of its childhood" groping for sexual release on his grandfather's front porch; " . . . this eleven-year-old, male, half-shaped child, pressing between the sharp hip bone and the floor my erection . . . sweating and shaking my head in a sexual and murderous anger and despair" (379–80).

Still, in spite of his inability to find pleasure in the anticipation of either copulation or simple genital emission (i.e., masturbation), his imagination, as if following the thread of its own psychic necessity, continues to seek the direction in which it obviously wants to go: from lust undifferentiated (with a stranger) to lust socialized (with an acquaintance) to lust introjected (with himself), his hunger and guilt have slowly devolved inward and backward in time, finally arriving at the root of his actual need in the envisionment of an idealized dream-companion—"a girl nearly new to me" ("she must not be a whore or a bitch," 382), a bastion erected against this "awful paralysis of Sunday and the sense of death"—whom he approaches less as a lover ("we would not try anything drastic") and more urgently as a heartsick and world-sick child questing maternal succor: " . . . putting my forehead against her cold throat and feeling against my face through her dress the balance and goodness of her breasts, knowing suddenly my weakness and the effort and ugliness and sorrow of the beautiful world, I should almost in silence cry the living blood out of myself" (383).

But the despair of ever finding such a figure ("where was I going to get her and would I want her if I had her," 384)—both loving mother and mothering lover, one who might staunch the tears of the grieving child just as she might bolster his "weakness" in her comfort and strength—initiates a hapless mental search for an equivalency. No longer ranging for prostitutes or sex partners, the central character now trashes amid the ruins of his personal domestic circumstances, firing off blank bullets of hemlock and self-pity (finally summarized as a "bad case of infantilism," 385). Before he is finished, however, Agee careens through his splintering marriage; his father, his grandfather, his "poor damned tragic, not unusually tragic, bitched family"; his bent toward suicide ("I could twist the car off the road, if possible into a good-sized oak"); finally in utter misery, cursing and virtually canceling himself and all his aspirations toward art: " . . . only the hard bastards come through, I'm not born and can't be that hard apparently and God—Genius and Works of Art anyway and who the hell am I, who in Jesus' name am I" (384–85).

It is at *this* point—the furthest extremity in his rush toward oblivion—as if in answer to the racking mysteries of passion, creation, and being itself ("who the hell am I"), as if having exhausted every possible avenue of hope and haven, he stumbles upon the solution that perhaps first suggested itself when he imagined Mrs. Ricketts's "gentling hand" setting the "little animal" free from its iron chain, that certainly exalts itself in the current reverie of the *femme inspiritrice* promising harmony and bounty in the "balance" and "goodness" of her breasts. Suddenly Agee realizes the direction in which his car has inadvertently been heading from the start: "The one I wanted to see was Gudger, to himself, or anyhow just with his family" (385).

The ride from Birmingham to Gudger dramatizes the powers of the unconscious discovering its special and irreducible needs in and through the blunderings of the outer mind, the one ineluctable object of recognition emerging amid counterfeits; from whore, to lover, to self-lover, to the Mother of All, lost as the family is lost and found as a surrogate is found: a new family wounded and imperiled, but forever more needed than needy—in the avid eye of one in need. Amid the whole astonishing anatomy of material want and economic deprivation depicted so scrupulously in this Depression classic, the one unequivocal "starving child" turns out to be Agee himself. It is the central character who burns brightest of all for the primal securities of the family nest, the emotional and spiritual cognates of "Food, Shelter, and Clothing" (xx). These code-words from one of the epigraphs to this book (opening lines from Louise Gudger's third-grade geography textbook) come back to remind us that beneath the sociomaterial truism stated in singsong for children, there resides a personal urgency, a rosary for the hungry heart: "Now everyone needs food, shelter, and clothing. The lives of most men on earth are spent in getting these things" (xx). "These things" are of course the mnemonics of Home, and it is the central character's very naked lack of and desire for "these things" that have all along submerged themselves under a welter of equivocal allegiances and outright "dissimulation"—so much so, that to suddenly acknowledge this lack and desire also entails a fundamental reorganization of priorities and estimates. He can now no longer even entertain the pretense (to the degree he ever needed to) of being a disinterested journalist who would write an article about someone else's social problem and economic ruin. He has become himself problem and ruin, and would now make a deeply biased work of personal art of how he and they resolved themselves in the home of his people. For he now has also discovered a new and special way to think of these people as particularly "his": that is, he too, in his abiding "weakness" and "ugliness," in his orphan's sense of uprootedness, in his grieving child's hunger for the body of the parent, in the now unsublimated intensity of his "separation anxiety" (using the clinician's lingo—but reluctantly), he too can at once join rank with the wretched and the dispossessed. In this light, all of his once blatant intellectual apartness and distinction from the impoverished farmer shrink, for the moment, to a cavil. It is now Gudger in his family adhesiveness, in his tiny knot of loyalty, rightness, and bonded blood, who has every advantage of his homeless, lovesick visitor from the North. Now Agee can properly begin to think of Gudger's world as not only his subject but his sanctuary, the "holy house" that might conceivably take him in, and the book he will write as not just a "study" of this world, but its epiphany and celebration. If the northern reporter in him asserts, as it will continue to assert, "this is an appalling situation and *something* must be done," the southern prodigal cries, "this is sacred space, touch nothing!" The central character may be something of both figures, but just now Alabama is everywhere and "the true tastes of home" (416) *as found* are in his mouth.

Upon the moment Agee realizes where he wants to be to get his version of the "things" he needs, the gloom that has settled about his head like a choking mist, from the opening of "July, 1936" through the heat of a Birmingham Sunday, slowly begins to evaporate. In spite of a subsequent number of sobering recognitions, his spiritual temperature never again drops to that annihilating level of isolation, paralysis, and abject self-pity that has marked virtually all of his initial gambits in Hale County.

Once he finds himself Gudger-bound, two heartening events follow in relatively short order: a revelation of the real reasons for his journey south, and, at least for the duration, a symbolic shedding of his Yankee Peddler persona. The first occurrence represents a mental act of visionary understanding, the second a physical and quasi-humorous rite of cultural purification. The dream vision arrives after stumbling upon Fred Ricketts and the right way to Gudger's farm, and incorporates the author's highest hopes for the Alabama venture in a delirium of liberations for captive soldiers, beleaguered farmers, and oppressed peoples everywhere, in-cluding the central character's own happy release in a return to childhood haunts (see "Two Reveries"). Agee then makes the first ("Introit") of his two consecutive visits to Gudger's farm in the midst of a ferocious late-afternoon rainstorm signifying the end of the hot spell and of his own emotional and spiritual drought, as well as literally bringing much needed replenishment to the farmers' crops; a good omen, then, for both host and visitor. But when Gudger urges Agee several times to spend the night, he refuses in "some paralyzing access of shyness before strong desire" (407). With that surfeit of self-awareness and irresolution that marks almost everything he does, Agee will come to Gudger but in his own time and manner; and this means largely in a semiconscious reflex of staged gesture—alone, on foot, stripped bare, silently in the night, like a stranger astray, a thief of dreams, a penitent at the altar of his expiation. (Later, for instance, when he approaches Gudger's house for the second time, he confesses that "I had half-contrived this," 411.)

But first he drives Fred Ricketts back to his home and then, half in innocence and half in effort, manages to run his car to a standstill in a muddy ditch ("Second Introit"); and there in his frozen, useless machine, he makes his first official obeisances to the rural landscape, as if resetting his human compass by a natural order of living things, each plant and tree actuated in alliance with "the work and living of some particular man and family." "I felt an exact traction with this country in each twig and clod of it as it stood, not as it stood past me from a car, but to be stood in the middle of, or drawn through, passed, on foot, in the plain rhythm of a human being in his basic relation to his country" (409). It is the "car" that fixes the driver behind a drifting landscape, that denies the proper "traction" between the sole of the foot and the skin of one's "country," that finally emblemizes the basic social disparity between the beneficiary of an urban industrialized economy and the victim of an old, ailing, agricultural one. In and of his car Agee remains, as it were, in William Faulkner's expression, "still tainted."[19] Before entering his "holy house," he must bid farewell to his now "tilted" and "helpless" technology, which at the moment also becomes symbolic of whatever remains of his Northern Slicker credentials and affiliations as Soft-Core Leftist, Salaried Employee of the Urban Glossies, Commissioned Snoop ("a spy," he reminds us repeatedly) for the agencies of Capitalist democracy: "I began to feel laughter toward it [his car] as if it were a new dealer, a county dietitian, an editor of Fortune, or an article in the New Republic" (410). He changes his shoes for sneakers, rolls his trousers to his knees, and as evening falls, treks across the darkening fields "in the plain rhythm of a human being in his basic relation to his country."

Now standing alone in Gudger's deserted yard, "vertical to the front center of the house" (411), James Agee achieves something very like his moment of consummation, an outlet and transfigurative climax for that great ache of erotic guilt and longing that has been building and subverting itself since the beginning of his journey from Birmingham: "and standing here, silently, in the demeanor of the house itself I grow full of shame and of reverence from the soles of my feet up my body to the crest of my skull and the leaves of my hands like a vessel quietly spread full of water which has sprung from in the middle of my chest" (411). This is an image worth holding, for in many respects it may be taken to prefigure the author's heightened condition of being throughout his stay at Gudger's home. At the most immediate and obvious level, the image suggests of course a kind of nocturnal emission; all day long Agee has been, as it were, simmering and simmering, and night entry into Gudger's space brings him to the proverbial boil. But this particular emission is of the heart ("the middle of my chest") and not of the loins, and privileges not one region of the body over another, but democratizes all (from "sole" to "crest"). Such an engulfment then represents less an expression of passion ejaculated (i.e., in a unidirectional stream toward a single object) than that of passion irrigated centrifugally throughout the extremities of the body (i.e., in a polymorphic spray toward a multiplicity of objects): an engorged being rather than an engorged genital, and, most significantly, one aroused not by any particular person or persons, but rather by the "demeanor of the house itself." At this moment, it is not necessarily or even visibly Gudger's house, but indeed just a "house" deep in the night, simply an evocative silhouette, "dead black . . . [it] just stands there, darker than its surroundings" (411): that is, the central character now stands before the shadow or archetypal suggestion of home, perhaps the one belonging to George and Annie Mae Gudger, or perhaps the one belonging to his grandfather, or perhaps the one that conjoins both, that permanent omnipresent refuge forged of memory and desire, the platonic idea of the great, good place.

Granted, it is eros that literally drives Agee out of Birmingham, and in some sense it is eros still that brings him to the "vertical" before the "front center" in Gudger's yard. But now, in this second surfacing, eros has taken on a different character; eros has been transfigured. I think this to be true even while we should probably always remember that, to some indefinable degree, Agee's entire relation with all three tenant families, even at its most reverential, seems to be mediated through a powerful and complicated field of preconscious hunger and shame that is often undeniably amorous in nature. His craving to be close to these men, women, and children, to watch, touch, lick, sniff, and in every sense *penetrate* their lives and possessions, is inseparable from a kind of all-pervasive erotic curiosity; and perhaps inseparable too from every good reason why he cannot linger with them one moment longer beyond the accomplishment of his legitimate aims for being there. For the most part, however, it is also clear that this curiosity is firmly held in check. Once, or perhaps at the outside, twice, it may express itself openly toward specific persons, notably and conveniently toward members of, so to speak, the "outer" family circle—such as Emma Woods, who when we first meet her is just leaving the "inner" core, and perhaps also, though less obviously, Ivy Woods, who has just recently entered it. But even these semiserious feelings remain strictly within the confines of whimsy, and not even this sort of half-hearted and innocuous fantasy is ever permitted in relation to any of the "core" members of the families. In general, entry into the "holy house" means entry into a stabilizing regimen of order, discipline, and enforced emotional quietude (conditions not at all dissimilar to those prevailing in Agee's own childhood home).[20] It is, he tells us explicitly, "a time of celibacy" (224), and as such inspires him to verbal accolades of the highest moral declension: "honor," "reverence," "love," "vigilance," "forbearance," etc. By contrast, later that night, again outside the house, alone in the dark, he only feels "lawless and lustful" (426).

In any event, I would also trust that "sensuality" is not exactly the quality most readers would readily want to attribute to this particular artist. Against any random sampling of important American writers, this author might conceivably rank among the least overtly erotic—hardly a single full-fledged "sex scene" is to be found anywhere in his published oeuvre—just as within the same sampling, he might also place among the most conspicuously and insinuatingly sensuous, all those lavish descriptions radiant with svelte and humanly alluring concrete detail. In the journey from Birmingham to Gudger, then, we witness the emotional process through which Agee evolves and ratifies that phase of his artistic character conducive to the production of some of his most dazzling literary effects; that process through which raw sensuality passes over to an erotically tinged sensuousness, and then sensuousness itself intimates a world beyond the senses; that process through which eros is first acknowledged ("I badly wanted, not to say needed, a piece of tail"), then focused, chastened, and extended to envelope the family nucleus ("Gudger was the one I wanted to see . . ."), and finally standing "vertical" before the Shadow-Home, defused and dispersed outward in the form of a full sensory alertness—an intensification of all the senses inseparable from consciousness itself, a kind of bodily thinking inclusive of memory and intellectual emission—in which the original erotic character has been fairly transmogrified in acts of sensate or purely mental entries, penetrations, and comminglings, with the extensions of a domestic space. In this manner, what appears to be an interruption of sex ("a time of celibacy"), a postponement or repression of eros, on one level is on another a radical clarification of one's erotic needs. What Agee isn't getting isn't really what he wants anyway, at least not in the form that he sometimes thinks he wants it (e.g., sex with Emma). What he actually wants *and* gets are ardent, plunging forays of perception and cognition, probing rooms with an inflamed eye, discriminating the cries of animals with tipped ears, caressing physical surfaces, walls and soft-textured garments, with sensitized fingers, devouring the voluptuous shapes of the night by "the starved brightness of the senses" (51). "The nakedness of this body which sleeps here before me," he explicitly informs us at the outset of his official investigation of Gudger's rooms (after the house has been temporarily vacated in "Shelter"), "this tabernacle upon whose desecration I so reverentially proceed . . . there is here no open sexual desire, no restiveness, nor despair: but the quietly *triumphant vigilance of the extended senses* before an intricate task of surgery, a deep stealthfulness, not for shame of the people, but *in fear and in honor of the house itself,* a knowledge of being at work" (137, italics mine).

It is clear that entry into Gudger's physical setting is at least as signifi-cant for Agee as meeting Gudger himself, and its effects upon his imag-inative life, as well as his emotional being, can hardly be overestimated. The encounter with the farmer's dwelling represents something very like an encounter with the ghost or structural outline of a lost ambit, the dream of an agrarian heritage corresponding to at least "half my blood": the entelechy of the paternal memory. The image of the central character standing "vertical" and alone in such a setting, flooded with "shame" and "reverence" in the night, is the image of a man confronting the ultimate mystery of who he is, a man moved to the keenest emotion by "dead black," unnameable, and unutterable presences in his immediate surroundings. It is above all the image of a man *inspired,* by "all that surrounded me, that silently strove in through my senses and stretched me full" (415). Gudger's great gift to his visitor from the North is the gift of inspiration, that escalation of consciousness by which all the ingredients of one's visual field—people, objects, structures, textures, tones and overtones, the points and the totalities—suddenly become potent, vivid, and meaningful, or as our author might have it, *actual* to the perceiving imagination. In such escalated condition, the contents of the farmer's space might conceivably spring to attention as force fields of symbol (Gudger's overalls, the lamp above Agee's writing table), signal (the javelin of light streaking through a knothole, passages found at random in the family Bible), and talismanic design (the print of a child's hand in whitewash, the brimmed "glory" of Annie Mae's hat, 286). Such potent ground enforces the discovery of powers within (like "extended senses") by submission to felt powers without (that "stretched me full"), and thus helps the central character find himself by passing beyond himself into "a world newly touched and beautiful to me" (427–28).

THE FURIES

For the rest, the presiding metaphor is predictably that of childhood—echoes, intimations, partial restorations. Drawn from their bed, the Gudgers welcome their night visitor, and Annie Mae fixes a dinner the eating of which, apart from posing difficult and complicated kinds of "enjoyment" for their guest, serves as an initiation rite into what is described as "the true tastes of home." Watching them in their surroundings, Agee feels as if he has been granted "a brief truancy into the sources of my life" (415); that after long "wandering and seeking," he now sits "at rest in my house"; and that "the wife my age exactly, the husband four years older, seemed not other than my own parents" (415). The second half of this statement flows oddly from the first unless we imagine that George and Annie Mae at their present ages, thirty-two and twenty-eight respectively, approximate the ages of Agee's own parents at that point in time when he would have been happiest to remember them, that is, as envisioned by a toddler's eye. Upon finishing his meal, he is escorted to the front room where he prepares for sleep on the mattress belonging to, and recently vacated by, the Gudger children (i.e., "the child-warmed bed," 419); and before turning in, thumbs through the family Bible ("In the Room: the Testament") making special note of the following lines (Malachi 4:6): "And he shall turn the heart of the fathers to the children, and the heart of the children to their fathers, lest I come and smite the earth with a curse" (422). And finally, hours later, at dawn ("In the Room: In Bed"), as he listens to the sounds of the family rising to ready for their morning chores, he sees "the wall of their room slit with yellow light, only with a deep and gentle sorrow, in some memory out of childhood which seemed now restored like the ghost of one beloved and dead" (428).

And so on: while the language and intent are sufficiently clear, the practical effects of both upon character may be less so. To what extent, that is, does "some memory of childhood"—indeed, the whole emotional and metaphorical evocation of the child's condition—effect the central character's credentials as artist inspired? We have in the previous pages been fairly lavish in our indulgence of the specialists' vocabulary, resorting to such terms and phrases as "polymorphous hunger," "separation anxiety," the "grieving child's hunger for the body of the parent," etc., to describe the quality of this character's evolving sensibility. Perhaps this then is the point to clarify that, in spite of the richness of his sea change, the figure who appears as "James Agee" never of course metamorphoses into a "child," the "spirit of childhood," or any sort of "infant consciousness," "polymorphous" or otherwise. His "rebirth," such as it is, has less to do with the time-honored and sentimental tradition of Romantic rejuvenation than with the intensities and refinements that ostensibly have taken place within the realm of experience itself. A sensuous and sensualized consciousness means precisely an accretion, not a diminishment, of consciousness, an amplification of thought and feeling to a presumptively advanced, and certainly different, frequency; and what Agee indicates by a set of "extended senses"—or what we have spoken of as an "inspired," "heightened," or empowered self—has probably less to do with that demimythic infant's paradise of spontaneity and unself-consciousness than with the mind's working linkage to the immediacy of its moments, a day-to-day intelligence of sensing and doing, and especially the body's sensing and doing in relation to the things that surround it. To be sure, in taking rooms with Gudger, Agee begins to resurrect many of those numinous and trancelike emotions we associate with our myths of childhood and the child's romance with the world about it (a romance sustained, and to some extent legitimated, much later in *A Death in the Family*). But he is never transformed into the infant naif, the Whitmanian hermaphrodite, the "greening" American, or even less into that guileless artist-maker absorbed in the heedless rapture of nonstop creation. He becomes what he has always been—only more so: a poet of consciousness, one who observes, combines, transmutes, and then self-reflexively interrogates—a moody and neurotic oracle at the house of Gudger whose triumphs of observation and perspicacity, of synthesis and unification, are always chastened by a complicated backlash of guilt, sexual shame, and self-consciousness; whose "silence of wonder" (425) and awareness of a world "newly touched and beautiful" (427) go hand in glove with his passionately held conviction that he has no right to be where he is, or partake in any way of one fraction of all the joy and good fortune that has come his way. Even in his approach to Gudger's yard, he initiates a chant that in one form or another will be reiterated throughout his stay: "I have no right, here, I have no real right, much as I want it, and could never earn it, and should I write of it, must defend it against my kind" (410).

If the torment of the earlier, pre-Gudger Agee was that of a man bereft, the result of something missing, an elusive connection fluttering just beyond his reach, the melancholy of this appreciably happier, more settled figure is that of a man rewarded beyond all justice and endeavor, of one who has been welcomed, fed, bedded, sheltered, and *illumined*. It is then a melancholy arising from the direct result of something acquired, the missing connection found, the heart's desire filled and filled to running over with rapture—and then some nameless, ponderous, restive weight, some yanking reflex of souring joy. Even in the verse serving as epigraph to "Inductions," as the poet approaches the "God of my joy and gladness," he also cries "why art thou so heavy my soul and why art thou so disquieted within me?" (360)

One version of the punishing side of Agee's "joy and gladness" dramatizes itself figuratively in the onslaught of bedbugs ("In the Room: In Bed") that infiltrates his first night's contentment upon his "altar of God"; so insistent is the attack that by morning he is fairly sure that he has never been to sleep at all. The incident becomes another one of many that occur through the book that seem to represent both what actually happened, as well as within context, what has been deliberately shaped for symbolic overtone. A brief bout of genital guilt initiates, perhaps even precipitates, this wildly comic seizure as Agee seems to experience another wave of "adult" libido: "I tried to imagine intercourse in this bed; I managed to imagine it fairly well. I began to feel sharp little piercings and crawlings all along the surface of my body" (425)—and the vermin, like Alabamian furies, are suddenly all over him. They literally shoo him from his beloved shelter, beyond the front porch into the middle of the dark yard, where he significantly feels alien in relation to the house, "like a special sort of burglar," keenly aware of his sexual promptings, "lawless and lustful" once again (426). The sequence represents a mock initiation rite that dims without eradicating the quasi-mystical aura already established by the serious initiation rite now digesting in his stomach, a farcical baptism that welcomes him to country living at the same time that it reminds him of the extent to which he must remain "outside" this way of life (i.e., in the yard, in the night). As emissaries from the fabric of a country child's intimate possession, the vermin bring him the sobering news (if reminding was what he needed) that he may not have any inherent right at all to this particular bed rest; that he is not a farmer, or a little boy, or, least of all, a born-again innocent; that the Gudgers may remind him of his parents, but that they are not his parents; and that in effect, he can, will, and perhaps must leave the house of his surrogate childhood, just as he left the house of his real childhood not so many years ago. I think all of this is implied in the expulsion from the home, for the vermin represent of course the "piercing and crawling" of his own "heavy" shame ("they were full of my blood," 425), of his awareness that he has no right to sustain such an intensity of contentment without some remorse of conscience, some reflex of retribution.

The bedbug sequence is the joker in the deck of happenings at Gudger's house, and the dissonant blue note within the relatively happy chord struck upon entry into the family context. It is also purest Agee, the lancing burden of his nostalgia, the deliciously necessary torments attendant upon all Agean transformation and renewal. Moreover, here and virtually everywhere throughout his work, the highest kinds of pleasure, the most ardent and saturated of emotional satisfactions, are frequently of this dappled, anomalous, melancholic variety, deepest joy authenticated only by its complicity with the sorrowful, the anxious, even the noxious and the repellent. Each mouthful, for example, of the never-to-be-forgotten first supper he enjoys at Gudger's table also reeks of "a sort of wateriness and discouraged tepidity, which combines to make the food seem unclear, sticky, and sallow with some sort of disease." "To a city palate," the warmth and odor of the milk are also "somehow dirty, and at the same time vital, as if one were drinking blood." Still, he affirms, "these are the true tastes of home . . . much as my reflexes are twitching in refusal of each mouthful a true homesick and simple fondness for it has so strong hold of me that in fact there is no fight to speak of and no faking of enjoyment at all" (416).

And so too with the itchy, alienating bedbugs ("I must admit that even in the vermin there was a certain amount of pleasure," 428). He urinates, returns to his room, bundles up in a swaddling of clothing, and still scratching and bleeding under the ceaseless ministrations of the surviving insects, reclaims his mattress and the complex rhythm of his irksome pleasure: "I don't exactly know why anyone should be 'happy' under these circumstances, but there's no use laboring the point: I was." So be it.

Child psychologist Melanie Klein has frequently described and analyzed the sadness and guilt experienced by certain children who feel they have received so much nutrition, comfort, and generosity from the body of the parent figure, and indeed later in life, from resources within the physical reality itself, that they are made despondent with the unappeasable need to repay the donor, to make "reparations," as if the donor had been in some way maltreated or damaged by the absence of what was taken from it. When one considers the manner in which so much of the central character's early behavior in Hale County seems to align itself with Kleinian patterns of childhood neuroses, it is equally difficult to resist the notion that Agee's raddled happiness frequently represents the need to make "reparations" of this kind.[21] In relation to Gudger's people, Agee often seems to quarantine and sometimes even curdle the milk of kindness received as the function of an overwhelming gratitude, his way of putting back in the form of a nagging contrition some smattering of all the good he has gotten of his benefactor.

But his need to repay goes far beyond this very characteristic (and admittedly lifelong) desire to don an emotional hairshirt. The need to repay also determines nothing less than his ultimate position and vocational identity at Gudger's home, not of course as family member (he does not dare), but as outrider and watchman, the custodian of Gudger's space and possessions, and guardian of his front yard. As one who has been granted comfort and protection, Agee will attempt payment in kind even if such a fiduciary relation has neither been requested nor in fact warranted by its intended recipient. Still, he insists upon comparing the house to "a little boat in the darkness, floated upon the night, far out on the steadiness of a vacant sea, whose crew slept while I kept needless watch, and felt the presence of the country round me and upon me" (421). Persisting in his nightly vigil, he and Evans eventually arrange sleeping quarters not in one of the rooms (a gesture perhaps too greedily familiar), but at a respectful distance on the front porch, which, as the structure of the text confirms, becomes Agee's personal creative base, his space beneath time and the habitation of his vision, the site through which the many shifting perspectives of the book seem to resolve themselves.[22] And while we continually learn of the other residents sleeping, we rarely see or hear of Agee nodding off—not until the last line of the last page, when virtually in mid-thought, his watch and his work are both officially terminated.

By stationing himself on the porch, Agee has also stationed himself on the equivocal borderline, the free zone—neither "in" nor "out"—that mediates between the two unalterable conditions of his identity, his home and the world, the point and the totality, the site of the southern child and that of the northern writer, the nourishing freedom-within-order of his past, sacred, celibate, and vulnerable, and the famished, anarchic rages of his present tense, dark, vast, and insatiable ("the country round me and upon me"), the machinery of time and circumstance, the relentless historical grind, that has both robbed him of his best and earliest joy and reduced Gudger to his present misery. At least part of Agee—northern intruder from a dark world dragging a southern household from its sleep—however unwilling, is part of this machinery, and in his guilty heart both he and it have taken from his surrogate parent (in the form of food, shelter, emotion) more than either can ever repay. So as he watches over the house of Gudger, he watches over himself watching the house ("and should I write of it, must defend it against my kind")—over that greedy, curious, devouring side of himself that might steal without so much as an attempt at reparation ("like a special sort of burglar")—now gliding through the petrified stage sets of Gudger's rooms with an eye not merely hungry and heightened, but responsible too (an ever-present sense of "vigilance . . . out of honor and fear of the house itself"). And as further tribute: his way of "guarding" the family expresses itself by actually creating his book on the porch (or such is the illusion), the truest fruit of his labor and offering of love to the farmer, the ultimate reparation by the only means available to him, the conversion of his recently discovered trove of emotion into art.

But is a man like Agee ever done with debt? His guilty passion binds him to his task and indeed well beyond it, chiding him in fact that art may not be enough, that one's reparations, unlike one's creative acts, may never be finished. This masterwork, this work of reminding what the world has either ceased to remember or ignored, this book may be Gudger's only ticket to immortality (not to speak of Agee's), but it may also be only a holding action against the nattering, everlasting disconsolations of a shameful heart. Was it not Agee who wished that his book be printed on the cheapest of paper so that in time it might whither like a flower, get lost like a child, be forgotten like a man or woman?[23] And did not the alleged "immortality" of art, for this art-driven, art-phobic artist, consist of little more than dusty preservation in libraries, mindless perpetuation in classrooms, treacly cooption by the bias and fashion of a future day—misread, misunderstood, and totally emasculated? And against this, who can say whether the writer at night on the porch was driven more by his zeal to fulfill his transcendent calling than more immediately by the private devils that tore away at his flesh like bedbugs?

The hunger and the knife, the grab and the melancholy, the piercing and the crawling, the delirium of the appetites amid recoils of shame—in the whole mortal shuffle in all the world over, these things, not art, may be the only madness that endures: these too, after all, are among "the true tastes of home."

4. GODS IN RUINS

Now this is the place to discuss the most immediate source of all Agee's guilt and joy, the source that helps him come to terms with his artistic identity, that shows him the way to his material, and through this material, to the mobilization and concentration of his creative forces; that is to say, this is the place to discuss the farmer.

OF PURITY AND CONSCIOUSNESS

Agee confronts the farmer—this then is the crux of the human drama, such as it is, "a meeting of the extremes of the race." And that which exists at the level of concrete fact also exists at the level of abstract debate: there the terms of the confrontation are between a shame-ridden intellect and an imperfect innocence, or, to use the terms preferred by the author (in "Education"), between "consciousness" and "purity." Insofar as this is the story of James Agee, it is the story of consciousness and its fate, its splendors and miseries, prodigious appetites, miracles of observation and penetration—and finally its abiding solitude. Insofar as this is the story of three tenant families, it is the story of purity and *its* fate, its sacred domain and imminent corruption, special graces, fierce beauties—and almost total defenselessness.

At one point in "Inductions," this colloquy of opposites shrinks to the size of a nocturnal tableau in which Agee eats the food the farmers have prepared for him and tries to imagine a poem that would suggest the major distinctions between the Gudgers and himself: "The form was one in which two plain people and one complex one who scarcely know each other discourse while one eats and the others wait for him to finish so they may get back to bed" (417).

The contrasts distilled within the image could not be more casual or inauspicious, or, as thematic configurations, more suggestive. Agee at Gudger's table embodies the destiny of consciousness at the altar of purity, and the fate of the hungry stranger is to enter and to take (i.e., to eat), just as the fate of his nurturing host is to receive and to provide. Or to push harder: a busy, devouring intellect sups at the site of a patient, heedless innocence while the latter awaits the completion of these activities in order to resume the rhythm of its uncomplicated constancy of being (i.e., to "get back to bed").

Consciousness seeks purity for the very plenitude of what it is, for its direct and unassuming thereness, for its sufficiency unto itself, which by contrast defines consciousness as parched, starving, and incomplete. The hungers of intellect, its notorious and "insatiable curiosity," are not simply a measure of its bottomless appetite, but also a gauge of its insufficiency, an index of its need to fill and fulfill itself through the incorporation of its passive and integral opposite. But this need is never to be satisfied: the discovery of purity by consciousness only brings consciousness close enough to purity to fully appreciate just how far away it really is, just as the move to merge with purity only reveals purity in its unassuming otherness. Making contact with Gudger only exposes Agee to the unbridgeable gulf that separates them:

> . . . by bland chance alone is my life so softened and sophis-
> ticated in the years of my defenselessness, and I am robbed of a
> royalty I can not only never claim, but never properly much desire
> or regret. And so in this quiet introit, and in all the time we have
> stayed in this house, and in all we have sought, and in each detail
> of it, there is so keen, sad, and precious a nostalgia as I can scarcely
> otherwise know; a knowledge of brief truancy into the sources of my
> life, whereto I have no rightful access, having paid no price beyond
> love and sorrow (415).

Agee's brief vision of his lost childhood, his "brief truancy into the sources" of his life, fill him with the awareness of just how immeasurably distant he still is from everything that he was or might have been; how largely through "bland chance" (presumably the death of his father, the eventual dispersion of his family, the subsequent history of a life cut off from its roots, etc.) he has become so different and estranged from his origins ("so softened and sophisticated") that he has no "right" to either claim, desire, or regret the legacy he has lost. He is simply engulfed by the "nostalgia" that arises from the gap between what he was—in his boyish potential, his "rightborn energy" (382)—and what he has become.[24] The failure of consciousness is not only that it can never fulfill or complete itself but also that it can never subtract from what it already is, can never undo or retrieve itself at an earlier stage of development. A "complex" man, "softened and sophisticated" as he has become, can fasten his mind to an immediate reality of simple feeling and direct sensation only through increments, not diminishments, of consciousness and self-awareness (cf., "The Furies").

Moreover, purity needs the very distance consciousness craves to abridge to preserve the sacred mysteries of its operation. Consciousness can gain full knowledge—incorporation and possession—of purity only at the risk of losing it forever. It is the inquiry itself that alters and endangers the condition of the suspect; and bridging the gap between purity and consciousness results not in the regeneration of the latter, but in the demystification and ultimate destruction of the former. One of the things Agee learns in reaffirming his powers as a creator is that the surest way of jeopardizing the integrity of Gudger's innocence is by making a book about him. The book as a mechanism of inquiry and understanding is, of course, the sharpest index of consciousness in action, just as it also represents the subjugation and annexation of its object, the pollution of its sacrosanct qualities, through incorporation into a demonstrably inaccurate and falsifying medium (c.f., "The Words"). Still, Agee cannot deny the hungers of consciousness, the need to enter and to take, any more than he can deny the claims of conscience, the need to restore and to anneal, the need, that is, to make reparations (c.f., "The Furies"): the moral art of his book becomes the equilibration of these conflicting needs. His text will be partly of and for the farmers (they will be the bearers of his dedication), but it will always keep them at a tactful distance. He will wander about them endlessly—their dwellings, their possessions; sequester them within a circle of tragic-heroism; even on one occasion (273), ascribe to them something very like the powers of emblem and medieval heraldry (comparing them to totemic beasts, Gudger as lion and ox, Ricketts as fox, etc.): but out of deference to everything they mean to him as vessels of fragile, perishable, and numinous force, he will never directly engage them as fully developed characters in a book.

By this reasoning, one finds oneself in curious and partial agreement with those critics who would admonish Agee for not presenting the farmers as "fully rounded" or "multidimensional" characters, for not developing them in a manner comparable to characters in successful works of modern fiction, such as, for instance, those southern farmers in the work of William Faulkner (e.g., Mink Snopes or Anse Bundren).[25] Agee's farmers are not in fact "fully rounded" or "multidimensional," and do not in fact have the moral or psychological depth of comparable characters in successful works of modern fiction (Faulkner's southern farmers being only the primary and most conspicuous examples). Our author has rendered his people with a vibrant and memorable sense of presence, but he has also refused to dramatize or seriously explore them, put them into a conflicted action, or even an extended conversation, so that we never get a sense of them as dynamic or "free" figures moving on their own terrain apart from his ministrations. On the other hand, I find nothing to admonish in this kid-gloved treatment: Agee *wants* his characters to be large-scaled but frozen and somewhat remote, grand but distant. Rather than view their presentation as a flaw in the author's technique, there is considerably more justice in learning to think of them—their rendering and effects—as the necessary results of a deliberate moral and artistic strategy. The farmers are not to be examined (and so judged) as segregated entities, but rather as part of a complementary relationship, the contrasting half of a conceptual dialogue with the central character himself: in this manner, each becomes the foil, measure, and counterweight of the other. As the farmers, for instance, are dignified and remote, the central character is confessional and self-indulgent; as they appear to be fixed and unchanging, he appears to be fluid and evolutionary; as they are "flat," he is "deep." Their gravity and silence balance the pandemonium of his language (that would encircle and evoke them); their fixity of being, the yardstick of his scramble to become; their grace and forbearance, the corrective to his gush and gaucherie; their wounds, the agenbite of his inwit; their supernal status as legend, the necessary counterpart to his all-too-human status as a bottomless muddle.

This calculated reticence in offering his subject to the reader, this strange tact and respectful hush, becomes Agee's ultimate tribute to, and reverence for, the sealed-off quality of lost time; his way of accepting his estrangement from his origins in purity, as well as whatever remnant of those origins are to be found in the farmer and his world. The dramatized exposé, the extended analysis, the intimate probe, become part of a dashed and forsaken paradise of unrealized longing, the ever-receding personal horizon line where the present moment converges with a lost home, an abandoned childhood, and a dead father.[26]

MARVELS

Here then is a nominal study of a specialized group in which we do not learn how members interact with one another as individuals, or interact as a group with other groups. The social and psychological profile that could emerge, and that Agee was particularly gifted to render (e.g., as in *A Death in the Family*)—the drama of personality, mix, exchange, and internal affair—is conspicuously absent. Thus we will not discover how Annie Mae Gudger and Sadie Ricketts socialize with each other, or how either of them might relate to Bud Woods's new wife, Ivy; nor will we observe how George Gudger or Fred Ricketts might bargain with their respective landlords; nor how Louise Gudger might get through a day in the classroom. In place of exploration of the farmer's personality, Agee gives us an extraordinary and exhaustive record of the conditions of his life. His most characteristic way of getting close to his human subject without violating its sanctity is to make an epical study of Alabamian architecture, furniture, clothing, tools, animals, labor, ecology, and topography; that is to say, he gives us the farmer's world as a substitute for the farmer himself. The prototypical "drama" of the book becomes a descriptive contretemps at the periphery, Agee's ecstatic evocation of the trappings of the farmer's life, and the peculiar vibrancy that resides at the heart of his inanimate objects. Each object becomes a kind of proxy for all the men, women, and children that have come into contact with it, "plain people" who live close to, and are defined by, sacred sources in nature (e.g., the foundation of Gudger's house slips into "a region prior to the youngest quaverings of creation," 21), and have left the imprint of these sources upon their instruments, garments, and spaces. "Age, use, and weather" (267), human and natural forces, have wrought extraordinary changes upon items that for the most part have originated as machine-made goods, and have converted the status of these goods from mechanical and inert to organic and expressive, and even beyond these, have transformed prosaic implements of use into "images and marvels" (267) of nature. Agee cherishes these "marvels" for themselves and for the special and extraordinary people that have recently vacated them, for the imprint left upon them by time and human circumstance, for everything that constitutes the felt absence of the object—that is, everything absent that charges everything present with the powers of an anaconic relic, the fleshy husks of spirits recently departed.

Such object-description provides Agee with his most spectacular occasions for hero-worship, allows him to say of the object what he would otherwise find vulgar, egregious, too intimate and familiar, or even sacrilegious, to say of the farmer himself. Understandably, many readers will not find these pages (and pages) of description to be any kind of proper or satisfactory substitute for character analysis, yet extraordinary and undeniable compensations abound. These idiosyncratic forms of analytic surgery and speculative lift-off may well represent something that Agee does better than any other American writer of his century. To this moment, one has yet to find his equal in pinpointing and expressing the brimmed-over busyness contained within the matchless singularity of the individual detail, the fascination of minutiae, contingencies, and manifold parts, the dense communities and swarmed orderings of texture and design. Nowhere else (even in Agee's other works) do we get such a graphic, meticulous, and exhilarating panorama of experience in the realm of "the extended senses," of the glowing intricacies of that kingdom available to a heightened but "unassisted and weaponless consciousness" (11). Put baldly: no one in American letters since Thoreau has found so much to say about so seemingly little.

And not just the "little," but also the obscure, the forgotten, and the despised; the worn, torn, patched, soiled, shredded, and wasted; the squalid, the abused, and the overlooked. It is only here, in and through these very long and sometimes obfuscating object-descriptions, that we discover Agee's covert but most determined plea for the transvaluation of received categories, specifically and most notably, for the recuperation of the farmer's fallen estate. Transformed through social, historical, and legendary reference and amplification, Gudger's overalls, for instance, are not just resonant with the force of Gudger himself, but with the whole collectivized strength and symbolic impetus of his yeoman class; they are the "standard or classical garment" of "the southern rural American working man"; "they arc his uniform, the badge and proclamation of his peasantry" (265).

> And in their whole stature: full covering of the cloven strength of the legs and thighs and of the loins; then nakedness and harnessing behind, naked along the flanks; and in front, the short, squarely tapered, powerful towers of the belly and chest to above the nipples.
>
> And on this façade, the cloven halls for the legs, the strong-seamed, structured opening for the genitals, the broad horizontal at the waist, the slant thigh pockets, the buttons at the point of each hip and on the breast, the geometric structures of the usages of the simpler trades—the complexed seams of utilitarian pockets which are so brightly picked out against darkness when the seam-threadings, double and triple stitched, are still white, so that a new suit of overalls has among its beauties those of a blueprint: and they are a map of a working man (266).

The overalls are of course the very mold of Gudger's form ("each man's garment wearing the shape and beauty of his induplicable body," 267), and Agee's hungry-eyed "uniform" inspection is one permissible way of evoking—of virtually touching and sculpting—and even exaggerating the body of Gudger (while avoiding the actual man), as well as un-abashedly rooting the source of his physical power in the almost topo-graphical sexual virility of his garment (and in this, there is a particular caressing of the parts of the lower anatomy, "of the legs and thighs and of the loins," of "the cloven halls for the legs," and of "the structural opening for the genitals"). But the grandiloquent and faintly biblical locution ("full covering of cloven strength"), the fabulous resonance of the antique diction ("cloven," "loins," "flesh," etc.), the muscular thrust of the hyperbole ("the nakedness and *harnessing* behind," "the *powerful towers* of belly and chest," "the cloven *halls* for the legs"), the sheer, great animal kinesis of the whole—and this fragment is typical of the extraordinary, and admittedly exhausting, energy of the entire four-page description—all this elevates Gudger from a potent man of the soil to the station of a natural folk monument, one of the soaring pillars of the "southern rural American" landscape. The closer the author's eye bears down upon its object the more exalted and far-reaching becomes the range of comparative reference (a tendency true for many of the object-descriptions); and as the passage proceeds, the "uniform" that began as an "emblem" of Gudger's heroic "peasantry" vaults upward in class as it ages through the years until the worn and repatched shoulders of his workshirt reveal "a fabric as intricate and fragile, and deeply in the honor of the reigning sun, as the feather mantle of a Toltec Prince" (268). And finally, in old age, at the outer limits of materiality itself, the outfit effervesces beyond class into its spiritual fume as an archetypal ancient of days, and takes on a kind of spectral music, a spun clear transfiguration beyond mortality into pure abstraction: the colors of wisdom, the secrets of structure, the spirit-life of texture: " . . . The blue is so vastly fainted and withdrawn it is discernible scarcely more as blue than as that most pacific silver which the bone wood of the houses and the visage of genius seem to shed, and is a color and cloth seeming ancient, veteran, composed, and patient to the source of being, as too the sleepings and the drifts of form . . ." (269).

The coopted or simply conventional eye may well see in all this—in Gudger's workshirt, or, for that matter, in any of his possessions—no smattering of "marvels" at all, but merely the old, the out-worn, or the dysfunctional. But for Agee, each demotion of the object as an instrument of utility only advances its status, and ensures its condition, as an object of spiritual and aesthetic satisfaction. Each scab and rent, the scars of time, the insignia of "age, use, and weather," become the very traces of gods in ruins, sacred remnants of a golden day and an ennobled order of being.[27]

And let us have no illusion about the very special and magisterial claims that Agee is making for both these objects and their owners. On the rather sticky issue of privilege, the author's metaphors, if not his explicit statements, are consistent, unstinting, and unequivocal. While well aware of his subject's substantial limitations (instances of bigotry toward blacks and unconscious brutality, particularly toward animals, do not go unspecified), Agee doesn't hesitate to implicate the entire category of southern backcountry poor, white *and* black, as not simply equal to every other category of peoples, but in fact slightly superior to them. So, not only does Gudger's aging workshirt become redolent of the "feathered mantle of a Toltec Prince," but even those unfortunate "clients of rehabilitation" (recall "At the Forks," from "July 1936")— the young farmer "with the lips of an Aegean exquisite," his wife with eyes revealing "the splendor of a monstrance"—sit on their porch as if "enthroned" (34) and the quality of their hate shines "scarcely short of a state of beatitude" (33). Emma Woods's build is "that of a young queen of a child's magic story" (59); Annie Mae's hat fits her like a "triumphal crown" (286); Agee's lost heritage compares with "royalty" purloined; and so on. In spite of his reiterated proclamation to the effect of the "holiness" of every living creature, etc., the Southern Agrarian creature may just be a little more "holy," a marginally more intense distillate of the spiritual liquor otherwise acknowledged to be in general distribution.

Let us allow that some small part of this bias represents one ploy of a subtle satiric strategy designed to tweak the knee-jerk egalitarianism of the author's socialist cronies and pasteurizing progressives everywhere; and that even some larger part derives from a lifelong instinctive habit of extolling his personal heroes and heroines (artists, historical figures, family members, etc.), regardless of regional background or ethnic origins, in the epochal, outsized, and often magical terms roughly analogous to a small crawling child's low-angled view of the tapering towers of the adult giants who love and watch over his arduous rambles (e.g., the four-year-old Rufus's reference to his parents as "my king and my queen"). But then let us also, and finally, acknowledge the dead-set earnestness of Agee's regional idealism; at least in Gudger's world, the author believes himself to be in the presence of something very like a natural, homegrown, moral aristocracy.

And one which really cannot be found anywhere but in the Agrarian South—an uncommon belief held in spite of his often formidable common sense that attempts, from time to time, to find similarities between his beloved tenants and workers everywhere and at any time.

Still, the exclusionist, possessive, and cloistered caste of his rural bias strives to protect his subject not only from the generalizing tendencies of the conventional northern liberal reader, but just as ardently from his own ecumenical hunt for a "common" humanity. Gudger's garments are not just those of any American working man, but particularly those of the "southern rural" variety; and while the work and Sunday clothing of country blacks may be the "expression of a genius distributed among almost the whole of a race" (264), he hastens to qualify in a footnote: "In all this on negroes, by the way, I am speaking strictly of small towns and of deep country. City negroes, even in the south, are modified; and those of the north are another thing again" (264). And when Louise Gudger attempts to pose her country purity for Evans's camera in an imitation town dress, Agee lets the tribal chauvinist cat out of its ethnic bag: " . . . you yourself gave it away, Louise, for your skin was a special quiet glowing gold color, which can never come upon the skin of nicely made little girls in towns and cities, but only to those who came straight out of the earth and are continually upon it in the shining of the sun, active and sweating, and toughening into work that has already made your clear ten-year-old mouth resolute and unquestioning of personal desire . . ." (367).

Obvious outcries of "elitism!" or "reverse snobbery!" may well be entirely beside the point here, particularly when almost every page of this masterpiece seems to derive its secret premise from this unwavering favoritism; such favoritism is not only responsible for the trumpeting sentimentalism of the Louise Gudger passage but also for some of the most stirring and brilliant writing in the book (e.g., the description of Gudger's overalls). More specifically, this passionate preference finds congruence with a politics that was always more emotional and visceral than principled and systematic; and one that completely underwrites the fact that however hard he tried, or however earnest his sympathies and convictions, Agee never could keep faith with the Communist party, or even for the length of a single book, walk the straight line as a fellow traveler ("I am a Communist by sympathy and conviction" [249]: a mid-text assertion later withdrawn—formally and finally—in "Intermissions," see "Teachers" below). For a time at least, Agee and the Marxists seemed to share the same enemies (i.e., Bourgeois Capitalism and its cultural by-products), and, too, a certain quick and deep fellow-feeling for the wretched and dispossessed everywhere. But where the Marxists' approach to human behavior was largely materialistic and socioeconomic, Agee's tended to be moral and spiritual; and where the Marxists confidently awaited the ultimate salvation of the race by means of the transcendental point-counterpoint of an implacable historical dialectic, Agee could only write convincingly about personal salvation, and even then, only through the intervention of much faith and a fair amount of family heroics—namely, maternal fathers, patristic mothers, and filial rebels and liberators. But just as crucial as any of these differences, his rural bias helps to explain why Agee, try as he might, never could successfully organize his consciousness along class lines; that is to say, under the spell of Gudger, he instinctively adopts the stance of one kind of traditional southerner, and more aptly represents the fruits of *caste*, not class, consciousness. And one of the more fascinating aspects of this book is the way in which this young investigator's "scientific" or "anthropological" fieldwork in farmer's "overhauls," skin tone, and the like, keeps confessing itself as a kind of genuine bone-bred mysticism based on deeply private, even subrational, responses to blood, breeding, and landscape.

Doubtless more than a few will find Agee's ennoblement of the Alabama farmer both willful and bookish, simply another specimen of the post-Appomattox sensibility of an unreconstructed Johnny Reb commingled with that of a young Harvard poet-taster's sip of several centuries of the Arcadian literary tradition. How in good conscience can one even begin to talk of "royalty," or for that matter "purity," in such debilitating circumstances as those which define the ongoing life of the farmer? Actually, Agee's writing on this issue is neither foggy nor quixotic: the concrete and evidentiary basis for Gudger's special elegance resides in the extraordinary aestheticized texture of his daily existence; no matter how dispiriting the circumstances, Agee never manages to compromise his unflagging awareness of, and insistence upon, the supernal *beauty* of the farmer himself, the many shapes and tints of his surroundings, and above all (once again), the many forms of his object-creation: "They live on land, and in houses, and under skies and seasons, which all happen to seem to me beautiful beyond almost anything else I know, and they themselves, and the clothes they wear, and their motions, and their speech, are beautiful in the same intense and final commonness and purity" (314). Much of Agee's book is devoted to a passionate and empirical demonstration of this judgment, and one most apparent in all those pages devoted to descriptions of the farmer's clothing, furniture, tools, exterior and interior design, and household appurtenances. Agee views these as specimens of a great "classical" art even though the men, women, and children who have made or inhabit these specimens do not understand them as such, nor do they mean them to be understood as such by others; nor in fact do they perceive these specimens to be in any way "beautiful." As already indicated, these forms come about almost entirely through an indeterminate and unforeseeable mix of practical and nonaesthetic human needs (i.e., they are objects for use, not aesthetic contemplation), and nonaesthetic natural forces (chance, time, and weather), and as such, are very much like the aesthetic forms found in nature itself; in fact, for the author, the two categories of form are often virtually indistinguishable, forms created by what Agee calls that "florid genius of nature which is incapable of error" (145). This "genius" also flows through the men, women, and children who suffer, struggle, and on occasion thrive, in almost smothering proximity to the earth (who "grow up straight out of the earth"), even though they may be deeply unaware of themselves as vehicles of its expression. In this manner, the things made or inhabited by these men, women, and children will embody the rich press of this "genius"—that is, a density and originality of power, sense, and design that bears little or no trace of the quaint or the charming or the "artsy," or even and especially the simplistic or the "folksy," but is rather complex, subtle, and rigorous; and Agee takes great pains to draw upon the masters of high culture—Bach, Beethoven, Cézanne, etc.—for the exact formal cognates of the farmer's creation. The makers themselves, however, remain utterly indifferent to its presence (i.e., that of "genius") and entirely ignorant of its import.

This utter indifference to one's creation, the felt absence of vanity and will, in itself constitutes a kind of "purity," a quality that may be perceived as part of the purity of the thing created. As such, the whole process of creation—both intention and act—is admired, cherished, even envied, not of course by the "plain" people who have engaged in it, but entirely by "complex" people of learning and sophistication, especially by that thoroughly familiar and most advanced development of modernist taste and sensibility profoundly sated with its own devices and brilliancies: the forced marches of the intellect, the appeasements and betrayals of the artist's ego, the fraudulent fires of the Archangels and the canned music of the Muses. Suddenly this taste and sensibility stands astonished before a maximum of aesthetic effect accomplished through a seeming minimum of deliberated effort, the achievement of a grace beyond the curse of mental labor, the restitution of something very like a lost Eden of creative innocence.

Agee's numerous object-descriptions begin to suggest the aesthetic framework for a thoroughly selfless art form, one beyond the taint of the personal ego and self-reflexivity, just as his numerous accounts of the simple decency and generosity of the three families begin to suggest the moral framework for a thoroughly selfless way of life, one "resolute and unquestioning of personal desire." And throughout the text his language has little difficulty shuttling back and forth from the aesthetic life of the thing made to the moral life of its maker; and frequently his sensible comprehension of moral perfection actually seems to originate in his sensible apprehension of aesthetic perfection. One senses this convergence particularly whenever the author feels compelled to draw upon his frequently reiterated term "classical" (or "classic" or "classicism," as in the "deep classicism" of Gudger's work outfit), or enlist any of those substantives that invariably adhere, or allude to, the "classical" condition—like "bareness," "cleanness," "sobriety," "stinginess," "simplicity," "symmetry," etc.—to describe everything from the gait of Gudger's mule, to the space that separates his bed from the wall, to the evanescence of the odor that permeates his rooms. In praising the farmer's possessions and spaces, Agee begins to sketch the rudiments of an American "classical" aesthetic, a thoroughly abstemious kind of beauty in which the sensuous flourish is everywhere chastened by, and made obedient to, a hand, however unconscious or inadvertent, that denotes impersonal rigor and a decorous ordering of parts.

In the light of the foregoing it isn't hard to see why Agee as artist could regret the loss of his upbringing among "plain people," or even anguish over the kind of maker he himself had become and the arduous path that his own art was clearly fated to follow: his best and most characteristic efforts (and efforts they were!)—romantic (not "classical"), extravagant, self-revealing, and self-aware—were of course the very opposite of everything represented by the virtually selfless creations of the farmer. One also has little trouble appreciating how his passionate experience of agrarian "classicism" could help form the basis of a lifelong aesthetic ideal, as well as the model for some of those rigorous moral and aesthetic critical standards by which he would later judge the work of others (e.g., films and filmmakers), and often find it and them wanting. One can even appreciate how qualities derived from his early inquiry into rural aesthetics helped to inspire the goals and practices of his own late creative manner, the studied lack of pretention, and the bone-plain, faux-naif stylizations of "A Mothers's Tale" and the Rufus material of *A Death in the Family.*

Perhaps it is altogether too glib to assert that Agee revered the farmer himself (as well as his works) for the very opposite of those qualities of character he found in his own person. Still: whatever it was to be a tenant, he could be fairly sure it was not to live within the crisis of consciousness, the almost intolerable insistencies of ego and intellect, by which he could virtually challenge and define himself all his life. However grim the present situation, the farmer, as Agee envisioned him, probably did not agonize over the ultimate value of his professional effects, the hopelessness of impossible aesthetic ambition, the validity of his thought and expression, the genuineness of his daily acts. Agee revered the men, women, and children who "came straight out of the earth" because he revered the earth and everything living closest to it as a kind of moral and spiritual absolute, and in this sense also "incapable of error." Of all the people he knew, and of all the people he would ever know, Agee looked to the farmers as those who lived closest to a way of life that *was* life at its most elemental and authentic, and therefore, the most decent, righteous, and unimpeachable life one could live—and of course the kind of life Agee himself did not live.

TEACHERS

There is, however, yet another side to the matter of "purity," just as there is always *another* side to almost any significant issue raised by this author. Agee's most extended awareness of the problems posed by "purity" and "consciousness" appears in "Education." This section concludes as follows:

> I would say too that there is a purity in this existence [i.e., the farmer's] *in* and *as* 'beauty,' which can so scarcely be conscious of itself and its world as such, which is inevitably lost in consciousness, and that this is a serious loss.
>
> But so are resourcefulness against deceit and against strangling: and so are pleasure, and joy, and love: and a human being who is deprived of these and of this consciousness is deprived almost of existence itself. (315)

The same lack of self-consciousness that was the source of so much envy and admiration was also the source of purity's deepest and perhaps most irremedial liability. If the failure of consciousness (the failure of Agee) was that it could neither leave nor make an end to itself, the failure of purity (the failure of the farmer) was that it could never know nor value what it was, and thus could never protect itself from what it was not (from, for instance, "deceit" and "strangling"). Accordingly, consciousness was agonized but enduring, while purity was perfect but perishable, and was in fact perishing even in the midst of one's envy and admiration for it. A triumph in the moral and aesthetic sphere, the farmer was a disaster in the political and socioeconomic sphere, and, like his sacred home, this paragon of aesthetic grace and moral forbearance was a "functional failure" (202), history's pawn, anybody's dupe, doomed to victimization by any and all the forces of consciousness deployed about him—anything from a drop in the stock market, a run on the bank, a war or a famine in Europe, to a landlord with a grudge, a schoolteacher with a tic, a government agent with a missionary's zeal, or perhaps just a young writer hungry for a subject. The major problem running through the brilliant and impassioned tangle of invective that is "Education" becomes how to educate purity, help it to help and protect itself, without changing and so corrupting its nature: and this, as Agee angles it, is a problem without any immediate or practical solution.

Put simply, purity cannot be "educated" without also transforming it into something other and thus immeasurably and irrevocably less than what it already is. Any action in the socioeconomic sphere portends a reaction—that is, a change—in an already attained perfection in the moral and aesthetic sphere.[28] Education may be the farmer's only "hope and cure" (307), but the author consistently finds its remedial powers more devastating than any problem to be remedied. For education too is a function of a paradoxical and double-edged consciousness and is, in fact, "the whole realm of human consciousness, action and possibility" (308); and this same educated consciousness, that might offer purity perhaps the only way out of its quandary, is also purity's "deadliest enemy and deceiver" (307) and the primary cause of all its problems. It is "responsible for every bondage I can conceive of and is the chief cause of this bondage" (308). Agee dimly tries to demonstrate how such an enlightened and activist consciousness might also be "guide of all hope and cure," but all he manages to offer is that the first duty of consciousness is to understand "its own nature" and learn to teach "all 'good' or 'wise' science, conduct, and religion" (308–9). Then he throws up his hands: "Oh, I am very well aware how adolescent this is and how easily laughable" (309). It is clear that Agee at this point in his career cannot find the language to extol consciousness to the degree that he feels he must, cannot expatiate upon it as "hope and cure," even though some part of him is convinced that that is what it is. For Agee to heap praise upon consciousness would also mean to heap praise upon the very position by which he has defined himself vis-a-vis purity, and this he cannot do without cataracts of remorse and equivocation; this author, as we know, would always be most creative and confident when pointing out flaws, not virtues, in his own position (and in the positions of others most like his own), and forever refocusing the terms of any problem so that the accusatory finger pointed inward. Accordingly, the rhetorical stress, if not the explicit statements, of "Education" insinuates that the problem of the pupil is really the problem of the teacher, the problem of purity that of consciousness, that while part of the farmer's morass may be inherent in himself, an even greater part may reside in persons like his putative benefactor, like, that is, James Agee.

Fainthearted and hollow in his advocacy of a renovative pedagogy and much more to his temperament, Agee memorably launches into a withering and richly specific indictment of the misuses of consciousness, and of the present educational system as an instrument for moral and intellectual annihilation ("I know only that murder is being done, against nearly every individual in the planet," 307, etc.). If one cannot approach the purity of the pure without altering its nature, one can at least agree to protect it from further misguided efforts to meddle and to "aid"; and the first duty of consciousness becomes not merely to refrain from aggravating the already near tragic condition of purity, but rather to understand itself through self-reflexive education against its own misuses. The lessons of "Education" implicitly plump for the reeducation of the educated; if the pure cannot be enlightened, then perhaps the enlightened can be purified.

But how is this to be accomplished? Who or what is responsible for the misuses of consciousness? If consciousness has actively become "enemy and deceiver," how can it also actively become "hope and cure"—if not for others, then at least for the best part of oneself?

The answers to these questions are not to be found in "Education," but actually in that curious, often underrated, but highly revealing cadenza known as "Intermission." "Education" tells us (at least on the level of abstract and didactic generalization) one reason why Agee must finally leave the farmer: he would only impinge upon, and thus further abet, an already perishing innocence. "Intermission" completes the "story," and shows us the degree to which his experience with the farmer has changed him, and further, what became of him—that is, specifically the kind of artist he became—after leaving Alabama and returning to his quondam home up north. In "Education," the author adopts the mannerisms of a social polemicist; in "Intermission," he speaks primarily as a personal, working artist adamant about the position and practice of his profession. Still, the political and artistic credo espoused in this brief section follows directly from, and in some respects resolves, the vision of a stymied and bifurcated consciousness (i.e., as both "enemy" and "cure") outlined in "Education." Usually ignored in discussions of *Famous Men,* perhaps because there are no obvious or overt references to the Alabama sojourn, this little interlude is neither arbitrary nor self-indulgent: it is in fact crucial to the book's overall structural design, and represents the culmination of the central character's moral and intellectual development; that is, the heightened consciousness and altered moral posture first crystallized in the summer of 1936 translates into a fully articulated social and artistic position three years later in Agee's brusque and vehement reply to a questionnaire sent him by the editors of the *Partisan Review*. The section includes both the journal's questions and the author's answers, along with footnotes dated as late as "1940" and "1941" respectively, defining it as one of the few dated episodes, and in terms of an unscrambled linear chronology, the very last installment of the narrative proper (only "Preface" and "Preamble" suggest similar late dates). Immediately preceded by and contrasted with "Work," which follows the farmer through the grueling ritual of picking and processing his cotton, "Intermission" reveals the author engaged in *his* characteristic line of "work," a presumably ongoing struggle with readers, colleagues, and ministers of his professional fate (i.e., magazine editors). The questionnaire itself is the relatively familiar kind that perennially surfaces (then and now) in little magazines and Sunday supplements asking the artist to state his views on the current social and political scene as a context for making art (e.g., in 1939, the imminent possibility of an international war), as well as his relation to the historical past, the dominant influences on his work, his sense of an audience, etc., etc. Hardly an unprecedented request: still, Agee seizes upon the occasion as an opportunity not only to savage the editors for the banality of their queries, but more importantly to sever himself officially from his earlier persona—that liberal, progressive, socially concerned, well-intentioned, self-lacerating, and somewhat patronizing young investigator that he had unofficially buried along with his stalled car in the Alabama mud. He mounts the equivalent of a funeral oration for this persona, and officially declares his independence from all of his former allegiances and commitments on both the left and right of the political and moral spectrum: to wit, Communism and Catholicism ("I felt less and less at ease with them and I am done with them," 355). And more than this: he formally segregates himself from all institutions, groups, movements, legislation, ideologies, parties, and programs—"I feel violent enmity and contempt toward all factions and all joiners" (356)—indeed, from the very idea of society itself: "A good artist is a deadly enemy of society; and the most dangerous thing that can happen to an enemy, no matter how cynical, is to become a beneficiary. No society, no matter how good, could be mature enough to support a real artist without mortal danger to that artist. Only no one need worry: for this same good artist is about the one sort of human being alive who can be trusted to take care of himself" (355).

"Intermission" everywhere implies that it is society itself that is responsible for the misuses of consciousness stipulated in "Education"; and it is here that society is officially determined as the central character's enemy, while he as artist—and this is the clearest and perhaps boldest declaration of himself as such—becomes the avowed enemy of it. In this light *Famous Men* presents, amidst all its other identities, a kind of political fable telling the tale of a northern journalist, a would-be leftist reformer and greenhorn activist, a very reluctant "spy," miserable in the knowledge that his socialist zeal has already been thoroughly compromised by his affiliations with corporate enterprise and governmental auspices, who goes down south to see what can be done to help the starving farmer. His subsequent experiences convince him that the starving farmer is less in need of help than he is, not the least of his problems being the fuzzy political notions and compromises that sent him traveling in the first place. This would-be leftist reformer ends up as a kind of nondogmatic, nonsectarian anarchist, an artist and visionary of radical individualism, veering sharply between Bakunian battle cries of full-scale subversion and Tolstoyan stillnesses of passive, nonviolent resistance, and from either position wielding a deep-seated contempt for all forms of civil procedure, compromise, halfway measures, and any and all instruments of practical remediation. We see here the first formal proclamation of a posture much like the one Agee would prescribe more than a decade later (in less personal and more stereotypical terms in writing of John Huston) as the profile for "perhaps five out of seven good artists who ever lived . . . a natural born anti-authoritarian, individualistic, libertarian, anarchist without portfolio" (*Agee on Film*, 325).

The Alabama experience has stabilized and solidified the central character's moral center, quickened his already ingrained taste for the absolute and his penchant for the quixotic: above all, it has provided him with a vision of the genuine and the pure, which in turn has provided him with a hoard of spiritual precepts by which to sniff out and excoriate the spurious and the corrupt, the deceptive apes and assassins of pure being. The farmer has entrusted him with a moral lens by which to

focus society and all its agencies as a united front, the nemesis of all
that is original, individual, natural, and sacred, and the primary cause
of false education. If nothing else, the farmer has helped the central
character to free himself from his former jailers, to take his stand (i.e.,
"to take care of himself") and continue his renovation of mind, by
insisting before all else on the primacy and necessity of "an unassisted and
weaponless" consciousness, of an "individual" and "anti-authoritarian"
consciousness, one that has been purged of its false upbringing at the
hands of bad teachers. All of this tells us why it is that when Agee
comes to write his "Preface" and "Preamble," he stresses this "free"
consciousness, beyond "the motionless camera and the printed word"
(i.e., "the immediate instruments," xiv), as the major instrument of
perception and understanding in our time ("the governing instrument,"
xiv), and how consciousness of this "free" consciousness constitutes
one of the unifying themes of his book: indeed, the "story" of this
consciousness, how and why this consciousness struggles into being—
comes to see the servitude of its former condition, as well as the necessity
of unchaining itself—is a considerable part of the story we have read.

Liberty for Agee, then, begins not with a vision of a free society,
but rather a vision of a free mind, a single integral self severed from
false values and distorting isms. Still: I do not believe that anyone can
really be deceived by his insistence upon a consciousness that is entirely
"weaponless" and "unassisted." Such claims for the completely cleansed
and ingenuous mind must, like many of the author's positions, also be
relegated to the realm of the aspirational ideal. Agee in actuality never
really stands alone, and his consciousness of course comes bulging with
a full arsenal of inherited attitudes and precepts, influences and models.
In defining society as the enemy, he automatically defines himself as an
independent and iconoclast, and, by his own definition, "a good artist,"
one who both identifies with and immediately makes applications to,
as it were, a select band of independents and iconoclasts, a company of
artists, visionaries, and moral renegades. These make up Agee's personal
pantheon of heroes and spiritual educators, (presumably) the right users
of consciousness, "members and liberators of the human race": "Christ:
Blake: Dostoyevsky: Brady's photographs: everybody's letters: family
albums: postcards: Whitman: Crane: Melville: Cummings: Kafka: Joyce:

Malraux: Gide: Mann: Beethoven: Eisenstein: Dovzchenko: Chaplin: Griffith: von Stroheim: Miller: Evans: Cartier: Levitt: Van Gogh: race records: Swift: Céline" (353).

The list itself of course immediately begs a mob of questions: how does one reconcile, for example, an emphasis on a "weaponless and unassisted" consciousness with such a population of spiritual props and heavy-duty intellectual ammunition? What principle of unity can possibly bind together such an aggressively heterogeneous list? In what sense can "Brady's photographs," or "everybody's letters" (to cite only two items), be considered "liberators of the human race"? Since when have "family albums" and "postcards," not to speak of "Cartier" or "Levitt," become an "enemy of society"?

The answers to these questions actually matter a good deal less than the fact that the central character is capable of assembling such a list in the first place. The "liberators" in themselves constitute no program or even fairly coherent position to juxtapose against all the isms, groups, and movements Agee has repudiated; the tenuous connections between them yield little in the way of a common ground for either action, discourse, or principle. What the list manages to do, however—and this is its primary function—is to plant us firmly in the mind and imagination of a now-unfettered protagonist, in the rich anomalies and arbitrariness of a single consciousness asserting itself against a society of the "deceived and the captured" (354); that is, a consciousness bursting at last with all the contents of its "right" and "good" education. Some of its teachers are among the regulation high priests of modernism (Joyce, Mann, Kafka, Eisenstein, Gide, etc.); some are heroes of the prophetic or visionary tradition (Blake, Whitman, Melville, Dostoyevsky, etc.); some emerge from a more sectarian stance (Christ, etc.); some are simply romantics with a mystical reverence for either innocence (Griffith, Chaplin) or nature (Beethoven, Dovzchenko); some are the Ageean champions of the Actual, conscious preservers, rather than creators, of the aesthetic forms found in nature (Brady, Evans, Levitt, etc.); and finally there are those works which represent the fruits of the Alabama experience (the farmer has *not* been forgotten),[29] those precious documents of unplanned and unintentional artwork by makers who are not artists or artisans, either professional or otherwise (letter, postcards, family albums, etc.). And these are the "weapons," the representatives and shapers of moral and aesthetic conviction, the stuff of a "free" consciousness, held in opposition to the hostile monolith that is society:

> Some you 'study'; some you learn from; some corroborate you; some 'stimulate' you; some are gods; some are brothers, much closer than colleagues or gods; some choke the heart out of you and make you dubious of ever reading or looking at work again: but in general, you know yourself to be at least by knowledge and feeling, of and among these, a member in a race which is much superior to any organization or Group or Movement or Affiliation, and the bloody enemy of all such, no matter what their 'sincerity', 'honesty', or 'good intentions.' (353–54)

Good teachers certainly, and much more: the passionate intimacy of the phrasing ("some are brothers, much closer than colleagues or gods; some choke the heart out of you . . ." etc.) tells us that Agee is still the orphan hungry for shelter; and apart from its function as both artistic credo and social protest, "Intermission" reveals the central character once again attempting to make entry into yet another "family," in this instance, a universal family of arts and letters and spiritual counselors. Within the confines of this book, it is perhaps the nearest the central character can come to reconciling who he is, that is, neither northern liberal nor southern sharecropper but a solitary and regionless artist of diverse sensibility, with what he wants, that is, union within a unique and exclusive circle of comfort and nourishment. He has extricated himself from within the ranks of the corrupt and the deceived, at the same time that he has found himself unworthy to enter permanently the home of the innocent and the pure; the farmers are members of an elite from which he had actually been excommunicated the moment he compromised the heritage of his own childhood family by leaving it. Now to some extent he compensates for both these losses, and perhaps even regains some fraction of his childhood legacy, by attempting to fulfill himself in art and identifying with a counter-family, an invisible republic of liberators and originators, a bundling, that is, unlike the farmer's family, imperishable, and unlike his own, impervious to the devastations of time. It is of course a properly Ageean and quite "impossible" gathering, one of his own devising and perhaps even born of his abiding isolation, a family of the mind, and (one may imagine) entered in despair of ever entering the family of the heart.

But good teachers certainly, and intellectual kin too, and yes finally, literally, famous men (or most nearly so): the heroic shapers of brain and spirit to balance against the heroic shapers of blood and body envisioned down south, the metaphorically famous men "who were our grandparents." But in either instance, whether looking inward or homeward, the present generation invariably seeks its solace and sustenance through contact with the generation of both the immediate and distant past. Did Agee ever title a book more aptly than this one? "Let us now praise famous men, and the *fathers* that begat us" (445, italics mine), is the opening line of the "Title Statement" from *Ecclesiasticus*. We recognize at once that the name of this work is no mere excrescence or ironic flourish, or, least of all, a harried author's eleventh-hour second-best choice. It is in fact this book's just and proper title, and best read straight (i.e., without bitterness or irony). Better than the original, working title, "Three Tenant Families," which placed emphasis on the farmer alone, the present title places emphasis on the visionary nature of Agee's quest: a search for the self in terms of founders and ancestral sources. The second half of the first line of the eulogy specifically links the "famous men" to "the fathers that begat us," and also helps us understand Agee's choice as an utterly devout evocation of the basis for his passionate kinship with the farmer; that is, a kinship based on remembrance of an idealized paternity that towers above the bowed heads of Agee and Gudger like some shared titanic ghost. Such a reading further helps us understand this book as no social documentary or species of para-journalese, but primarily a great family testament, a lyrical record of the silent communion between the generations, between parents and children, and the ways in which the latter discover and fortify themselves within common memory of the former:

> And some there be which have no memorial; who perished, as though they had never been; and are become as though they had never been born; and their children after them.
> But these were merciful men, whose righteousness hath not been forgotten.

With their seed shall continually remain a good inheritance, and
their children are within the covenant.
Their seed standeth fast, and their children for their sakes. Their
seed shall remain for ever, and their glory shall not be blotted out.
(445)

These lines in particular finally help underscore the secret bias behind
Agee's curious treatment of the farmer's "problem," why time and again
he so vehemently refuses to view the farmer as either a member of the
"Underprivileged" or a ready-made symbol of the Depression. Agee's
people are not representative men and women, but avatars and legatees
of "famous men." They are the chosen ones and a breed apart, members of
a sacred "covenant," inheritors of a moral heroism (i.e., however obscure
or neglected, the mercy and "righteousness" of the fathers "hath not
been forgotten") that embodies every exaltation Agee ever dreamt of
childhood, and his father and his father's people, and perhaps even by
implication, of all the lost farming men "of that last war in which there
was much nobility." These are the private gods of Agee's landscape and the
guardians of the enchanted circle of his earliest glory, the jade bullfrog
and the watering gardeners of the Knoxville twilight, the felt absence
that hovers like some ineffable dew about the inhabitants and holdings
of Gudger's farm (in the vision of the flame in the coal oil lamp, in the
glowing phial and the rod of light, in the cries of foxes), and of course
about the language of the artist who would render this nimbus with any
hope of exactitude. In the shadow of these gods and in the intoxication
of this language, in a time of hunger and wretchedness, in the anguish of
the "heart's need," whether in Alabama or New York, Gudger and Agee,
purity and consciousness, "standeth fast."

CHAPTER FOUR

THE MILK OF
PARADISE

Agee on Film

O ANY OF US ACTUALLY NEED reminding at this late date that film criticism in America did not originate with the advent of James Agee, that there were other ardent and articulate cinephiles writing regularly long before, and of course during, Agee's movie regime who were just as important to the development of the film critical eye in this country as he was—and a few of these perhaps more so? If prompting is needed, let me reiterate that he was not the first, or even the second or fifth, critic in America to write intelligently, perhaps even brilliantly, about the movies; or the first, second, or fifth to take them seriously as art, or invoke them in a lofty and sibylline manner. Nor was he anything like a pioneer among the intelligentsia in his high-diving plunge into the gym pool of the popular arts or in the perception that at least one of them might represent an authentic expression of the social consciousness of a whole people. Nor did he stand anywhere near the front rank of ocular sharpshooters who learned to appropriate the uniqueness of the film medium through the uniqueness of its form, to cull concept from image, and evince the thrust of a movie through the uses of the camera, the deployment of light, editorial rhythm, the somatics of posture and gesture, etc. All of these by now thoroughly familiar attitudes and approaches had either been suggested or fully elaborated by others before Agee started reviewing in 1941.[1]

Nor did he initiate the many hot topics, and frequently irresolvable debates, that until recently had long constituted the polemical life of cinematic discourse both here and abroad: those time-honored controversies focusing on, say, the respective merits of silent film as against sound, color against black-and-white, filmed theater against "pure" cinema, European "film" versus American "movies," personal art versus mass entertainment, the silent Chaplin against Chaplin talking, Eisenstein under Lenin and then Stalin, Lubitsch early and late, and so on and on. As one might imagine, most of these concerns are also voiced by Agee, some of them emphatically, some glancingly; little or none of them, however, derive from his work. The terms and limits of many of film criticism's almost "axiomatic" disputes had been started, extended, and all but anatomized inside and out by those critics, scholars, theoreticians, and pop culture historians, who preceded Agee by some years and many, many words: persons such as Vachel Lindsay, Hugo Münsterberg, Kenneth Macgowan, Robert E. Sherwood, Gilbert Seldes, Alexander Bakshy, Harry Alan Potamkin, Pare Lorentz, Welford Beaton, Andre Sennwald, Mark van Doren, William Troy, Seymour Stern, Iris Barry, Paul Goodman, Lewis Jacobs, Meyer Levin, Robert Stebbins, (a very young) Dwight Macdonald, and (the still underrated) Otis Ferguson.[2]

Until recently, however, no one would think to make a fuss about most of these figures: for many people, making a fuss about anyone's film commentaries usually began with commentaries by Agee. Even during the forties the concerned public, if so inclined, could have given at least some of its allegiance to the two, or possibly three, brilliant, and utterly unique, film critics who emerged not long after Agee began his tour of duty at *Time* and the *Nation,* that is, Manny Farber, Robert Warshow, and perhaps even Parker Tyler. Yet each of these three had to wait at least a decade after the death of the *Time/Nation* reviewer before beginning to achieve anything like a proper recognition and estimate in the annals of the intellectual community beyond that of film specialists.[3]

Nor was it simply a matter of the clear-cut superiority of Agee's critical credentials as against those of his predecessors and contemporaries. There was in fact nothing clear-cut about them. His film savvy was without doubt—and not to put too fine a point on it—eminently satisfactory. But then Harry Alan Potamkin (1929–1933, *New Masses, Close Up, Hound and Horn,* and elsewhere), for example, was a more vigorous theorist, futurist, and aesthetician of film than Agee ever was (and perhaps ever would have wanted to be).[4] Otis Ferguson (1934–1942, *New Republic*) was a more thorough and unequivocal populist than Agee, and eventually developed a more original slant on the power and influence of Hollywood movies, viewing them neither as an expression of a director's vision or a studio's taste, but primarily as a subconscious mandate from the folk-swarm, impervious to either morality or intellect, and certainly immune to the ordinary judgments of film criticism as commonly practiced at the time. The advantage of Robert Warshow (1946–1952, *Commentary, Partisan Review,* and elsewhere) over all other film critics (including Agee) was an exquisite sense of the deployments and interlocking of the American social and political scheme, and the relation of these to the moral life of the private moviegoer. And for sheer quirkiness, irreverence, and high-voltage temperament, who needed Agee when one could have read Manny Farber (primarily 1943–1969, *New Republic, Nation, Commentary,* and *Art Forum*). Painter as well as film critic, Farber sprayed his imploded prose in a gaudy and aggressive array of splatter-and-drip sensuous effects, transforming a deeply ingrained and seemingly relentless crankiness (a matter of sensibility, not ideology) into a rampage of near murderous elation. But beyond the tiny and embattled perimeters of the cultural shoe box in which most film specialists appeared to reside, no one before or immediately after Agee's critical tenure seemed to be paying much attention to any of these lively and significant figures; in Ferguson's case, for instance, his death was followed by a virtual thirty-year moratorium on his work.[5] As far as many in the greater intellectual community were concerned, after some seventy years of film reviewing in America—from the earliest notice of the short film program playing at Koster and Baily's Music Hall in 1896 to the efflorescence of what has widely been called the "film generation" in the mid-sixties, and a concomitant publishing explosion of film criticism, history, biography, and theory—James Agee might just as well have been the only person in America who ever bothered to write deeply and passionately about the movies.[6]

His reviewing term technically entailed a nine-year run, going full stride from 1942 through 1947, visibly flagging in 1948 and 1949, and finally ambling to a virtual halt by the end of the decade. Within this timeframe, Agee managed to compile a record of reviews and essays—most lucratively in *Time,* most brilliantly in the *Nation,* and perhaps most famously in *Life* (particularly one long, influential, and much-quoted resurrection of the silent comedians, "Comedy's Greatest Era")—that blazed more brightly than any other comparable record made in America before, during, and immediately after its appearance. In 1958 much of this compilation comprised perhaps the first collection of one American's film reviews ever to be gathered and preserved in book form, and in this manner, *Agee on Film* jump-started, by less than a decade, an entire generation's omnivorous concern for searching commentary about the movies. Agee may not have been the first critic in America to write seriously about film, but he was indubitably the first critic in America to make substantial numbers of serious people think seriously about practical film criticism, to make them respect and even celebrate the enterprise of the film critic; precisely, to stir them by the performances of the film critic the way they might presumably have been stirred by the performances the critic was writing about. Perhaps it is this accomplishment that offers us a clue to the reason for Agee's extraordinary preeminence over his gifted colleagues and predecessors. Permit me to advance this perfectly obvious and unastonishing explanation (which for all that strikes me as entirely just): that Agee "ruled" the film critical scene for as long as he did precisely because of his mind and manner; because of the force of his own remarkable persona in prose. "What he says is of such profound interest, expressed with such extraordinary wit and felicity," wrote W. H. Auden, in a well-known fan letter to the editors of the *Nation* after Agee had been their film reviewer for little more than two years, "and so transcends its ostensible—to me rather unimportant—subject, that his articles belong in that very select class—the music critiques of Berlioz and Shaw are the only other members I know—of newspaper work which has permanent literary value." Sidestepping for a moment Auden's dismissal of an entire medium (revealing in itself), his judgments are still worth repeating, for even now this exalted estimate of Agee and his criticism seem to me as exact as anything that has ever been said about him or it. In addition, and just as important, Auden's letter still has value in signaling to us the kind of impact Agee may have had on the intelligent reader of his day, and even perhaps to some (lesser) extent, the kind of reader he may characteristically have had; that is, a sophisticated and fastidious reader, but also an amateur and nonspecialist who, in reading Agee on film, might have begun to segregate a cult of the writer apart from an interest in the writer's subject—which in itself, even for the nonspecialist, must still have been more considerable and positive than Auden's: "I do not care for the movies," he also declares in the same letter, "and I rarely see them." It is abundantly clear that an interest in Agee did not promote in Auden an equivalent interest in film: on the contrary, reading Agee has promoted an interest in Agee, and Agee only. Again Auden: "I find myself not only reading Mr. Agee before I read anyone else in the *Nation* but also consciously looking forward all week to reading him again. In my opinion, his column is the most remarkable regular event in journalism today." James Agee may not have been the greatest film critic we have ever had in this country (however one fumigates *that* hornet's nest), but he was without question the most powerful and imaginative prose writer in America—that is to say, the greatest American artist in prose—ever to write regularly about the movies; and it is his authority as a writer that has made all the difference in determining his authority as a writer on film. The creative element is in fact so pronounced in his criticism that one is continually tempted to position Agee as the first American in the whole history of the craft to raise writing about the movies to a level of art independent of its subject.[7]

Naturally, I do not mean that his subject needed in any way to be transcended, or that Agee himself felt that such transcendence was in any way necessary, or least of all, that such a subject could or should be advanced as a conduit or camouflage for another, different, "better" subject. After all, any subject that could gather within its wide embrace such works as *Zero for Conduct, Monsieur Verdoux, Ivan the Terrible* (Part One), *Day of Wrath, Children of Paradise, Farrebique, The Battle of San Pietro, Notorious, The Miracle of Morgan's Creek, They Were*

Expendable, The Southerner, Henry V, Great Expectations, Odd Man Out, Black Narcissus, Meet Me in St. Louis, The Big Sleep, The Best Years of Our Lives, and *The Treasure of Sierra Madre;* that could include the earliest freshets from the broad wave of Italian Neo-Realism (e.g., *Shoeshine, Open City*); that could sustain the advent of some of the richest inspirations of the Hollywood B-film (e.g., the Val Lewton chiller series for R.K.O.); that could oversee the emergence of a new dark, brooding, style-conscious strain of domestic thriller (e.g., *Shadow of a Doubt, Double Indemnity*) that a quarter century later came generally to be known as *film noir*—any subject such as this, that is to say, the substantive gist of Agee's film watch, was not a subject to be "transcended," rerouted, dodged, or, pace Auden, patronized. On the contrary, even when the forties film under review is ostensibly without any redeeming qualities, Agee is so completely engaged by his material, so deeply immersed in it, that he discovers his self-fulfilling structures of wit, insight, and verbal flighting not apart from or beyond his subject, but thoroughly within it: any "independence" that may result from this effort derives from the unique scale and quality of these achieved structures, but certainly not by ducking the matter at hand. When Agee and film found each other in print, it was a meeting, so to speak, of mutual excitation: the glamour of the movies and the glow of Agee's persona. Reviewing current films on a regular basis lent his writing a charismatic timeliness, and inspired the writer to some of his worldliest, wittiest, and most sumptuous utterances, where the show of intellect itself became as glittery and alluring as any of the glittery and alluring subjects embraced by it. And Agee gave as good as he got: no critic before him had ever brought such a stylistics of ennobled emotion to bear upon this subject, or made the creation of film seem such an utterly honorific enterprise, such a high moral, even chivalric, calling, but also one riven through with mortal risks of the deepest shame and the darkest disgrace.

Now I realize that I have been making certain grand claims about Agee and this particular branch of his work, and in the following discussion, I'd like to ratify with example the burden of these claims; to explore one of his most singular and perhaps durable contributions to discursive writing in America: the sound of Agee talking about the movies.

1. PERFORMANCES: THE CRITIC AS ARTIST

As everyone knows, the act of the critic usually emerges in response to, and in this sense is inextricably bound up with, and dependent upon, another prior act in which the critic in no way participates, and that of course is the act of an artist. Without this act—let us call it the primary act—the critic's act could not, strictly speaking, come into existence at all. Because the critical act usually exists in such a necessarily subordinate and secondary capacity—and let us call *this* act the secondary act—to the artistic act, we are usually quite right not to consider, demand, or even begin to anticipate, the work of the critic as an independent work of art. But under certain special circumstances we have a demonstrable right to think differently about a critic and his work, and that is obviously when the critic is himself an artist, or at least (what amounts to the same thing), performs as one in making his criticism: secondary acts become primary acts when the one who acts makes, as it were, the part his own (like any good performer at a concert, play, or movie), and converts the given according to a transformative design. In what sense is Agee such an artist, and what are the notable features of his critical art?

I would suggest that the most salient, even daunting, quality that distinguishes Agee's work from that of any other film reviewer is the way the highest degree of intellectual and imaginative pressure has been brought to bear at each and every point in the developing argument, from the smallest detail contributing to the shape of the phrase and the sentence to the overall structure of any given review. The general effect of this consciousness-beaming is a prose texture of unflagging density, intensity, and sheer concern, impacted with Ageean ministration and verbal stitchery, ceaselessly "busy" in the resource and singularity of the point-by-point rhetorical invention. In the best Agee reviews (i.e., the *Nation* reviews), mental concentration itself, maximized and unremitting, becomes an active part of the critical drama, and in some instances—particularly when the film itself, or the issues raised by it, are of minimal interest for the reader—the most indelible part. If genius indeed be the infinite capacity for taking pains, the evidence of its effects are to be found everywhere in the oak knot concentration of these *Nation* reviews, and reason enough to ensure their permanence.

The effects of imaginative pressure become particularly conspicuous in those areas that would seemingly represent the most standardized and mechanical requirements of the regular reviewer's chores; that is, precisely those areas where Agee—if he were some other reviewer and not his utterly original self—has every reason to sound exactly like any one of his colleagues. But does he? For instance, what reviewer at some point during his beat has not had occasion to apologize in print for bungling someone's name? Here's Agee: "In the issue of July 3 I suggested that those interested in the movie subscription society Cinema 16 write the secretary, Alex Vogel, 59 Park Avenue. The name is Amos. I hereby apologize to Mr. Vogel and to you; and sadly join company with an Aunt of mine who used to refer to Sacco and Vanetsi, and with all those who call me Aggie, Ad'ji, Adjeé, Uhjeé, and Eigh'geeé" (311). Was ever routine less routinized? Or what regular reviewer has not found himself in the position of having to catch up with a film only after its initial run is over (or nowadays, has outflanked the theatrical circuit altogether)? Again Agee: "Tardily, I arch my back and purr deep-throated approval of *The Curse of the Cat People,* which I caught by pure chance, one evening, on a reviewer's holiday" (85). Need I point out how the first word dangles in front of the sentence like the tail of the animal described? Or how the whole short sequence of four comma splices actually manages to "ripple" the sentence to its conclusion like delicate muscles under fur? Everywhere one finds that the writer's language characteristically shapes itself less in the manner of an observation applied from without than in the manner of an original entity, an autonomous construct; here a tiny cat-thing, seeming to emerge from within the subject itself (that is, cats, not the actual film, which has relatively little to do with them).

In the following construct, Agee reflects the concern any reviewer might feel when he changes his mind about a previously expressed judgment, in this case Claude Rains's portrayal of Caesar in *Caesar and Cleopatra.* Any honest reviewer will of course readily admit such changes of mind and Agee did so all the time, but how many could also couch such admission in a contretemps as extravagantly ingenious as the following?

> In an elevator the other day—a hell of a place to bring such
> a thing up—an acquaintance rebuked me for liking *Caesar and*

THE MILK OF PARADISE

Cleopatra. As it turned out, he simply doesn't like the play much, whereas I simply do; and he minded the gaudiness, whereas I still don't; but I found I was close to agreeing with him about Claude Rains. He flatly thought Rains was a ham. I think he is, but has a saving ironic understanding of his hamminess; I also think Shaw's Caesar is, among other things, a conscious ham. Watching Rains again as Caesar, I realize that he plays nearly everything much too broad, to be as right for the role as I had thought. I now think he was adequate, and skillful, and amusing, but in second gear.

I speak of this now partly out of my duty toward myself, my God, and my neighbor, chiefly because I was unable to do anything but mumble about it in the elevator. Ground floor. (216)

One sees immediately that in Agee's satiric replay of a ping-pong argument with his "acquaintance," he chides not only the finical nature of the dispute but also the small-spirited obsessiveness, that rage-over-a-lost-penny quality, of critical pedants and die-hard buffs in general. Naturally the brunt of the comic butt has been reserved for his witty recreation of himself as reviewer-on-the-defensive, a sort of dupe of intellect, armed with a garrison of explanations, rebuttals, and self-justifications. He was right, you see, even where he appeared to be wrong; Rains *is* a ham, but a knowing one, and thus correct in his interpretation of Shaw's Caesar who is also a ham. Then only after this way of being right is appreciated, does he freely admit how and where he was wrong; that is, even as a knowing ham, Rains overdid it, and he (Agee) was probably wrong to praise him for it. So as it turns out, he was very right in analyzing Shaw's intent, but merely, you see, oversold Rains's execution of it. (O.K.?) All of this is presented in the form of professional overkill, both making and mocking his points, and no more so than in the sarcasm of the concluding paragraph, the last two words of which, curt and no-nonsense, definitively shut down the conversation, the elevator ride, the pretentions of the critics, and the column itself.

A performance artist, not to belabor the matter, is interested in just that: performance; he seizes whatever occasion presents itself, however dog-eared or trivial, as potential for the creative act, for showmanship, for applause. What Agee gives to the most jog-trot tasks of the reviewer are also given, as one might imagine, to those tasks that are the most serious and essential: the business of discriminating and understanding the work at hand. Agee's evaluations, meticulously graded, infinitely shaded, hair-line calibrated, perhaps to a fanatical degree, would be singular and noteworthy when applied to any art form, but when applied to popular movies, they were simply unprecedented in their time and place. Turn virtually at random to any page in the *Nation* collection, and find neurosurgical rankings similar to the following: "At his best [Danny] Kaye suggests that he might be a much better comedian than he has yet become; at his loudest and blurriest he suggests that he may never become that good; but even at his worst he is more than good enough" (169). One sees too, in these scrupulous placements, how Agee's elevator set-piece exaggerates the actual and habitual case only slightly. Witness the little interdisciplinary taxonomy brought to bear upon an unsatisfactory presentation of the Don Juan archetype in *The Notorious Gentleman:*

> But it takes a great artist to present such a man . . . Mozart presented him in *Don Giovanni,* and Byron, more spottily, in *Don Juan;* on a high, though less inspired level Shaw has been doing it most of his life. But smaller people seldom get away with it. Waugh did, by reducing the type to pure meeching horror in *A Handful of Dust,* but the reality of Basil Seal becomes as arguable as the uses he is put to in *Put Out More Flags.* The people who made *The Notorious Gentleman* are much farther below Waugh than he is below Mozart or even Byron. Considering how supremely this job has been done a few times, and how often it has been done much better than here, how can anyone care for this version? (221)

The effect is that of a plethora of bristling parts, each with its own individuality (e.g., that wonderful Uriah Heepish "meeching"), presented as the function of a unified whole. The entire cultural ladder is created rung by rung in descending order, distinctions nailed, ramifications (Waugh) and exceptions (*A Handful of Dust*) attached, and *The Notorious Gentleman* is unwaveringly placed (bottom rung). An exacting set of critical standards became of course endemic to Agee's critical manner, but even more important, the application of such standards to what many people considered—and in some quarters, still consider today—to be a "throwaway" art made each film, good or bad, seem worthy of the most strenuous kinds of concern; and if one bad film mattered this much, so did all films; and if they mattered that much, so did criticism of film.

The *Nation* reviews represent the most confident and intricate writing Agee ever accomplished; *A Death in the Family,* equally confident, isn't intricate; *Famous Men,* immensely intricate, derives from a welter of doubt; and nothing is more confident or intricate or characteristic of his critical skill than the high-wire mastery and overriding elegance of his dialectics. Agee's extraordinary force of concentration invariably ferrets out opposition among the parts of his developing stance, and his artistry often resides in apprehending, controlling, and sustaining the warring polarities as the interlacing joints of a single, seemingly indivisible and expressive organism. The marshaling, for instance, of the variegated details in the following commentary on Olivier's reading of Henry V's St. Crispin's Day speech (from *Henry V*), as well as the conflicted nature of these details, into a grandly operatic and internally combustible synthesis is probably without parallel in the film criticism of its day; Warshow wouldn't have bothered with the detail; Farber, with the synthesis; Parker Tyler, with making himself understood.

> . . . His Crispin's Day oration is not just a brilliant bugle-blat: it is the calculated yet self-exceeding improvisation, at once self-enjoying and selfless, of a young and sleepless leader, rising to a situation wholly dangerous and glamorous, and wholly new to him. Only one of the many beauties of the speech as he gives it is the way in which the King seems now to exploit his sincerity, now to be possessed by it, riding like an unexpectedly mounting wave the astounding size of his sudden proud awareness of the country morning, of his moment in history, of his responsibility and competence, of being full-bloodedly alive, and of being about to die. (211–12)

One could fairly extrapolate a little essay on the phenomenology of Early Renaissance kingship simply from the phrase referring to "the astounding size of" the sleepless young monarch's "sudden proud awareness of the country morning," as one can fairly extrapolate many essays from the myriad of figurative condensations strewn lavishly throughout these reviews. But just as important is the way in which Agee's double-edged interpretation of Olivier's reading—Henry's speech is both sincere and calculating, selfless and self-aware, exploitative of the moment yet possessed of something larger, finer—how all this is contained and disciplined in the rising tide of the eloquent, and eloquently modulated, second and concluding sentence that at once evokes and imitates in its overall shape the rising pitch of Henry's call to battle, as well as pinpointing precisely the infinitely delicate tussle of emotions that compose it; how the sentence itself becomes a "mounting wave" of jostled yet completely articulated passion (i.e., again, not just an observation, but an embodiment); introduced by that gentle, rocking to and fro water motion of "now to exploit" against "now to be possessed," and followed by that long, lovely, streaming conceit, "riding like an unexpectedly mounting wave the astounding size of his sudden proud awareness of the country morning," providing the ground base for the steep ascent of the incremental buildup; and how this is whipped higher, higher, and higher still, by the repetition of the three short phrases following—"of his moment in history, of his responsibility and completeness, of being full-bloodedly alive"—the last of the three slightly amended ("of his" becoming "of being"), and thus cresting in anticipation of the sudden, saddening change and falling away of the fourth phrase, "of being about to die," the tip of the wave, as it were, furling over upon itself, preparing for its massive glide downward . And this is what Auden called "newspaper work."

Readers experiencing the unprecedented density of the *Nation* reviews for the first time may be puzzled, and perhaps a little irritated, to discover how draining, and on occasion "inaccessible," some of these concise columns can prove to be. Particularly if one has been weaned on contemporary standards of even very good newspaper and magazine reviewing, how strange and unfamiliar Agee's sentences may sound with their faintly biblical and Elizabethan locutions, hot-wire diction, and gyral syntax; how slowly they may read with their hesitating, veering, turn-and-turn-about arguments; how little they seem to contain of what one may still want to call (even today) "ordinary" writing or "common" discourse (i.e., simple coordinated sentences compacted of educated high middle- to lower upper-class colloquialism); how little one gets of that easy, lulling, off-white to gray conversational fluency channeled to evaporate with the transmission of its thought. Agee's prose is built from first to last of extraordinary writing and uncommon discourse, the optimum reverse of prose that does not demand to linger in the memory, or call attention to itself, or to the singular and personal urgencies of the writer of whom it is the embodiment.

Perhaps to best appreciate the difference between authentic Agee-talk and the more familiar and accessible brand of medium to very good opinion journalism, one has only to compare the *Nation* reviews with the writing Agee himself did for *Time* (or what we may imagine to be his, intermingled, as is customary, with a managing editor's cuts, rewrites, and additions).[8] The *Time* sentences are short, spiffy, and relentlessly crisp. They are not without clichés or smarminess (e.g., "Benjamin Stoloff's direction is gingersnappy"), or their requisite share of Timese (e.g., "cinemaddicts," for film fans, appears numerous times). They are not dense, not difficult, and certainly not pretentious, but they aren't much else either. Often the tone comes remarkably close to that of the disc jockey, the sportscaster, or, more aptly, the press agent; that is, some mechanical voicebox neither analyzing, nor judging, nor even ostensibly thinking, but rather, as it were, selling its wares, convincing the reader that the latest occurrence is news, that something has validly *happened,* and of course promoting its own motoric accessibility and occupational perkiness. The average review consists of about 40 percent plot summary and 40 percent "background" information—biographical profiles of stars, directors, or producers, striking or unusual pre- or post-production anecdotes, any warm factoid or "newsworthy" tie-in with the film. The *Time* review of *Since You Went Away,* for instance, runs ten trim paragraphs, six of which rehash the story, and another—the longest—spotlights David Selznick's career as showman-producer:

> The duck that hatched a swan was lucky compared to David Oliver Selznick. He hatched *Gone With the Wind* and has been trying to hatch another ever since. Last week he punctuated four pictureless years with *Since You Went Away,* a marathon of home-front genre-filming. Sure enough, it was no *Gone With the Wind. The Wind* blew for four solid hours; *Went* goes on for ten minutes short of three. *The Wind* cost $4,000,000 to make; *Went,* a mere $2,400,000. *The Wind* was photographed in some of the most florid Technicolor ever seen; *Went* is in Quaker black and white

and Hollywood's pearliest mezzotones. *The Wind* was perhaps the greatest entertainment natural in screen history; *Went,* though its appeal is likely to be broad, is essentially a "woman's picture." But it is obviously, in every foot, the work of one of Hollywood's smartest producers. (349–50)

A second newsy thread tenses over Shirley Temple's promotion from child-star to teen-star: "Chief reason U.S. cinemaddicts have breathlessly awaited *Since you Went Away* was to see Miss Temple in her first grownup part." Verdict: "She is charming" (350). And so on. The rest, to be sure, is criticism.

Agee of course could do nothing without at least partial commitment, some smattering of wit, vividness, or trenchancy, and the *Time* reviews are not without these qualities (*vide* directly above); and the longer features on, say, *Hamlet* or *Henry V* actually begin to strike up an argument and develop a position. But even the well-known set-piece on *Hamlet* stops dead in its well-oiled tracks for a quick, two-page, time-out profile of Olivier's "discovery," his new Ophelia, a seventeen-year-old stunner named Jean Simmons. These mass-marketed sound bites manage not only to disguise the authentic Agee accent and emphasis, but finally may also misrepresent his full and carefully graded judgments. In the then official *Time* manner, the first person singular is almost never used (in the *Nation* no review is without it), and, as some have pointed out, the specific evaluations of certain films differ from the judgments on these same films advanced in the *Nation*—not drastically, but palpably. At *Time,* Agee often seems to mesh what he thinks of a film "personally" with his intuitive sense of the tastes and biases of his large readership (and perhaps those of his editor as well), so that the resulting review frequently represents less the emphatic mark of the reviewer than a print-out or impersonation of what he thinks his traffic is likely to bear. The culturally nutritious *Henry V,* for example, the first major motion picture to make the Bard both attractive and accessible to a mass audience, obviously has a chance of being a real crowd pleaser, and Agee pushes much harder for it in *Time* than in the *Nation,* where he also admires the film (e.g., as in the excerpt above), but within a severely qualified framework. A personal favorite, however, such as the bleak, brilliant, and unregenerate *Monsieur*

Verdoux by the then unpopular Chaplin, isn't going, nor does it seem to want, to make a lot of friends. So in the *Nation,* where he tells you what he thinks as opposed to what he thinks you might think, he doesn't hesitate to elucidate and argue for a "masterpiece" (in three separate columns!). In *Time,* he also praises the film, but sifts and muzzles his enthusiasm in serving his sense of an audience. His work for the *Nation* was one-of-a-kind, enriched the moral and aesthetic caliber of the craft, and established benchmarks by which to measure comparable work, past and future. His work for *Time* was little more than that: a job well done, but not that much better than some others could have done it, and one that did not necessarily need Agee to do it. To prefer the *Time* reviews to the *Nation*'s, as some have (e.g., see Manny Farber's response), is not just perverse, but is to prefer journalistic surfaces to critical and artistic depths; it is also to prefer the superficial aspects of movies to the real thing.[9]

I should further point out that none of the foregoing excerpts from the *Nation,* intriguing and thoroughly characteristic as they are, represent instances of what critics of Agee on film usually single out for praise: that is, for instance, his impressive powers of visual evocation or the passionate intensity of his moral commitments, qualities to be found everywhere in his writing, including of course in his writing about the movies. But even this very modest sampling of quotation should help us to see that Agee's rich and extensive range of effects cannot be constricted to those of the "visual" or the "moral" critic, or to any other facile pigeonholes.[10] The grand and lasting impression of his commentaries is one of a completely disarming individuality, a wonderfully various, un-predictable, and thoroughly elusive humanness that should legitimately drive conscientious critical classifiers to dithers of allocation. Sometimes in reading one of these little *Nation* columns, you may feel as if you had never read a review before, or more aptly (and it is pleasing to imagine this), that the reviewer hadn't read one either; that he is making up the rules for reviewing—what should or should not be done in a review— as he goes along; and that if he is ever aware of any rule prior to his invention of it, he will promptly stand it on its head. There is simply no way of foreknowing the different turns any given Agee review will take, or the infinite clusters of oddments and special interests he might pry loose from any seemingly ordinary movie. It is simply fascinating, for instance, how often the *Nation* columns will ignore the mainline attraction of the moment, the box office bonanza playing at the Roxy or the Radio City Music Hall, or simply relegate this to an aside (see the marginal offhanded receptions tossed at *Casablanca, Mrs. Miniver,* etc.); and focus instead on a documentary or a newsreel (*Agee on Film* never lets you forget that there is a war on); or an interesting B-movie (such as William Castle's *When Strangers Marry*); or an experimental film (such as Deren's *Meshes in the Afternoon*); or a Warner Brothers cartoon (such as Freleng's *Rhapsody Rabbit*). Sometimes he will springboard off a movie into a euphemistically "loosely related" topic, such as a little tangent on the mostly male Times Square audience, or one on the ethics of celibacy, or another on the obscenity of current child-rearing manuals, or the Catholic Church's inquiries into the private life of movie stars, or the future of Hollywood after the HUAC investigations, or the fate of Humanism in a post-atomic era.

The truth is that no matter how much Agee ever tells you about a movie, his credentials as a wild card and artist-at-large invariably supersede those of the film critic. He is just about as unclassifiable a movie reviewer as he is a journalist, fictionalist, and screenwriter; and by "unclassifiable" here, I am simply referring to the eruptive way this writer's assertions of self invariably stampede the conventions of the form in which he elects to work. Often Agee's way of being a film critic is to explore the many different ways that in fact a film critic can be. His taking up and casting off the different roles of the critic's theater is one of the major means available to him of imposing the largesse, surprise, and variousness of who he is. His largely successful attempts to exercise a variety of critical approaches allows him to demonstrate all the different things he can do with a movie without ever ceasing to sound like himself. So if one reads his analysis and castigation of the montage patterns in *Wake Island* or *For Whom the Bell Tolls,* one witnesses in "praxis" a formal aesthetician of film rhythm and syntax. If one turns to his review of *Tender Comrade* or *Since You Went Away* (in the *Nation*), one confronts the ardent social critic, a prober and deconstructionist of class fantasies as politically astute and undeceivable as any George Orwell or Robert Warshow. By contrast, his exhaustive investigation of Henri

Verdoux's criminal motivations are entirely the effusions of the gifted amateur psychologist, just as his largely descriptive responses to *Meet Me in St. Louis* or the different kinds of gag-structure and hurtling bodies in silent comedy ("Comedy's Greatest Era") are among the most exact and resonant specimens of visual impressionism to be found anywhere in American film writing. On the other hand, at the paler ends of the tonal spectrum, his reviews of *Shoeshine* and *The Notorious Gentleman* canter so grandly on the high horse of his moral humanist sermonizing that he won't dismount long enough even to pretend to look at the movie at all, let alone evoke a single visual image. But then, finally, when frivolity does strike, he is perfectly capable of presenting himself as the hit-and-run kind of young fop-reviewer, targeting just those sitting ducks that will allow him to turn a conceit, wittle his wit, and leave "responsible" analysis to someone like Bosley Crowther (as in, say, his entire four-word snit on the five-word title, *You Were Meant For Me:* "That's what you think," 296).

All of which brings me to the second distinctive and distinguishing quality of Agee's criticism (and one may position this as, in some ways, the polar opposite of his quality of concentration), and that is, the sharp ozone of liberty, and sometimes even misrule, that energizes his writing for the *Nation,* and along with this, the accompanying sense of discovery and risk, and even on occasion the lure of recklessness and flagrant disregard. One may experience these qualities most intimately, less perhaps in his impressive range of subject matter or striking eclecticism of method, than in the exhilarating texture of what he actually wrote. When in the mood for some irreverent fun, Agee, for instance, could bang out a sentence that traveled like a yard-built jalopy souped up with a brilliant assortment of anomalous parts, freaky paints, and left-field fittings, and if one wanted to get on board, one prepared for plenty of bounce and din—as in the following reaction to an interethnic marriage in *Carnival in Costa Rica:* "I was also interested to see that Ann Revere, as a Kansan, was shown to be happily married to J. Carroll Naish, as a thoroughly Costa Rican coffee planter. If this sort of un-American propaganda takes decent hold in Hollywood, the day will come when the husband of a high-bridged daughter of the Confederacy will shag into the scuppernong arbor playing ootchmagootch to a slice of watermelon and reciting *Ballad for Americans,* between spat seeds, in an Oxford accent" (252). I can't account for your taste, but for mine just about every choice and ordering in the main clause of the second sentence registers as an almost complete and tonic surprise. Perhaps it (i.e., the surprise) resides in the way that the fake-slum "shag" slouches up against the fake-fanciness of "scuppernong arbor"; or in the way that the blue-blood image gets farcically pumped up and revitalized by the watermelon image from an old racist joke; or in the way that the monosyllabics of "spat seeds" snipe at the reader like bullets; or in the way that "ootchmagootch" evokes the pure bliss of an idiot's delight, a supreme silliness beyond analysis. Perhaps it is simply in the joining and cybernetics of the varied particulars, not just the mischief in the touch but the steerage in the turns, the way in which every shift within the nearly indigestible conceit is commandeered down to the final period. Whatever the precise reason, the amusement that runs through the line manages to merge the habitual grip and fastidiousness of the self-conscious artist with the raucous and the willfully coarse, an urban sophisticate's knowing evocation of a naughty country boy's redneck rowdiness. Only the most controlled yet audacious of stylists could stick his aesthetic neck out this far, just beyond the borders of good taste, then—"ootchmagootch"—chop it off, only to return as whole, tame, and orderly as any Jack back in his box.

The following description of Bugs Bunny at the concert piano fashions another kind of original construct from seeming chaos as it races up the comic evolutionary scale, grade by grade, from the physical farcical to the cream-of-the-jest cerebral, starting with Keystone slapstick and tailing off with an almost "Shavian" (*vide* Auden) inversion:

> I could hardly illustrate without musical quotation; but there is a passage in which the music goes up with an arrogant wrenching of slammed chords—Ronk, *Ronk*, RONK (G-B-E)—then prisses downward on a broken scale—which Bugs takes (a) with all four feet, charging madly, scowling like a rocking horse late for a date at stud, (b) friskily tiptoe, proudly smirking, like a dog toe-dancing through his own misdemeanor or the return of an I-Was-There journalist, a man above fear or favor who knows precisely which sleeping dogs to lie about. (218)

The opening lines seem to thrust us up to the ears in pure noise ("RONK"), but by the time we reach "Bugs," a shaped creature emerges from all the primal racket (i.e., onomatopoiesis, neologisms)—not a bunny, but a lusty equine, part hobby-part horse, a cyborgean sex machine, immediately transformed, one notch up, to a natural canine pirouetting above the scene of his crime (that "misdemeanor" politely distancing his mess); and finally top notch, there appears a faintly Kilroyan human figure, but a tawdry one, just up from the mutt and his mire, whose true imposture cannot be fully savored unless one does a swift double take on Agee's deft compression and transposition of clichés (i.e., notably, where-the-bodies-are-buried, and where-sleeping-dogs-lie). The whole Darwinian contraption—that is, Darwin by way of Rube Goldberg—sustains itself at each stage, from the acoustical ooze to the infractious quadrupeds to the seedy primate, by a nervous facade of would-be decorousness teetering precariously above the brink of an irredeemable scurrility.

Like many of the poets, fictionalists, musicians, and painters of the wartime forties who doubled with equal brilliance and commitment as regular critics—such as, at random, Randall Jarrell (poetry) at the *Nation,* Virgil Thompson (music) and Edwin Denby (ballet) at the *Herald Tribune,* Mary McCarthy (theater, film) and Delmore Schwartz (poetry) at the *Partisan Review,* Manny Farber (film) and Edmund Wilson (literature) at the *New Republic,* among others—and who helped determine that undervalued period as a kind of "golden age" of reviewing, Agee's primary means of expository analysis, of compacting and fine-tuning his insights as well as taking his pleasure, was usually by way of the conceit. But even within a critical era notable for its verbal precocity, Agee's similes, for instance, must surely have been among the most exuberant and outrageous in the business—also the longest. I would venture to imagine that for sheer size, stamina, and cyclonic dazzle one would have to time-travel back to the Mermaid Tavern to flush out the metaphorical superior of the following twister:

> *Till the Clouds Roll By* is a little like sitting down to a soda-fountain de luxe atomic special of maple nut on vanilla on burnt almond on strawberry on butter pecan on coffee on raspberry sherbet on tutti frutti with hot fudge, butterscotch, marshmallow, filberts, pistachios, shredded pineapple, and rainbow sprills on top, go double on the whipped cream. Some of the nuts, it turns out, are a little stale, and wandering throughout the confection is a long

bleached-golden hair, probably all right in its place but, here, just a little more than you can swallow. This hair, in the difficult technical language of certain members of the Screen Writers Guild who exult in my nonprofessionalism—political as well as cinematic—would, I suppose, be called the "story-line." (234)

Perhaps nothing is more indicative of the very personal and free-wheeling critical game Agee is playing than the superabundance of this conceit, not just the flow of the confection, but the overflow. As in a typical character description by Dickens or a Chaplin mime-dance—to cite just two other connoisseurs of superflux—Agee also gives you more than he needs to make his point: but in all these instances, more really is more, the genuine artist self-enchanted by the torrent of his own fecundity; and one notes with delight the way the first sentence piles preposition "on" preposition so that the effect literally doubles the condiments themselves; and the way the precious novelty of words such as "filberts" and "sprills" add divine decadence to the already overdressed cap of the sundae; and the way "go double on the whipped cream" tops the topping by breaking pace, voice, and syntax with a rough and satisfying flop into the vulgate. One further reflects how any ordinary writer might well have rejected the comparison itself (i.e., gaudy film production, ice cream sundae) as trite beyond salvation, or how, having risked it, might have been more than pleased with himself to have dropped it after the unexpected success of the first sentence—and how deeply in error he then would have been: for it is the second sentence that really fixes the critical focus and undercuts whatever aura of innocence might have adhered to the fruit and creamed plenitude of the first, by further extending an already overextended figure to indicate not just plenitude, but criminal, or at least fraudulent, excess (e.g., the nuts are "stale," a "hair" threads throughout—not just "long," but "bleached," etc.). In this manner, the overstuffed conceit becomes not merely entirely apposite of an extravaganza gone sour, but the perfect embodiment (that *juste* word again!) of what has often been meant by the expression "pure Hollywood" (here a big studio musical of the forties) as a sybarite's embarrassment of corrupt riches.

Nor should we pass over the passing distinction posed between the professional and the nonprofessional; here and throughout his criticism,

Agee's libertarian aesthetics unhesitatingly pushed him in the direction of the latter. Embracing the stance of "nonprofessionalism" was this writer's way of endorsing a personal margin of openness, flexibility, and self-determination within an occupational arena rife with regulation and procedural requirement. It was also his way of applying for the moral and intellectual license to certify the artistic license habitually exercised in the wild-cat wit, cantilevered conceits, gnarly textures, and, most of all, in the unstoppable effusions of personal sensibility; that is, a doctrine of "nonprofessionalism" blew a smokescreen of thought-out polemics over what at bottom was, in all likelihood, an incorrigible case of creative fire. But just as vital as any of these reasons, the mask of the nonprofessional provided Agee with the necessary myth to establish continuity between his personal past and present, between what had happened to him in the summer of 1936, and his continuing search for who he was. Accordingly, in his first column for the *Nation,* he takes pains to establish his credentials as a "would-be" or "amateur critic," specifically disassociating himself from the expertise and privileges of the professional filmmaker.

> That my own judgment, and yours, is that of an amateur, is only in part a handicap. It is also a definition. It can even be an advantage, of a sort, in so far as a professional's preoccupation with technique, with the box-office, with bad traditions, or simply with work, can blur, or alter the angle of, his own judgment . . . If I were a professional . . . my realization of the complexity of making any film would be so much clarified that I would be much warier than most critics can be in assigning either credit or blame. Indeed, if you follow out all the causes of that sort of high-serious failure, you would be involved as much in the analysis of an industry, a form of government, and the temper of a civilization, as in the analysis of a film. (23)

Let's assume that in promoting these relatively modest distinctions, Agee is not simply recycling the familiar, and more or less self-evident, tension emanating between the autonomous critic and the company creator, or, equally familiar, between the honest outsider sans excuses against the self-deceiving insider cocooned in alibis (e.g., "the industry made me do it," etc.). Rather, in his own way, and in terms appropriate to the new situation, he continues to cultivate, to refine and concentrate, the artistic profile first proclaimed in the "Intermission" section of *Famous Men*. In distancing himself from the studio regular he is indicting more than the work of a filmmaker, but once again by implication "an industry, a form of government, and the temper of a civilization." Once more he is contrasting the original and independent mind, the "individual and anti-authoritative mind" (i.e., "an amateur"), with one that has already been coopted and coerced (i.e., "a professional"), whose membership within a system and assimilated knowledge of its "technique . . . box-office . . . bad traditions . . . or . . . work" has made him, however unwilling, a beneficiary of that "technique . . . box office . . ." etc.; and, however unwitting, hesitant in exercising his judgment in relation to the continuance of such "technique . . . box office . . ." etc; and so, however passive, complicitous in furthering their ends. Recall that a "good artist" is, or should be, the "deadly enemy of society," and "the most dangerous thing that can happen to any enemy . . . is to become a beneficiary." As against membership in such a system and acquiescence to such "technique . . . box office . . ." Agee now projects a new film critical version of the "unassisted and weaponless consciousness" in terms of the amateur film critic's self-reliance of "eye" and "mind": "As an amateur, then, I must as well as I can simultaneously recognize my own ignorance and feel no apology for what my eyes tell me as I watch any given screen, where the proof is caught irrelevant to excuse, and available in proportion to the eye which sees it, and the mind which uses it" (23).

It's important to reiterate that, in the same column, Agee refers to himself not simply as "an amateur," but pointedly as a "would-be" or "amateur *critic*" (italics mine), thus explicitly extricating himself not only from the ranks of the professional filmmaker, but from those of the professional critic as well. Divesting himself of any professional uniform—particularly the one he was already wearing—represented this writer's assertion of fidelity to his own best self, his most romantic and heroic sense of who he was, or at least wanted to be: that is to say, the "good artist," a category of being incompatible with anything less or other than a posture of defiant autonomy and recusant creativity. And for this writer, the most expeditious way of reconciling his almost religious need to be the "good artist" with the practical and very immediate need to be the good critic was to be an artist in his criticism. But whenever the heterodoxies of his faith collided with the orthodoxies of his profession, there was never any doubt where his primary allegiance resided. As responsible as he was to the demands of his present chores—and Agee frequently practiced his craft as if no one beneath the rank of Recording Angel exercised greater scruple than he—his deepest responsibility clung to the personal principles of art, morality, and soft-core anarchism evolved in the afterglow of the Hale County experience; and sporadically these principles could push his criticism to the verge of what appeared to be a noncritical or even anticritical position. Even long-standing admirers of his commentaries may squirm as they recall the notorious instance (in the "Folk Art" essay for *Partisan Review,* Spring 1944) when after vigorously slating theatricals such as *Oklahoma, Carmen Jones,* and the then current production of *Othello* (with Paul Robeson), he added an in-text "Postscript: I should explain that I have not seen *Othello, Carmen Jones* or *Oklahoma,* because I felt sure they would be bad. People who spoke well of the shows have reinforced me in this feeling and have helped give it detail. People who spoke ill of them, I regarded as even more trustworthy" (408). Now without exactly elevating such rash practice into general critical policy, let me suggest that Agee's real point (and true effrontery) may reside not simply in reviewing (and reviling) productions that he hasn't seen, but in actually advertising the fact. Such vaunting irresponsibility may be the critic's most efficient way of nailing the critical point: that, in effect, he cares so little for even the *idea* of these productions that he would deny them the courtesy, not to speak of the fairness or decency, of a responsible review.

But the critical point may also finally matter less than the personal point: that Agee's responsibility to the image of himself as the "good," that is, the free, artist takes precedence over everything, even, and most particularly, over his discipline as a professional critic; and in the "Folk Art" essay, he willfully asserts his allegiance to the former even at the extreme expense of undermining his credentials as the latter. The assertion of a radical self and full liberty demand the expression of everything that the critic-as-artist has within him, all his energies, not just the creative and "constructive" ones, but also what may be perceived as the willful, miscreant, and foolhardy ones too.

So when all is said and done, the practice of criticism may not have always allowed Agee the widest possible latitude for the practice of his art; indeed, in the last year or more of his reviewer's shift, it can hardly be denied that he was already impatient to be doing other things (e.g., writing fiction or making movies). Still, in view of the time expended on it, and everything he consistently brought to it—the force, the passion, the transformative fuel—the criticism in the *Nation* must stand as one of this writer's supreme achievements in art; and equally significant, in no way an interlude between or a departure from, the more overtly "personal" and "imaginative" creation that came before or after it. As already intimated, the authorial persona exercised in the criticism, as well as the themes and attitudes present throughout, are in every way consistent with the artistic profile, stresses, and preoccupations evidenced in *Famous Men* and *A Death in the Family*. A full investigation of these matters will bear further, if not altogether stranger, fruit below.

2. THE TESTAMENT OF ENDYMION

"Cold critics" (288), he called them, and Agee had little trouble in consistently relegating disinterested analysis to such frosty professionals. For himself, he had no hesitation in confessing a commitment to films, good and bad, that reflected his obsessions, or films, good and bad, whose full interest was revealed only when the critic brought "special attitudes of mind" to bear upon them. On January 10, 1948 (in the *Nation*) he writes, "André Malraux's *Man's Hope* is probably a very fine and moving film only for those who, like myself, bring special attitudes of mind to it . . . Right or wrong, I care a great deal for work which requires special attitudes of those who will fully appreciate it" (288). In this light, one can, if so inclined (though as you will see I am not) and with considerable justice, sift through Agee's reviews exploring what seems to me an extraordinary number of films—regardless of their quality, and regardless too, of the general level of disapproval he often brings to many of them—that are clutched at with a special fervor, an intensity of regard, solely because they coincide with the lifelong, private passions of the critic. These would include, for instance, the large number of responses devoted to films of rural life and peasant ethnography; not just searching inspections of generally admired work such as *The Southerner, To Live in Peace,* and *Farrebique* (i.e., films interesting to many critics without Agee's bias), but equally extensive and meticulous critiques of weak, or at least problematic, or simply arcane and far-flung items such as *Dragon Seed, The Well Digger's Daughter, The Pearl, 48 Hours, The Silent Village,* etc. Consider too the special kind of protracted and persnickety concern he brings to the many movies depicting American family life; again, not just the "mainstream" choices (which he nevertheless manages to guard and inventory like his private preserves), such as *The Best Years of Our Lives, Meet Me in St. Louis, National Velvet, A Tree Grows in Brooklyn* (among others), but those more likely to require "special attitudes," such as *The Human Comedy, The Happy Land, A Medal for Benny, Sunday Dinner for a Soldier, Kiss and Tell, Tender Comrade, Our Vines Have Tender Grapes* (and many more).[11] And even more sharply revealing, a vital tributary of this familial focus, there is the almost unconscionable fuss over child stars, and in general the treatment of children in movies everywhere; beginning with loving ruminations on the underage actors in all the aforementioned family films (Rooney, Taylor, O'Brien, Butch Jenkins, Peggy Ann Garner, etc.); extending to needlepoint probes of slop he readily admits to be inconsequential save in this one area (reviews of *The Lost Angel, The Canterville Ghost*); sometimes interposing itself in virtual fits of proprietary rage, as in "She [Margaret O'Brien] is an uncannily talented child, and it is infuriating to see her handled, and gradually being ruined, by oafs" (106); sometimes bursting into unabashed but touching, funny valentines, as in "Ever since I first saw the child [Elizabeth Taylor] . . . I have been choked with the peculiar sort of adoration I might have felt if we were both in the same grade of primary school" (132); reaching its epiphany in 1947 in his stirring apostrophe to the "child-worship" and "anarchic fury" (264) of Jean Vigo's *Zero for Conduct,* a film placed even above his personal favorite, *Monsieur Verdoux.* Then (still within the family nexus) there are the virtually predictable Ageean ecstatics lavished upon numerous celluloid portrayals of strong and protective father figures—the wise salts, grizzled patrons of the earth, careworn heroes of command, and stoical caretakers of the flock; such as Robert Mitchum's young captain in *The Story of*

G. I. Joe, whose death scene "seems to me a war poem as great as any of Whitman's" (173); Robert Montgomery's P.T. boat commander in *They Were Expendable,* "the one perfection to turn up in movies during the year [1945]" (185); Aldo Fabrizi's peasant in *To Live in Peace,* "one of the few towering archetypes I have seen on the screen" (284); Walter Huston's prospector in *The Treasure of the Sierra Madre,* "this performance crowns a lifetime" (292); the face of Toscanini, "as good a record of human existence near its utmost as we are likely to see" (200); and a near mystical response—i.e., in Agee's most filial, that is, most reverential idiom—to the ravaged features of a mortally ill Franklin Roosevelt (in newsreel footage of the Yalta and Teheran conferences): the "quality of heroism emergent at last upon its highest and grandest prospect" (159).

It isn't my intent to deliberate over these cathectic clusters of home-grown emotion, but simply to insist that they are very eminently there in the weekly, on-cue, "newspaper" utterances, just as they are there in his more obviously private, and allegedly more "creative," efforts. But far more instructive than the specific subjects he chooses to fret over, or even the very personal bias he brings to them, is the poetic melodrama he manages to construe out of his general field survey of the history and ontology of film as art, a tale whose tragic shape and fate, as he determines to contrive it, was nearly as sorrowing and deracinated as his own fall from the mottled heaven of his childhood, and in some ways directly collateral to it. The silent luminescence of the early film, the "wild animal innocence and glorious vitality" (6) of its nascent expression, its shackled and ambiguous devolvement as a "talking picture," along with the embattled fate of the men who made the movies—none of this was conceived in the manner of the film scholar or the historian of fact. Rather, Agee envisioned the origins and development of the movies as legend, and in terms roughly homologous to the legend told of himself. Freely projecting an Ageean cinema, then, we begin once more with an Edenic age of virtually spontaneous creation, and yet another gathering of artist demiurges (c.f., the watering row of Knoxville fathers, the Hale County farmers as "classical" folk artisans), another "family" of fecund founders and free-makers, such as Sennett, Griffith, Chaplin, Keaton, and Stroheim in the first, purest, and nearly indigenous flowering; and then in close temporal proximity—actually the haloed moment nearing its end—a second harvest of personal heroes from foreign shores, including Eisenstein, Dovzhenko, Lubitsch, Murnau, and Clair. With the consolidation of the major studios, however, this period of golden silence shatters in sound. What follows represents a steady decline into the present tense of big company wartime foundries making contracts with the current confusion of lonely, uprooted, well-intentioned, but thoroughly encumbered and conflicted filmmakers; some of them, such as Chaplin, Eisenstein, and Clair, actually holdovers from the lost heroic age working now in diminished and severely anguished circumstances; some of them, such as John Huston and Geroges Rouquier, members of a new "orphan" generation frozen in postures of rebellious "intransigence," "undirectable" directors pitted against deeply entrenched, antagonistic, and "difficult odds" (290); still others, such as Hitchcock, Wyler, Wilder, Olivier (and many more), making partial alliance with those "difficult odds," and as a consequence producing hopeful, even brilliant, but also uneven, compromised, and in some instances "housebroken," art. Struggling in the wake of a vanished radiance, all of these harried figures now seek to discover themselves in terms of a proper, fearful ambit pledged not to liberty and creation, but to "safe-playing" (31), "genteelism" (73), the front-office, and the ordinances of the censor.

Agee may not have had a settled theory of the movies, or a systematic means of resolving their anomalies, or even a ready answer to the question "What is cinema?" But he did have a very distinct, highly personal, and severely discriminating sense of film history and the moral life of film form—specifically, what the movies were, what they had become, what had gone wrong, and what or who was to blame—and this sense promoted, in turn, certain deeply felt general attitudes about the current film scene. The essential outlines of these general attitudes not only scarcely wavered, but seemed to hold fast even when specific evidence compiled by nine years of close reviewing of individual movies often urged him to other, or even contrary, attitudes. His genius may have been for a rhetoric of equivocation and hesitation, a dramatics of self-consciousness, but about certain estimates and predisposals concerning his cherished art, he held the line to the end. These included: (1) A forever finished period of silent filmmaking towers above the present one. (2) The present period characterizes itself in terms of timidity, routine, and every variety of

artistic strangulation and unadventurousness. (3) In the current situation, a "great" movie can still be made, but only by "a good artist" in the
Ageean sense, that is, a radical individualist ("Trust only the individualist
in art" [239], "a dangerous sort of man" [139]). (4) The likelihood of
such a man getting a chance to make such a movie in the current situation
remains exceedingly small. (5) If such a movie does get made, however,
it will change nothing; the current situation will remain the same. (6) If
the current situation does change, it will be for the worse.

I have presented these attitudes as a bill of particulars, which of course
they were not, nor did they appear as such in his writing. Still, there was
nothing covert or even veiled about the judgments inspired by such
primal predilections. In his first column for the *Nation*, for example, he
begins his first review of the current cinema: "The best picture I saw all
year was *The Gold Rush*" (23) made in 1925. One year later (1943) when
Lubitsch's *Heaven Can Wait* appears, it brings "back a time when people
really made good movies; it was so good I half believed Lubitsch could still
do as well as the best he ever did if he had half a chance. *Heaven Can Wait*
is not up to his best; nothing has been for the past twenty years" (49). (In
other comparisons to the historical past, this number would occasionally
diminish to "fifteen years" or even "ten years or more," as in "the whole
industry has been dying for ten years or more"; but in the early reviews,
"twenty" seems to be the preferred number, as in "the average American
filmmaker" has been acting toward "the general audience" like "a housebroken Nazi for the past twenty years" [134].) When an old master, such
as Lubitsch, Clair, or Eisenstein, emerges in the present, his new film
invariably dwarfs the current scene just as surely as the new work in its
turn is dwarfed by the director's earlier accomplishments (e.g., reviews of
Clair's *Man About Town* or Eisenstein's *Ivan the Terrible*). Even Chaplin's
Monsieur Verdoux, the only possible exception to this tendency, "is not
the best of Chaplin," only the most "endlessly interesting" (288). When
a fresh find by a young filmmaker does appear, Agee can think of no
compliment greater than to compare it with work from an era of golden
silence; "*The Treasure of the Sierra Madre*," for instance, "is one of the few
movies made since 1927 which I am sure will stand up in the memory and
esteem of qualified people alongside the best of silent movies" (290); or
of *Zero for Conduct* (which he first catches up with in 1947), "it extended
the possibilities of style and expression as brilliantly, and germinally as

the best work of Griffith, Chaplin, Eisenstein, Dovzchenko, and Murnau. It was made fourteen or fifteen years ago, and nothing so adventurous in terms of pure movie expression has been made since" (287).

In contrast to his golden day, it is the contemporary scene that inspires his most dire and stricken formulations. In 1941, he refers to contemporary filmmaking as part of a "decaying tradition" (57). In 1945, "it is a time of artistic cowardice and cynicism, and despair" (144); again in 1945, "when an art is sick unto death, only men of the most murderous creative passion can hope to save it . . . I wonder whether it is any longer possible, anywhere on earth, for such a man to work in films. I am almost certain it is not possible, and is not ever going to be, in this country" (139). In 1947, he laments the constrictions placed upon "our men of genius. In Russia we make corpses of them, living or genuine; here we drown them in cream" (238); again in 1947, "the art of moving pictures has been sick for so long, the most it can do for itself is to shift unceasingly from one bed sore to the next" (255). In 1948, writing in the shadow of the HUAC investigations, "it is now an absolute certainty that every most hopeful thing that has been stirring in Hollywood is petrified more grimly than ever before. The firing of the Ten Contemptuous Men was merely the most conspicuous death spasm; I doubt that from now on—for how long it is impossible to imagine—anyone in Hollywood will dare even to breathe loudly" (290). And again in 1948, when he comes to write his last column for the *Nation,* it is with full poetic justice on the death of the oldest and grandest of old grand masters, D. W. Griffith: "Hollywood and, to a great extent, movies in general grew down from him rather than up past him; audiences, and the whole eye and feeling of the world, have suffered the same degeneration" (317).

Now, I don't mean to argue the truth or falsity of any of Agee's general assessments of the forties film scene, or his various contentions concerning the relative merits of individual movies and moviemakers, past and present. Such arguments would only take us deeper into movies, not deeper into Agee's view of them. Naturally, to spotlight just two of his more prominent attitudes, he hardly stood alone among the critics, historians, and aestheticians of his day in his generalized disdain for the more oppressive aspects of the studio system (though his sweeping condemnation extended to far more than just those aspects), or in his near deification of the first generation of American filmmakers (though for Agee virtually anyone working in silence seemed ripe for reverence), who for a short time at least seemed to flourish freely while the corporate hegemony struggled for consolidation. Suffice it to say, that many just, evidence-crammed, and persuasive arguments (Agee too is persuasive) could be rallied in defense or in repudiation of any part or all of Agee's position. Nowadays, the sentimental majority would doubtless uphold a view diametrically opposed to his; particularly when so many critics, scholars, and the media itself tend to interpret his era of factory filmmaking as by no means "sick unto death," but in fact another "golden age"—the last one before the rise of television and the breakup of the studio power structure in the late fifties. Nowadays our movie mavens are frequently heard to proclaim "the genius of the system," and how contract directors actually thrived within the formulas of the studio-approved genre film, as well as within the efficiency, discipline, and security of the studio-imposed divisions of labor. (For more on the current film scene vis a vis Agee, see "Obligations.")

But I do think it valuable to understand, and pursue further, the foundations of Agee's tenaciously held values and priorities. Where, why, and how did these fiery strictures emerge? Whatever "it" was that this one critic may have wanted from the movies, I think it was abundantly apparent that the specific films he reviewed—most of the ones deemed good, and sometimes even the precious few deemed great—were not giving "it" to him. Whatever it was that Agee may have believed about the movies, such beliefs in all likelihood were formed (as we should attempt to argue) entirely anterior to, and not as a result of, all the movies he saw as a critic. At times one feels that even if the movies of the present had been immeasurably different or better than they were, they still could not compare to movies of his childhood and early youth simply because they were not those movies. But what was the basis for such a curious predisposition? What did the movies really mean to a man like Agee anyway—or he to them?

COMMUNIONS: MOVIES AT THE MAJESTIC

The nature and origin of Agee's "special attitudes" concerning the motion picture, as well as the seeds of his disenchantment, reveal themselves not in the film criticism per se, but substantially in the evocation of early moviegoing, and the silent film itself, that appears in the opening chapter of *A Death in the Family*. Turn then to Knoxville, 1916, as Jay takes his six-year-old son Rufus to see Charlie Chaplin and William S. Hart at the Majestic Theater for what proves to be the last time (on the night of the following day, Jay will be dead). Love of movies is a passion held in common by father and son, and going to the movies a repeated ritual that binds one to the other, and that very explicitly separate both from Rufus's mother, Mary, who does not accompany them on these outings and significantly does not approve of Chaplin. "Oh, Jay! . . . That horrid little man!," Mary says of the Tramp, "He's so *nasty!* . . . So *vulgar!* With his nasty little cane; hooking up skirts and things, and that nasty little walk!" (11). And "nasty" and "vulgar" is precisely what the movies are not only for Mary, but for Jay and Rufus too: and desirable for those very reasons. Accordingly, father and son find their way to their seats amid "the exhilarating smell of stale tobacco, rank sweat, perfume and dirty drawers, while the piano played fast music and galloping horses raised a grandiose flag of dust" (11). For Agee, part of the religion of early movies was the power generated by participation in a unified experience composed of what was seen (thrilling motions), how it was seen (wordless images, fast music) and, above all, who was seeing it: his father, himself, and a rowdy crowd characterized by its freedom from inhibition. And part of the excitement of early moviegoing was the excitement of entry into the raffish company of what he later called "unrespectable people" (*Agee on Film*, 7), and of soaking in all the disreputable things those "unrespectable people" had come to see: "And there was William S. Hart with both guns blazing and his long, horse face and his long, hard lip, and the great country rode away behind him as wide as the world" (12). The Majestic Theater is the place where one begins one's education in the rich teeming existence outside the home—"nasty," "vulgar," and "exhilarating" too—where one discovers what Agee would later refer to (praising certain wartime documentaries) as "irreplaceable pieces of teaching" (*Agee on Film*, 56); where an ordinary, proper, curious American child could gaze in wondering discovery of the world's dappled things, an endless treasure of improper disclosures and taboos split wide; precise "teaching" in, say, hard conduct (e.g., an ocean of male action), violent death (e.g., cowboys with "blazing" guns), startling vistas (e.g., space "as wide as the world" exploding everywhere); and subsequently, in the Chaplin film, amorous improprieties and the secrets of bodily function. A genteel mother's worst fears are realized as Chaplin flirts with "a pretty woman . . . he flicked hold of the straight end of his cane, and with the crooked end, hooked up her skirt to the knee, in exactly the way that disgusted Mama, looking very eagerly at her legs, and everybody laughed very loudly . . . Then he twirled his cane and suddenly squatted, bending the cane and hitching up his pants, and again hooked up her skirt so that you could see the panties she wore, ruffled almost like the edges of curtains, and everybody whooped with laughter . . ." (12–13).

This "laughter" might well have been the best laughter Agee ever knew—the most powerful and the most purifying, "as violent and steady and deafening as standing under a waterfall" (*Agee on Film*, 7)— for it not only included him in the community of his father, but as the direct antiphonal response to the scandals on the screen bestowed the authority of its blessing on all manner of infraction unacceptable, and perhaps even unknown, within the purview of the family enclave. Seconds later, when Charlie sits down on a handful of stolen eggs hidden in his trousers and drenches his seat, and Rufus is reminded of the time he peed in his pants—"when it ran down out of the pants-legs and showed all over your stockings and you had to walk home that way with people looking" (13)—even here, the great audience gathers up his shame and squeamishness in the might of its violent toleration, the near animal glee of its recognitions and acceptances. Charlie's mess helps Rufus accommodate his own by means of a shared embarrassment; and the wordless roar of the crowd provides final absolution for both; and particularly for Rufus, a flood of remission from the miserable isolation of his self-pity: " . . . Rufus' father nearly tore his head off laughing and so did everybody else, and Rufus was sorry for Charlie, having been so recently in a similar predicament, but the contagion of the laughter was too much for him, and he laughed too" (13).

In this manner, the early silents became part of Agee's secular church in life, the primary fount of the innocent eye's instruction in worldly goods and earth's traffic, including lessons in violence, sensuality, indelicacy, and sprawl: each jolt administered within the provenance of a revered father, arraigned, as it were, within the diocese of his consent and that of his parish, a flock of "unrespectable people." Obviously much of what this critic disliked about the movies of his maturity as opposed to those of his youth derived from his sense that the unruly sacrament of his childhood had begun to spruce up and demystify itself in the pursuit of decorousness and respectability. In 1944, for example, discussing the deficiencies in an attempted work of religious art (*The Song of Bernadette*), he notes, "The limits are those of middle-class twentieth-century genteelism, a fungus which by now all but chokes the life out of any hope from Hollywood and which threatens any vivid appetite in Hollywood's audience" (*Agee on Film*, 73). For Agee, filmmaking in the forties had little in common with the permissive religion of the rough crowd, had become in fact something closer to the innocuous pastime of proper people, closer in spirit, that is, to the polite curtailments of his mother as against the abrasive enthusiasms of his father. Worst of all, the moving image itself had lost more than a palpable share of both its power and glory—the hypnotic enigma and trancelike purity of its silent envelopments.

Throughout their moviegoing adventure, father and son take the most intimate soundings of each other within the near mystical conditions of almost total dumb show, a series of virtually unmediated and indelible communications beyond "the frauds, compromises, and artful dodges" of the word. Attending the film is only the first phase in a complex rite of nonverbal bonding; the somnambular journey homewards is the second, both rhyming and intensifying the first, as the subconscious eloquence that resides at the aesthetic core of the silent movie is replicated in a wordless duet of parent and child, a dreamy ceremonial of motions and hesitations, glances and gestures. First, as Jay and Rufus stroll past "the deaf and dumb asylum," "deep and silent among the shadow of the trees," there is the "crossing of the viaduct" (17); then the anticipation of the corner; then, walking very slowly and nearing the corner, there is the pause "at the edge of the sidewalk"; and then, without speaking, they step into the "dark lot" and sit down "on the rock" (18). Now they are gazing not at the images of Chaplin and Hart, but at the "trembling lanterns of the universe" (20) and the map of lights that is Knoxville itself; once more, that is, they reside before another space "as wide as the world," another (literal) "Majestic Theater."

It is here, as Rufus first communes with the full paradox of his father's distraction—with the "loneliness" (19) and the homesickness at the heart of his contentment and well-being—that the stipulation against verbal communication becomes critical, an explicit diminishment of the immediate "pleasure of their privacy" (21), and their intimate divination of each other. Rufus felt that

> He knew these things very distinctly, but not, of course, in any such way as we have of suggesting them in words. There were no words, or even ideas, or formed emotions, of the kind that have been suggested here, no more in the man than in the boy child. These realizations moved clearly through the senses, the memory, the feelings, the mere feeling of the place they paused at. . . . Sometimes on these evenings his father would hum a little and the humming would break open into a word or two, but he never finished even a part of a tune, for silence was even more pleasurable, and sometimes he would say a few words, of very little consequence, but would never seek to say much, or to finish what he was saying, or to listen for a reply; for silence again was even more pleasurable. (20)

Within this rapture of silence and before an audience of stars, it is now father and son who become primary players; the language of pantomime entirely subsuming the language of words; the public euphoria of union with the moviegoers echoed and refined by the private euphoria of a union for two (i.e., "the unity that was so firm and assured," 19). Now the tracings of film gesture erupt into living human gesture as Jay and Rufus perform a gravid semaphore of hands and heads, ribs and shoulders, the silent forging of an Ageean "chain of flesh" (in this context—last movie, last walk—the final consecration of the Adamic son with his father creator):[12]

> Rufus felt his father's hand settle, without groping or clumsiness, on the top of his bare head: it took his forehead and smoothed it, and pushed the hair backward from his forehead, and held the back of his head while Rufus pressed his head backward against the firm hand, and, in reply to that pressure, clasped over his right ear and cheek, over the whole side of the head, and drew Rufus' head quietly and strongly against the sharp cloth that covered his father's body, through which Rufus could feel the breathing ribs;

then relinquished him, and Rufus sat upright, while the hand lay strongly on his shoulder, and he saw that his father's eyes had become still more clear and grave and that the deep lines around his mouth were satisfied; and looked up at what his father was so steadily looking at, at the leaves which silently breathed and at the stars which beat like hearts. (21)

Here in Knoxville we view an enactment of the rudiments of silent film gesture. Years later, Agee would reformulate the matter more flatly and abstractly for the readers of the *Nation:* "Somewhere close to the essence of the power of moving pictures is the fact that they can give you things to look at, clear of urging or comment, and so ordered that they are radiant with illimitable suggestions of meaning and mystery" (*Agee on Film,* 164). For Agee, the language of the silent film—by definition unencumbered by "urging or comment"—would forever be a direct pipeline to an "illimitable" ocean of nonverbal vastation, a convocation of "the senses, the memory" and "the feelings," the validity of which could only be sullied, diminished or debunked, by language. To the degree we honor the depiction in *A Death in the Family,* we also recognize that this silent tongue was inseparable from the form, the very kinesthetics, of the privileged moments between his father and himself. Such moments help us to appreciate not only Agee's lifelong reverence for the authority of the silent gesture, but also his equal compliment of lifelong ambivalence about those methods and technologies (i.e., "the talkies") that muzzled, mollified, or in any way delimited the full spread of that authority. What exactly did those raw visual images, "clear of urging or comment," mean to him personally? His evocative rendering of early moviegoing makes it emphatically clear that whatever else they did, those images could crack the circle of his self-absorption and pull him out of himself— out of his fear, confusion, hesitancy, his abiding sense of softness and inadequacy—and into direct contact with forces vastly greater, harsher, more valid, and more "actual" than he could ever imagine himself to be: into contact with the whole booming universe of brash and unfettered happenings depicted in those images; into contact with the swarmlife of the feculent throng who worshiped at the shrine of those images, and for whom those images were summoned into existence; and through both of those contacts, into ecstatic "union" with the great sheltering hand of the supreme man of the image-loving throng, the father himself, who, through that blessed hand, could usher his son to perhaps a glimpse, or even merely a sense, of that great beating heart (as in, "the stars which beat like hearts"), the *Creator Spiritus* in nature, the point of origin of the human chain, that procreant demiurge of whom the father and the world of the father—both the teeming image and the roaring throng—were but the avatars. What did those early images mean to the "boy child" who grew to become one of the most remarkable moviegoers of his day? They were not less than conduits to his very sentiment of being, and to his last, most precious recollections (and perhaps all he would ever know) of divinity in being.

ART AND BRAVERY

Now we should always try to remember that Agee could be, and often was, as aware as the most passionate enthusiast of the "talkies" of the enormous potential represented by the sound principle as both legitimate aural companion to the image and as a natural extension, even advancement, of its expressive powers. For instance, he usually had nothing but praise for the creative use of sound effects in film, that is, for the successful ordering of nonverbal audibles—as in, say, Minnelli's *The Clock* (*Agee on Film*, 165)—resulting in a sea of reverberation readily comparable to the resonance of the silent image. From time to time, he was even pleased to extol the employment of music in certain efforts (e.g., Dovzchenko's *Frontier*, the score composed for Griffith's *Birth of a Nation*). But in this area his sympathies were severely quarantined. In general he felt the "greatest possibilities [of music] have hardly yet been touched . . . Music is just as damaging to nearly all fiction film as to nearly all fact film, as it is generally used in both today . . . It sells far too cheaply and far too sensually all the things it is the business of the screen itself to present" (164). Agee was in fact instantly inhospitable to almost anything that might coerce or qualify, certainly usurp, or sometimes merely even challenge the primacy and power of the visual image itself, silent or otherwise; sometimes "anything" meant music; sometimes it meant music and words; most often, however, it meant just words.

Agee's emphatic preference for visual comedy is of course well known (c.f., "Comedy's Greatest Era"), but actually this preference could be extended to virtually anything visual over anything verbal. For example, "I wish this twenty-year old show were revived," he writes of Lubitsch's *Forbidden Paradise* (1924) in comparison to Preminger's remake, *A Royal Scandal* (1945), "both for its own sake as I remember it, and because between the two versions one could get a pretty good measure of the difference between talking and silent pictures. I realize, of course, that talking pictures can be better than *A Royal Scandal,* and as good as anything silent, and conceivably even better; but in order even to try to be so, they have to know the value of pantomime, and they have to know when to shut up" (155). He was also particularly adamant about the correct use of the voiceover in newsreels and documentaries; "I wish I might see a newsreel or a longer film which first presented its images in the most powerful order and weaving possible, without a word of explanation; then got down, with diagrams and with recapitulated shots, to explanation. I am interested in explanations, but a thousand times more interested that an image have its full power" (100). On one occasion, his animus went so far as to begin to create the impression of relegating the indigenous parlance itself to simply another golden calf for certain categories of Middle-Americans: "The normal native commentary [in the average American documentary], well measuring our loss of cinematic instinct, heckles and humiliates the screen image, and pounds it, like the nagging of a shrew, a salesman, a preacher, a demagogue, a pimp, or all five combined; we use films to illustrate the rotten words we worship" (34).

This of course was hardly the first time that a preening of the verbal afflatus could fill him with disdain (c.f., "The Words"). Still, "rotten words" were strong words for a regular employer, even for a reputed master, of words; and one for whom words, for good or ill, were the sole, shining means of entry to and presentation of everything within him; and as far as any reader could know, everything that he was. For surely if language was privileged to anyone, it was privileged to him, and an open attack on language by Agee was also a covert attack, by design or not, on his own special ambit of accomplishment and self-display. If the image was numinous and totemic, the insignia of "meaning and mystery," and if an aesthetic ordering of such images could be the primary means of conveyance to a silent, refulgent other (compare "the trembling lanterns of the universe" to "the cruel radiance of what is"), then just as surely the word was capricious and self-reflexive, and a vain ordering of such words could be an index to a demoralized artist's pattern of self-enchantment, a lethal plunge into the perfumed cell of the self. Born as they must be in pride of rumination, in dream, whim, and unrequited yearning, in the mirror-lined crib of Narcissus—even as the child is born in the swaddling of the home, regulated and caressed at the line of his mother's ankle, tucked far away from the hurley of the crowd and the harsh, infinite bower of the father's palm—even so, the pampered word easily devolves into the "rotten" word, and the "worship" of "rotten words" may simply be another way of hoisting the spoiled and timorous self onto the altar of false idols.

Among the highest, and sometimes hardest, of Ageean artistic ideals—for himself and other practitioners (interpreted in the light of the self)—was the courage for self-immolation, an aesthetic ordinance compelling a near absolute humbling of the self and its selfish imperatives—the prophylaxis of an addled ego—in utter deference to an ineffable object (*nadryv* is the corrupt counterfeit of this). Even as far back as Knoxville, 1916, Rufus painfully recalls and rehearses, on at least two central occasions, the final lesson of his father to him, as a kind of boy's primer in self-abnegation. This lesson emerges from the moment, just after the movies and just before the silent journey homewards, when Jay stops off at the local bar for a drink, and Rufus notes the "hollowness" in his voice when he boasts to the other men of his son's ability to read at an early age; and promptly Rufus fills with an "anguish of shame" (*A Death in the Family*, 16). He subsequently reflects (as they walk toward the vacant lot), "If I could fight, thought Rufus. If I were brave; he would never brag how I could read. Brag. Of course. 'Don't you brag.' That was it. What it meant. Don't brag you're smart if you're not brave. You've got nothing to brag about. Don't you brag" (17). This is the very last piece of officially reflected advice ("Don't you brag") attributed by Rufus to his father before his death, and its connotations continue to haunt his actions throughout the book. And beyond: into the moral life of the man who continued to view certain acts of self-assertion and expression, most famously his own, in at the very least a fervor of double-mindedness.

At the simplest level, of course, Rufus's reflection represents a version of the traditional American male parent's traditional preachment to his American son: the extolment of physical courage and brave deeds undertaken in silence and stoicism, with the explicit caution against vanity of intellect (precocious reading, acting "smart," etc.) and loose talk ("brag") as dubious distinctions, at best lesser forms of accomplishment. But after Jay's death, we learn how this same anxiety over bragging and self-display (i.e., the "showing-off" sequence, 263–81, where Rufus tries to gain favor with the older boys by exploiting his father's accident) takes on greater importance, as the guilt and shame attendant upon "brag" provide the basis for a virulent onslaught of conscience ("But if his father's soul was around . . . it could sit and look at him and be ashamed of him" [280]), one that would eventuate in a lifelong reflex of self-chastisement; and in the film critic, a legion of raging scruples that incessantly took arms against all forms of creative indulgence advanced in the name of self-interest. Echoes of Jay's last lesson to his son resonate still in the critic's admonition to the "talking picture" to learn "the value of pantomime" (silent action over "smart" dialogue) and "when to shut up" ("Don't you brag"); but even more significantly it helps us understand the critic's lasting preference for adjudicating the acts of the artist in film largely as a problem in personal valor (perhaps the only major film critic to regularly do so). Rarely did he speak of such acts as determined, say, by greater or lesser degrees of talent, but most characteristically, by an exercise in spiritual grit; often, that is, a film was both the result and measure of the fortitude (or turpitude) of its maker. In this respect, *Monsieur Verdoux* of course becomes an act of "moral and artistic heroism" (*Agee on Film*, 254), "one of the purest and most courageous works I know" (261); or of Georges Rouquier, he typically writes, "it seems as if the man is hardly alive any more who is fit to look another man in the eye. But this man is" (297). Rouquier's audience too must muster a strength of character similar to that of the director in order to properly respond to his work; thus, *Farrebique* is for "those who have eyes capable of seeing what is before them and minds and hearts capable of caring for what they see" (298). But then, if neither maker nor viewer is up to the mark—"When you can make such a picture," he writes of a failed Russian film (*The Rainbow*), "or watch with untroubled approval, some crucially important moral nerve, has, I believe, gone dead in you" (125).

Such an ethos of daring and dedication became the focal point of his much discussed, and much misunderstood, concept of "realism" in film, his ardent advocacy of an "uninvented" or "unaltered" reality. During the war it was indeed the documentary form (i.e., "fact film," "film of record") that impressed him most (e.g., *The Battle of San Pietro, Desert Victory*). And after the war, he was pleased to note certain fiction films— from Italy (e.g., *Shoeshine, Open City*) and then from America (e.g., *Boomerang, Call Northside 777*)—appropriating certain documentary approaches to their varied ends. But as in the case of *Famous Men*, the subject of an "unaltered reality," also a leitmotif throughout these film pieces, did not always promote his most cogent or original vein of reflection. He often wrote, as did others, about the need for taking fiction films outside the studio, etc.; for replacing trained actors with nonprofessionals, etc.; and that he was, in other words, perfectly capable of sounding as hasty and superficial as anyone else who rattled on in this fashion—frequently creating the false impression that merely a change in venue or performer provided in itself an automatic guarantee of authenticity in film, an instant antidote to the presumed poison of Hollywood artifice and Big Studio methodology. As against these push-button promotionals for the "real" this or that, however, we should recall that most of his heroes in film—Sennett, Griffith, Chaplin, Keaton, Dovzchenko, Murnau, Clair, Vigo—could hardly be described as "realists" either in Agee's, or probably anyone else's, usage; nor did he usually seek to describe them as such. Actually, in his more searching phases, he could be found ready to march his obsession for "unaltered reality" into considerably more probative, less chartered, regions. "Since I think so highly of both films," he writes of *Open City* and *The Raiders,*

> I should take special care to make clear that this is not *because* they use non-actors or are semi-documentary, or are "realistic." It is rather that they show a livelier moral and aesthetic respect for reality—which "realism" can as readily smother as liberate— than most fictional films, commercial investments in professional reliability, ever manage to. If they are helped to this—as they are— by their concern for actual people and places, that is more than can

be said for most documentaries; which by average are as dismally hostile to reality as most fiction films. (237).

Not simply, then, "actual people and places," but rather a "livelier moral and aesthetic respect" for those "actual people and places." But what, then, constitutes such "respect"? Actually, more than one might imagine. Actually, "respect" may not be nearly enough, as we see in the following instance concerning the relative failure of the actors in Renoir's *The Southerner* (a film he generally admired) to portray sharecroppers:

> Betty Field clearly and deeply cares for the kind of regional exactness I too care for; but her efforts to disguise the fact that she is an intelligent, sincere young artist who feels sympathy and respect for a farmer's wife are as embarrassing as mine would be if I tried to play Jeeter Lester. Beulah Bondi, an actress I generally admire, demonstrates merely how massively misguided, and how swarmed with unconscious patronage, the whole attitude of the theater has always been toward peasants. I don't want to go on. I am afraid that in my objection to this kind of inaccuracy there are streaks of parochial pedantry and snobbery. But mainly, so far as I know, my objection comes out of a respect for people. If you are going to try to show real people, in a real place, I think that you have to know how their posture and speech and facial structure can alter even within the width of one country; that you have to communicate the exact beauty of those minute particulars without their ever becoming more pointed to the audience than to the people portrayed, and without a single false tone; that if you don't you are in grave danger of unconscious patronage, you don't see or appreciate or understand your subjects as well as you think you do, you stand likely therefore to be swamped by your mere affection or respect, and so perhaps should give up the whole idea. (167–68)

By this line of reasoning, "unaltered reality" and "realism" itself reveal themselves as having less to do with an exhibition of "actual people and places" than with the erasure of the artist's personality and a showing forth of a virtually selfless production—a standard that, in this instance as in most others, proves beyond the reach of the merely dedicated. All the goodwill and serious intentions in the actor's arsenal, all the "affection and respect," etc., may only be the outward forms of vanity slumming at its own masked ball, every conscious and heartfelt attempt to embody the raw innocence of an elusive other undermined by an unconscious allegiance to the devices and defenses of a cosseted self. It is further hinted that even the critic who criticizes such allegiance may be guilty of a form of it himself, as Agee balances the actor's "unconscious patronage" against his own possible "parochial pedantry and snobbery."

This passage, and there are many others like it, represents a thoroughly characteristic instance of the politely relentless way our writer could skewer an artist with a scruple; and then boomerang the spike. No cinephile has ever been better than he in calculating the various measures that a filmmaker, or a film critic, might take to inoculate himself against a full commitment to his subject. No analyst of the interior has ever been more persuasive in exposing the almost bottomless forms of evasion and self-deceit of the craven ego in art, especially when entangled in service to decent causes. His uncanny success in this area flowed, in all probability, from his own pitiless propensity for self-interrogation. He had a guilt detector that knew how to track the enemy who did not always reside in the front offices at MGM, but more familiarly in one's own mirror where the face of compromise and "safe-playing" could always be found if one was, as he was, always looking. Wasn't this face born and bred as much of his mother's "genteelism"—the decorousness, studied proficiencies, theological armory, and virtuous withdrawals—as of his father's courage, independence, and immersion in the senses? And as a practicing critic, couldn't he attempt a creative solution to his divided legacy? He was "smart" just as his father knew he was, but in his own way he could try to be "brave" too; and his bravery would consist in naming the vices and subterfuges of "smart" people like himself. This gauge of the artist's moral temperature, this grand critical inquisition into the secret heart of valiants and varlets, became Agee's special brand of working out his contrition in public.

MOONGLOW

For both critic and filmmaker, the implied form of penance for the debauched ego was generally the same: a flagellation of the self in devotion to one's project. And Agee could carry this standard like a burning cross pushing both artist and work to quixotic altitudes not only beyond self-interest but at times seemingly beyond the humanly possible—at least, beyond the practically feasible. After all, what is it that he is asking of the players in *The Southerner*? Not just "affection and respect" for "real people, in a real place," which he allows they have already demonstrated. Isn't he actually asking for something very like that near voodoo of inhabitation, of objects, people, and places, that characterized his own "failed" exertions in *Famous Men*? That actors stop acting and start *being* the persons they attempt to imitate? And might not this form of self-immolation actually entail apart from all considerations of talent and intelligence, and imagining for the moment such transportation to be even halfway possible—an entire reconstruction of "minds and hearts," a wholesale reborning of the spirit? At its furthest reaches, then, Agee's stand against the craven self gives every impression of becoming a stand against the self in its entirety.

We are sometimes told that Agee's exacting standards represent the passions of a frustrated filmmaker, that he remade in his mind the movies that he saw in the theater because he was denied access to making them in person. Perhaps so—but then let's also entertain the possibility that such a position can only be seriously maintained by someone who is not, and never has been, an actual filmmaker.[13] The fact remains that not one page of the film criticism reveals the mental outlook or actual practice of the would-be director. One is hard pressed, indeed, to imagine any tough-minded artisan of the trade finding more than a handful of this critic's suggestions for the "improvement" of specific films as something other than the rarest grain of angeldust, simply too good to be entirely true. "Of the material we have seen," he writes, for instance, of the nonfiction film, "it is clear that nearly always, when there has been a chance to prepare for the shot through the mind and the mind's eye rather than the eye purely of courage and of the camera, the mind has been painfully inferior to the possibility offered. The presentation invariably has been worse" (65). Now how can one conceive of an "eye purely of courage and of the camera," but not of the "mind" as well? How can one sever "eye" and "camera" from at least some vestige of "mind"? And how can one oppose such categories against each other, as if they represented right ("eye" and "camera") and wrong ("mind" and "mind's eye") sides of some moral/aesthetic dispute (and what is an eye "purely of courage," anyway)?

The point here is not simply (or only) the utter human impracticality of such a position; the "impossible" was as much a stimulus for this writer as the "actual," and for the most part he managed to envision both, in the most vital ways, as joined at the hip. The point rather is the near Draconian measures to which the passionate intensity of his commitment to that raw visual field first introduced to him by his father—and in this, its purest form, forever associated with his father, a field of talismanic imagery that could free him from the everlasting shame of who he was—the frenzied measures to which such commitment could frequently compel him. The near absolutism of these expectations, the systolic rhythm of the reviewer's aspiration/disillusion, was not that of a maker frustrated by blocked entry to his craft, but that of a young man forever frustrated by memory and reverie; a young man true to himself because true to his dream of perfection and the grip of an engulfing nostalgia; one who had drunk of the milk of paradise in the first six years of life, and thereafter could never take of any other drink without awareness of some hint of taint, each sip at best just off its taste in the reflected remembrance of an immortal brew. If the operative legend of *Famous Men* was that of Antaeus, the presiding sign that drives the currents of the film criticism—and especially the final years of reviewing (i.e., 1948–1950)—is that of Endymion, moon-drunk and dream-driven, beloved of the Goddess Diana, the young shepherd who left his flock and worldly goods to the ministration of the Moon Queen, while he slept and dreamt furiously in the beams of her divinity. "Why did they bother to make the film at all?" he writes of *The Human Comedy* in the rhetoric of the exacting critic, but then adds in Endymionic extremity the attenuated accents of the shepherd boy ruled by the extravagant wail of impossible phantoms: "Why, for that matter, do they bother to make any? Surely, not twice in any hundred thousand feet can they flatter themselves that they qualify to" (33).

Not exactly, then, a would-be filmmaker; nor exactly "the man who loved the movies" either (that other tag-line frequently affixed to his name).[14] To describe the allegiance he felt to the movies he cared about, especially those of his childhood and young manhood, "love" is perhaps too flip, faint, and saddle-sore a term. To describe the majority of the movies he reviewed from 1942–1948, however, "love," to paraphrase a famous lady of the thirties, had nothing to do with it. For the many bad movies he saw, he either found highly imaginative ways to excoriate them, or equally imaginative ways to offer them an Olympian biscuit by finding some concept, moment, or series of moments (a performance, an image, etc.) to savor amid the general ruin, and sometimes to do so at great and dazzling length. As for the surprisingly substantial number of films that filled him with fleeting enthusiasm, and his pen with superlatives, there is not one of these that is without some blemish, however minor. Even within, for example, that small sanctified circle of contemporary favorites—films that represent the very summits of celebration in his tenure at the *Nation*—he makes space to note that the verbal achievement of *Monsieur Verdoux* is inferior to the visual achievement; that the portraiture in *Zero for Conduct* tends to fetishize, and finally sentimentalize, only one kind of child, and thus its depiction of youth lacks variety; that the record of the family economy in *Farrebique* is incomplete, and that some of the montage patterns (i.e., the length and order of the shots) do not achieve "the eloquence of the highest kinds of poetry" (299); *The Treasure of the Sierra Madre* would have been better without music, and, even though he gives the best performance of his career, without a superstar like Bogart in a central role (for in every other respect, the movie is "selfless" [293]), and so on. Every fault found adds another note of luster to the gleaming perfection of that last boyhood night in Knoxville when "the lanterns of the universe" trembled and the stars "beat like hearts."

He begins his last phase of reviewing for the *Nation* weary with disillusion. The current social scene fills him with as little hope as the current situation in film; the atom bomb has already been dropped (and he writes of this event with great foreboding for *Time*); the HUAC investigation of Communist activity in Hollywood has already begun. These two events are enough for him to initiate a period of mourning for the death of all humanist ideals, and compound an indictment of the contemporary social scene that may well have been compiled in his deepest mind many years before. Social practice now confirms in fact what the heart always seems to have known by instinct. In the December 27, 1947, issue of the *Nation* he writes cryptically, as if some nameless war had long ago been lost without ever really having been fought (the context here is the HUAC investigations):

Those whom I regard as friends and fellow-soldiers, many of them conscious and unimaginable millions of them never to become conscious, have already lost. And those whom I regard as enemies are already so securely in charge, throughout the governing of the world and throughout the so-called opposition groups, that one can care very little who fends off or dislodges whom, or which laws and principles, long insulted and injured, are at last officially put out of their misery—very little except in the tragicomic intelligence and in a small but acute personal way. (287)

And he concludes by predicting the end of civilization in its present form:

I doubt that it [civilization] will continue. It has been rotting above ground, on its feet, legally classified as alive, for a long while already, and will destroy itself either by failure to shut out enough of its enemies, or by definitively violating its own nature in its primordial efforts to defend itself, or by shutting out, along with some of the more conspicuous of its enemies, all those who might conceivably preserve within it some last flicker of humanistic sanity. (287)

In 1948 he contributes only eleven columns to the *Nation,* fewer than ever before. Three films richly, but briefly, revive his spirits—*The Treasure of the Sierra Madre, Farrebique,* and *Day of Wrath*—and he devotes one full column to each. Of the remaining eight entries, six are round-up reviews in each of which a cynical, sated Agee typically corrals about twenty or so movies, lists them alphabetically, and then ticks them off one by one, often in a scintillant sentence or two. He calls one such column "mid-winter clearance" (294); begins another, "here are twenty-five more of them" (300). As interest in the current scene sours, so too does his initial enthusiasm for recent films and filmmakers. He feels, for instance, just about everybody, including himself, "flagrantly overrated" (288) *Shoeshine* and *To Live in Peace;* or after warmly praising Rossellini's *Open City,* he has already turned cold a few months later when reviewing the director's latest effort, *Paisan* (e.g., "The best of this movie is the best that has come out of Italy; highly gratifying and exciting; the worst is sycophantic, vulgar, lick-spittle stuff which could begin to be forgivable only in a man of, say, D. W. Griffith's size" [301]).

The one American director who finishes the year burning bright, with all of Agee's hope and goodwill intact, is of course John Huston. But 1948 also represents the zenith of Agee's expectations where this director is concerned. Following the glowing review of *The Treasure*, he spends many months struggling to finish a profile of the filmmaker for *Life*, and when "The Undirectable Director" finally appears in September 1950, his conclusions clearly reduce Huston from demiurge to merely major artist. While still "the most inventive director of his generation" (330), he is unequivocally precluded from the ranks of the Ageean immortals: "To date, however, his work on the whole is not on a level with the finest and most deeply imaginative work that has been done in movies—the work of Chaplin, Dovzchenko, Eisenstein, Griffith, the late Jean Vigo" (330). Huston, shockingly for Agee, lets studio technicians cut his films, "a startling irresponsibility in so good an artist" (330, where had Agee been all this time?); and "conceivably Huston lacks the deepest kind of creative impulse and that intense self-critical skepticism without which the stature of a great artist is rarely achieved" (331).

For the rest, his late writing dreams fast in the arms of the past. His memorial for D. W. Griffith is arguably the best of his columns for the year 1948. His longest and perhaps most famous film essay, "Comedy's Greatest Era," appears a year later (in *Life*) and renews interest in the work of the silent clowns—Sennett, Chaplin, Keaton, Lloyd, and Langdon—for a generation that seemed to have forgotten. He returns to the present for one final film review (for *Films in Review;* reprinted in *Sight & Sound*) and it is of *Sunset Boulevard,* aptly the story of an affair between a young contemporary script writer and an aging silent film star, that is, a black comic agon between word and image. Naturally the affair is doomed, and between the two there is little doubt where Agee's sympathy lies even though it may not coincide with that of the filmmakers: "Largely through what is done with Miss Swanson, the silent era, and art, are granted a kind of barbarous grandeur and intensity, but the inference seems to be that they were also a good deal hammier than they actually were at their best. Further inference appears to be that the movies have come a long way since then. In many ways they have; in many other and important ways, this is open to argument and no such argument appears in this picture" (414).

In these late years his most significant writing is invariably devoted to the dead or the forgotten, to what he calls (in the *Sunset* review) "lost people": Swanson, Sennett, Keaton, Langdon, Lloyd, Lincoln, Gauguin, his father, the families of Knoxville, 1916, himself as youth and child. While he may have been one of the finest American occasional writers this century has produced, his specialty within this area was—and no surprise to anyone—the elegy, public and private, the indelible memorial for personages vanished recently (FDR, Griffith), or long ago (everyone else). Nobody mourned better.

3. OBLIGATIONS

By now Agee's film criticism has become so much a part of the established history of American film culture that there may not be a need for the present generation to get excited about what he actually said. Like Kane's sled and Dorothy's slippers, Agee's reviews have become for many part of that airless, timeless zone occupied by movie relics, something to be savored under glass, all operative functions suspended.

Too bad: He gave us what is perhaps the best and most-rounded portrait of movies and moviegoing in the forties, and anyone who writes of filmmaking in that era will—one hopes—still feel obliged to consult *Agee on Film*. He is also an endlessly quotable critic, and quotation may still be the most just and revealing way to appreciate his accomplishment in this area; and critics presumably will continue to quote him. It would also be a literary crime if he is not read by everyone on the planet with even the faintest interest in what can be done with the Anglo-American tongue in a discursive format. And *that,* many would feel, is more than enough, the most that could be hoped for regarding the afterlife of anyone's critical remarks.

As for his actual critical currency—that is, his ability to impact upon the cultural life of the moment—most of today's film students seem to have departed so far from the concerns of his period, as well as from the individual bent of his tastes and priorities, that one may legitimately wonder whether an esteemed place in the movie museum of the contemporary mind isn't great, good fortune enough for one dead film reviewer. The current film/literature wing of the academic constabulary, for instance, can scarcely have any use for him because they are mad for theory and Agee did not have one. There is little in his work—so personal, so idiosyncratic—that could even be appended, let alone assimilated, to the fashionable theoretical models already fully functional (and by now even showing some gray)—namely the Lacanian, feminist, and deconstructionist systems that seem to be employed by the most fashionable, if not the best, academicians. To the academy, one might say that Agee had something better than a theory of movies: he had a vision of life, and movies were a vital part of that; and more important, that the example of his criticism dramatically serves to remind scholars and teachers hooked into the cyborgean arcana of University exegesis in its present form of what a thoroughly human (and humane) activity intense and concentrated thinking about art and culture can be.

As for the larger film community—critics, reviewers, buffs, historians, culture generalists, and ordinary moviegoers everywhere—Agee's criticism will doubtless talk at them in the estranged accents of the historically passé. Responding to his stand on individual directors, for instance, film folk nowadays will probably feel that, in spite of his numerous reservations, he still overrated filmmakers such as John Huston, William Wyler, and Rene Clair (will anyone ever again think as well of him as Agee did?); that he underrated Ford and Welles, the former often appeared too studied for his taste (e.g., *The Fugitive*), the latter presumably too much the addled ego (perhaps that is why he only had kind words for *The Stranger*, the least personal of Welles's films). They will doubtless also feel that he admired Hitchcock, Sturges, Walsh, and the Val Lewton productions pretty much as we do today, but that in spite of all his respect for *Notorious* and *Shadow of a Doubt*, he seemed to prefer the British Hitchcock to the American (a generational preference; c.f., his critical brother-in-arms, Dwight Macdonald), while nowadays we tend to reverse these priorities; and that he also had serious qualms about Sturges's spasmodic deconstruction of his comedic forms, while these concerns, if true, bother us much less in a period of postmodernist dismantlements. Many today look upon the whole era in which Agee wrote as virtually blinding with golden age glitter; while our man was there to testify that there was more brass than gold in those Hollywood hills, more glitz than glitter.

Aside from the fact that the values and preferences of any generation are never engraved in bronze, but are, to paraphrase current film taste, written on the wind, and that our sons and daughters will doubtless find us as odd and accountably nearsighted as some of us now find critics like Agee—aside from all this, the major difference that separates the film generation today from the whole tenor of Agee's work in film is that we have become "professionals" and "specialists" of the movies in a way that would doubtless have distressed this confirmed "amateur critic," this proponent of individual liberty and the "unaided eye." We are crazy about the movies and hunger without discrimination for all there is to know about them. We dive into them as if into a diving bell and leave the rest of the world, the world outside of film, to look to itself. Good and great movies, and many bad ones too, take us deeper into the aura and magical content of all movies, into the whole Movie Idea itself: into the history of films, their technology and production, into the lives of stars and directors (as if they too were stars), into everything great and small in and around the movies; the gossip and the rot; the money and the deals; the office memos and the early versions of the script. Nowadays we really think we have learned something when we discover that most of the story and dialogue of *Citizen Kane* can be attributed to Herman J. Mankiewicz and not to Orson Welles; but that Welles was most responsible for the film's originality of form and technique; but that he could not have executed his ideas without the presence of his master cinematographer and lens developer, Gregg Toland. Well, what have we learned (or have I still not got it right)? Scholarship is scholarship and a fact is a fact: but if what we know about the making of *Citizen Kane* is a fact, isn't it also a fact that fastidious Vivien Leigh did not welcome the kisses of her dentured leading man, Clark Gable, in *Gone with the Wind*? Now isn't *that* a fact too, and if so, what have we learned? Nowadays, movies take us deeper into movies—and maybe little else—and deeper into our insular fantasies about them. And that apparently is where we want to be: deep into ourselves with everything we know about the movies.

Now for Agee, of course, good and great movies could and should do just the opposite of what they do for a generation of "specialists." They could and should take you not deeper into yourself, or even exclusively into the movies, but out of yourself and deep into contact with some aspect of the "actual," the great thrumming arena of the not-self. He championed individual actors and directors, just as we do; and was deeply interested in what went on behind the scenes in making movies, just as we are: but above all else, he celebrated film for the power of its imagery to further the education of the eye of the beholder, not in relation to some private fantasy but in relation to what used to be called the ways of the world. Everything he spoke of in *Famous Men*—the need for proper "education," the restoration and development of individual consciousness through immediate visual experience (the stress upon the camera and the human retina)—is continued and heightened in the film criticism. Good and great films can be "irreplaceable pieces of teaching," an affront to one's vanity, a repudiation of ignorance, navel-gazing, and the indulgences of consciousness.

"And that's *all*?" the present film generation responds, "Is it *all* just a matter of 'teaching,' of 'education'? Will there be no more pleasure? Where is our *pleasure*?" For "pleasure" is all we seem to ask now of movies and our moviegoing experience. "Was Agee's movie-going so virtuous," asks Pauline Kael, our foremost pleasure specialist, our reigning queen of fun, "or did he perhaps now and then, like the rest of us, enjoy decadent, sleazy, slick commercial pictures?"[15] He certainly did and made no secret of it; he could enjoy what was good in a bad movie and what was bad in it too; and he could pick and choose among "decadent, slick, sleazy commercial pictures" as well as almost anyone (but not as well as Pauline Kael). But he did this—as it is perhaps the best way to do it—undefensively, unself-consciously (for once), and generally without sermonizing; that is, he could enjoy "fun films" and "movie movies" without inflating frivolity into a metaphysic, or even so much as a fixed attitude; without, say, encoding his tastes into some oxymoronic doctrine of "trash art," "pop masterpieces," "good bad movies," "guilty pleasures," and the like; and above all, without using any of these tastes and categories as a club with which to beat serious, non-"decadent," non-"slick," non-"sleazy" art to death.

Nor did he try to fetishize his pleasures—as does Pauline Kael—by calibrating and enumerating the various kinds of "kicks" and "highs" that a film could give him or his audience. Kael's audience, however, apparently feels the need for this sort of fetishized pleasure, for it gives every impression of a disgruntled crowd deeply down and out with the grind of mere dailyness. For such an audience the calibrated pleasures of the movies, as well as the critic's evocation of such pleasures, represent a ripe rebuke to the daily funk we all presumably endure. (Kael once called film "the sullen art of displaced persons.")[16] For Agee, the life of an ordinary day was no grind, but a glaring miracle; and his problem was always how to keep faith with the pulse of that miracle. If film helped him make that contact, he took it seriously because he took that miracle seriously. And he presumed that his audience would want to follow him in the direction of his passion.

At least he wrote as if he did and as if they would. And this idealism was perhaps this critic's greatest gift to his *Nation* reader and perhaps his most precious legacy for us today. He wrote as if his *Nation* reader was as decent, generous, patient, tolerant, serious, intelligent, and challengeable as he consistently conjured him to be. He wrote as if a selfless devotion to art and humanity and individual freedom mattered more to this reader than the pleasures of escape, more even than one's self-enchanted dream of the movies. When he wrote for *Time,* on the other hand, few of these exalted qualities and possibilities were evoked. Now every vestige of common sense tells us that the *Nation* reader was no more noble or selfless than the *Time* reader, and no more noble or selfless than we are today. But among Agee's many moral and aesthetic achievements in his writing for the *Nation* was the ability to sustain the *illusion* of a virtuous reader. In this manner, he gave his actual reader, then and now, a taste of what it might be like to be better than he was. Agee's way of educating himself was by going to the movies, and imagining a virtuous reader was his way of educating his audience, of teaching it how to participate in the terms by which he wanted his view of film to be understood.

"Excessive virtue," says Pauline Kael, "may have been Agee's worst critical vice," just as an uncontrollable itch for the enjoyably corrupt in movies may have been Kael's.[17] But she has her point. Just as some readers may find the self-absorption of the young Agee (in *Famous Men*) off-putting, so some may find the high-minded quest for selflessness of a more mature Agee—the film critic who has grown beyond the orbit of his early indulgences and into the larger world of surrounding images—equally off-putting. On more than one occasion, he could ride high and hard on his moral nag and not look back. But this quality of "excessive virtue" is also a quality of his idealism, the source of a genuine exaltation in his work, and one that has probably become more crucial for us as time goes on. What's a critic for anyway? Agee tells us: " . . . the desire of any critic, like that of any artist, who has the right to even try to defend or practice an art—as perhaps of any human being who has the right to try to defend or practice living—cannot be satisfied short of perfect liberty, discipline, and achievement . . ." (188).

Movie critics write for us today as if this kind of perfection has nothing to do with movies, just as it has nothing to do with living either. But Agee's richest vein of critical expression is often his most "excessive," and appeals to our best and perhaps most hidden aspirations, those virtually "impossible" and least immediate of contemporary needs—the need for perfection of life and perfection of work; not to what we are or even have to be, but to what we want to be if we want to be better than we are or even possibly could be. Like perhaps only the greatest of critics—and in many ways he is one of them—Agee leads us into an ideal model of art and culture populated by only the most morally and aesthetically invigorating ideas, works, artists, and audiences, and teaches us what it might be like to become citizens of that ideal republic of art and ideas. He doesn't try to sell us a fun-fix, the hot pitchman's hypodermic that will help us pass the time, or get through the sludge of the day. He works in a realm where individuals and their creations can be made better and better still; and his obligations are to the laws of a perfection that may well be of another order, unknown and "invisible." What are the obligations of the critic? What are the obligations of the artist? I'm going to conclude by yielding to an even more high-minded critic and artist than Agee, Marcel Proust—who, however, like Agee was both artist in his criticism and critical in his art—and let Proust attempt to answer these questions and elucidate this position on my behalf:

> All that we can say is that everything is arranged in this life as though we entered it carrying the burden of obligations contracted in a former life; there is no reason inherent in the conditions of

life on this earth that can make us consider ourselves obliged to do good, to be fastidious, to be polite even, nor make the talented artist consider himself obliged to begin over again a score of times a piece of work the admiration aroused by which will matter little to his body devoured by worms, like the patch of yellow wall painted with so much knowledge and skill by an artist who must for ever remain unknown and is barely identified under the name Vermeer. All these obligations which have not their sanction in our present life seem to belong to a different world, founded upon kindness, scrupulosity, self-sacrifice, a world entirely different from this, which we leave in order to be born into this world, before perhaps returning to the other to live once again beneath the sway of those unknown laws which we have obeyed because we bore their precepts in our hearts, knowing not whose hand had traced them there—those laws to which every profound work of the intellect brings us nearer and which are invisible only—and still!—to fools.[18]

CHAPTER FIVE

CHAINS OF FLESH

The Morning Watch and
A Death in the Family

I have been fashioned on a chain of flesh
—AGEE, SONNET IV

N HIS LAST SEVEN YEARS, Agee divided most of his creative life between writing fiction and writing for the movies.

Many critics find this latter activity of greater value and significance than I do, and I refer the reader to those critics if she wishes to find more detailed and generous accounts of Agee's work for the screen and television than she will find here.[1] Peace to those critics, those interested readers—and perhaps to Agee himself—as I continue to wrestle with the conviction that the chief value and purport of his screenplays was to give him the time and cash necessary to write the two books that constitute his major artistic accomplishments during this final period.

Now we know that Agee greatly valued his work for the screen, and that he gave unstintingly of himself to each of his film projects. We know that he had long wished to involve himself deeply and directly in virtually any part of the whole process and atmosphere of making movies, and that when the opportunity of doing so finally presented itself, he was ready—and then some.

He wrote; he acted (in *The Bride Comes to Yellow Sky*, in the *Lincoln* project); he scouted locations (for *Lincoln*); he sported and socialized with industry regulars (e.g., tennis with John Huston); and if asked to do more—and if capable of doing more—there is little doubt that more he would have done. Further: we also know that a reading of even the least of the screenplays is not entirely devoid of certain aesthetic satisfactions. As everyone agrees by now, this writer was never observed to do anything by half measures; and there is pleasure, and wisdom too, to be found in virtually everything he wrote largely because *he* wrote it. The effects of his sensibility, the intensity of focus and special uses of the language, are readily apparent even in the most seemingly inauspicious of his undertakings; that making the perfunctory seem fecund was one of his many gifts (and one among the tenets of his faith); and that the impress of his mark can be found even in such anomalies as an assigned article on furs and furriers for *Fortune;* a midnight letter to Father Flye; or the screen adaptation of a book he did not write for a film he did not direct.

None of the foregoing is disputed. I don't find the screenplays of great value and significance largely because they are "screenplays," blueprints for art works, not the works of art themselves, and so cannot either be appreciated or judged as self-contained entities. And while I have little doubt that Agee gave this form everything it demanded of him, I seriously doubt that it—by its very nature—demanded of him everything that he had to give.

Compare these last seven or eight years with the previous six: for the better part of 1941–1947, Agee did not need to divide his time between his film criticism and his "personal" creation because for all intents and purposes, his film criticism was his personal creation. While it is true that reviewing for two journals simultaneously took up much of his time, it is equally true that much of the time, Agee, consciously or otherwise, allowed it to do so. Screenwriting possibly offered him an even better wage than reviewing (though one less regular and dependable), but it also took, I'm inclined to think, far less out of him.

Consider the format: no matter how pungent the dialogue or evocative the descriptions of character, motions, and settings, the central expressive life of even the most filled in and scrupulously realized of

Agee's screenplays—say, *Noa Noa* or *The Blue Hotel*—as in virtually all screenplays, resides, as it must, elsewhere; that is, beyond the text, beyond the writer writing. It is an expressive life that at best can only be hinted at by words like "close-up" and "long shot," abbreviations like "int." or "ext.", or such technical instructions as (from *The Blue Hotel*) "cut or lap dissolve to medium two shot—facade of Hotel—door at the center. The camera is still creeping, lowering quietly to eye height. O.s. sounds of walking on icy boards" (395); and so on. Now all of these instructions and abbreviations *as written* have little or no qualitative or aesthetic status either as literature or even perhaps as cinema. These mechanical insignia represent relatively neutral pointers or indicators for a series of artistic choices and enactments that occur beyond the written page in another time and space when the film itself is made by cameras shooting and actors acting. The actual experience and full effect of words like "door," or "facade," or "cut or lap dissolve" cannot be predetermined, or even properly envisioned until transferred to celluloid. The actual movement of the camera, for instance, may perhaps turn out to be something very like Agee's "creeping" and "lowering quietly," or perhaps something marginally different, or perhaps something altogether different. In no instance can a verbal description of a camera's movement embody or even anticipate either the experience or effect of an actual camera's movement, even when such movement explicitly attempts to follow the verbal directions exactly as written. It is of course the sum total of these filmed enactments—not "cut" or "close up" as written—that constitute the actual artistic event that was merely alluded to—as it were, requested but not granted, indicated but not enacted—by the verbal treatment.

What then are the practical uses of the screenplay? For the filmmaker, it may serve as an invaluable tool, an outline or sketch-pad for his work. For the book publisher, it is by now the long outmoded marketing phenomenon of a pre-videotape era through which the film buff may indulge the ersatz thrill of annexing "the movie" into his library. But for the reader reading, an encounter with the screenplay represents a species of what may be called "participation art" ("art" is the moot term here) in which desultory and fragmented literary pleasures may be derived from the dialogue and brief descriptions of action (in Agee's screenplays not so brief, and often quite remarkable). But when it comes to terms like "close-up," "cut or lap dissolve," and the like, here as in do-it-yourself novel kits, the reader must help the writer construct his work by imagining all those expressive enactments that do not exist on the page. Granted, there is a niggling cinematic satisfaction to be culled from a perusal of these parts, and reading a good script for some may be more engaging than viewing a failed film, but such satisfactions even at best can never be much more than inspirations induced by suggestive scraps, not by a realized whole: a fully achieved "cinema of the mind" can only be authored by a precocious reader, not by an assiduous screenwriter, not even by an overachieving screenwriter, such as Agee.

In any event, for the critic—as opposed to all these other worthies, and to make an end where I have begun—the screenplay does not offer the experience of a unified work of art, and so does not offer either the integrity or the autonomy by which such works have customarily come to be assimilated, digested, and finally estimated. In brief: when it comes to screenplays, the critic, if interested, will be out of luck; and if wise, out to lunch.[2]

1. NEW VOICES

Since I have already adopted both the tone and manner of the spoiler, let me grumble on for a moment longer in this vein, and raise the ante somewhat, by suggesting—but in no way insisting upon—a general, relative decline in the power and originality of *all* of Agee's production in these last seven years of his creative life; that is, a decline relative to the previous twelve. By this, I refer specifically to the period beginning in the summer of 1936 with Evans and the tenant families in Alabama, and ending in the fall of 1948 with Griffith and his last film column for the *Nation*. I hope it has been made abundantly clear from everything I have urged and argued thus far that the period of his most important, and, I trust, most enduring creation resides within this time frame.

Generally speaking, I do not perceive Agee as primarily—and in the most received and conventional sense of the term—a fiction writer, either for the screen or for the novel; and I continue to find sentence

by sentence—indeed, sometimes word by word—more freedom, excitement, astonishment, and invention—and, yes, more "fiction" too—in
his essay manner than in his fiction proper. That is why it seems to me
that among the greatest losses of this late period is that of the early Agee
persona, the extraordinary sound and manner of Gudger's porch-poet,
that late-night rambling man, talker and visionary, that inflammatory
intellect on the prowl: knotty, intense, confessional, combative, lyrical,
seditious, mystical, rowdy, elegant, disarming, dangerous, decent, devout, contrite, indulgent, embarrassing, chivalric, heroic, equivocal—
utterly individual. I take the voice of this persona to represent the most
concentrated and exuberant display of nonstop discursiveness of his
generation—and perhaps of ours too. In this late period, that voice is
effectually modulated and, in some ways, altogether pacified by another
voice: one more conciliatory and serene, more mellifluous and "mature,"
sometimes acutely plain (as in *A Death in the Family*), sometimes calcu-
latedly fancy (as in *The Morning Watch*)—the voice of Agee, the novelist.
The murmur of this new voice now takes its cue from the sensibility of
newly created characters, predominantly young boys and children; its
range and orchestration determined largely by newly imagined settings
and contexts fixed in the distant past.

The early persona is now set to pasture and with it goes another great
loss in these final years; and that is, the immediacy of the present tense,
the drama and urgency of the social moment that gave stimulus to the
early persona and of which the early persona was in many ways the
expression—the teeming indeterminacy of the ongoing historical crisis
(e.g., farmers in trouble), the very nick and currency of the cultural
ferment (e.g., Chaplin's latest creation). Boiling urgency now gives way
to nostalgia and humidity; cutting edge, to distant music; dramatic
moments, to the croon of remembrance, to fond and aching things
caught up in the wallow of long ago and far away. In abandoning criticism
for fiction, Agee was exchanging a clock-bound, experiential, open-
ended art of impermanence (i.e., daily reviewing) for one of symmetry
and transcendence (i.e., the art of the novel) in pursuit of those twin
chimera of liberal humanist aesthetics, "timelessness" and "universality."
As a critic, he had become, or made of himself, a master in his element: as
a novelist, he was also lavishly gifted, but still, in some ways, an outlander.

All of this may be respectfully suggested of Agee's late efforts as opposed to his earlier ones. Once delivered of these suggestions, however, one is then free to judge this late work on its own immensely absorbing terms. If one knows Agee only by the *The Morning Watch* or *A Death in the Family,* and remains ignorant of everything else, one may readily find much that is remarkable and admirable, and, particularly in the posthumous novel, extraordinary and cherishable. One can savor these qualities, as well as the real solidity and permanence of both of these fictions, without ever deciding either to be entirely successful in every department, or without noticeably observing that the author himself had been born to write in this form and this form only.

ART NOVEL: THE MACULATE HAND

A Death in the Family, even in its somewhat unfinished state, remains Agee's most immediately accessible and congenial work, perhaps the only one of his books that can truly be called popular, and for better and worse, deservedly so (more of this work in subsequent sections). *The Morning Watch,* however, is another matter: terse, dense, by turns psychologically adroit and theologically abstruse, this difficult and problematic tale seems to have found its most devoted admirers largely among the Ageeans; its slender, delicate, autobiographical materials all but submerged under a barrage of literary artifice, bipolar symbolism, and emblematic detail, testing and stretching the devotion of even those already committed.

Still, *The Morning Watch* bears the distinction of being the one full-sized fiction brought to completion by the author himself, and the only one ever to be published in his lifetime. Moreover, the work, even on its own straitened terms, commands attention. The high ambition and seriousness of the project are never in doubt, nor are the great gifts of the writer. For better or worse, there isn't a single slack, casual, or untuned utterance to be found anywhere throughout its entire length. In the first two of its three sections, Agee's grading and control of a young Anglo-Catholic boy's thought patterns—the ironies, humorous self-deceptions, and unwitting bad faith of a Christ-intoxicated mind in process—are masterly. In the final section, depictions of certain actions in a natural setting—the dive into and ascent from an icy, murky pond, the stoning of a snake—have much of the nuanced power and sensuous detail that, even beneath the thick impasto of allegorical appliqué, one has always associated with this author at his characteristic best. The workmanship is indeed so close and meticulous that the more time one spends with the book, the more one comes to respect it—without ever quite coming to like or enjoy it. It's never easy to take full satisfaction in such a drawn-tight, uptight, art-proud construct in which hardly a single moment ever breaks free of the grip of its author's predetermined designs.

Yet the tale itself is disarming in the simplicity of its outlines: a twelve-year-old boy finds his freedom and young manhood by sneaking off from a church service with two companions, trekking into the woods, swimming at a nearby pond, killing a snake, and then heading back to the chapel. Even this crude summary will be sufficient to ring a familiar set of chimes in the ears of readers attuned to the classic strains of hallowed American themes: They will perhaps suggest the flight from social and public ordinance, the tutorials in nature, the all-boy youth gangs, the rites of passage in contact with a beast of the forest (e.g., *The Bear, Why are We in Vietnam?* etc.); in other words, many of the immemorial pastimes of a traditional, quasi-rural, literary American boyhood. All these motifs are implicit in Agee's story, and constitute some essential part of its meaning as he elects to tell it.

Nevertheless, the way in which the tale presents itself consorts oddly with the indigenous American materials. The clotted stateliness of Agee's language—diction, syntax, rhythm—seems to draw inspiration primarily from an Anglo-Irish, high-Latinate and grandiloquent tradition of Art Catholicism (Newman, Pater, etc.); and particularly from that special incense and mortification apparatus for depicting Catholic guilt invented and patented by James Joyce in *A Portrait of the Artist as a Young Man.* Joyce had long been one of Agee's front-ranking literary deities, and the American writer doubtless saw the immediate similarities between the background and spiritual crisis of his very young hero Richard and those of Joyce's somewhat older Stephen Dedalus: the religious schooling, the power of the "Fathers," the Satanic defiance, the remorse of conscience, the arrogant identification with the masochistic strain implicit in Christian sacrifice, the incompatibility of a public and institutionalized faith with the growth of the individual "soul," etc.[3] A random sampling:

> And imagining that moment he felt a tearing spasm of anguish in the center of each palm and with an instant dazzling of amazed delight, remembering pictures of great saints, shouted within himself, *I've got the Wounds!* and even as he caught himself opening his palms and his eyes to peer and see if this were so he realized that once again this night, and even more blasphemously and absurdly than before, he had sinned in the proud imagination of his heart. *O my God,* his heart moaned, *O my God! My God how can You forgive me! I'll have to confess it,* he realized. *I can't. Not this. How can I confess this!* (77)

This is Agee, of course, not Joyce; still, all of that internalized scenery-chewing (e.g., he "shouted within himself," "his heart moaned," etc.), the soap operatics of adolescent vanity (compare Richard's "proud imagination" with Stephen's "proud sovereignity") sound a lot like more direct, less alliterative versions of rented property from the holdings of Joyce's self-impressed hero.[4] Stephen's melos, however, is characteristically more pumped, lush, and arty:

> He could still leave the chapel. He could stand up, put one foot before the other and walk out softly and then run, run, run swiftly through the dark streets. He could still escape from the shame. Had it been any terrible crime but that one sin! Had it been murder! Little fiery flakes fell and touched him at all points, shameful thoughts, shameful words, shameful acts. Shame covered him wholly like fine glowing ashes falling continually. To say it in words! His soul, stifling and helpless, would cease to be.[5]

Can these rhetorical postures also be comfortably occupied by a twelve-year-old American boy? Yes, to an extent; Agee successfully manages a more modest plain-speech equivalent of Stephen's *furioso* as long as Richard suffers, as he does above, in church. But when he enters the woods and the author wants to give his protagonist (and us) a sense of release, the epiphanic patter becomes even more aggressive and hermetic. Nature becomes a scholarly charade of itself as sheets of allegorical erudition hang like lead napkins about the necks of every twig, bole, and locust shell in the landscape. Here Richard inspects the latter:

> He turned it again and held it near his eyes: the eyes looked into his. Yes even the eyes were there, blind silver globes which had so perfectly contained the living eyes: even the small rudimentary face in its convulsed and fierce expression, the face of a human embryo, he could remember the engraving in a book of his grandfather's, a paroxysm of armor, frowning, scowling, glaring, very serious, angry, remote, dead, a devil, older, stranger than devils, as early, ancient of days, primordial, as trilobites. Dinosaurs heaved and strove; a pterodactyl, cold-winged, skated on miasmic air, ferns sprang, to make coal in these very coves, more huge than the grandest chestnuts. Silurian, Mesozoic, Protozoic, Jurassic, all the planet one featureless and smoky marsh, Crowns, Thrones, Dominions, Principalities, Archaeozoic, through all ranks and kingdoms, to the central height, armed in the radiant cruelty of immortal patience, Ages and Angels marched clanging in his soul. (98–99)

Is *this* an American child's sensibility, even a very bright one, or the boot-legged import of his older, more flamboyant, and esoteric Irish Jesuitical benefactor?[6]

Moreover, throughout the tale Agee's language may be dangerously overblown not just in proportion to Richard's age and breeding, but especially to the scale of his sins and actual defection from church dogma. Stephen Dedalus earns the apocalyptic elevation of a language grounded in a two-thousand-year-old high church insistence upon the drama of the immortal soul's acquisition of either eternal glory or everlasting damnation in its daily acts; verbal grandeur becomes the necessary corollary of a titanic struggle in which the consequences are omnipresent and absolute. In one famous instance, Joyce immerses the reader in the terrors and devastation of an epic-length Hellfire sermon that promises an eternity of torment for misspent youth; and in those vivid moments, fear of God, the Devil, and the immortal risks involved in human choice become artistically available even to nonbelievers. Richard's Anglo-Catholicism, on the other hand, in spite of its misleading nomenclature, is really much closer to American Protestantism; and if other members of this sect worry about rewards and punishments in the afterlife, Richard in the course of his story hardly ever does; nor was his creator ever known to entertain any vivid imagination of Hell. Richard's internal condition may be ingeniously dramatized, and his behavior during the Easter service genuinely dismaying to altar boys everywhere, but nonsectarians may legitimately find the whole weight and extent of his agonizing disproportionate to his actual deeds. Stephen at least visits prostitutes; Richard walks, swims, and stones a snake, and many readers will be at some pains to learn how his debauch in the woods differs radically from simply playing hooky.

These problems and others help determine *The Morning Watch* as perhaps the most worried and overelaborated of Agee's works since the needlepoint of his sonnet cycle stitched at Harvard. But make no mistake: this novella, unlike the poetry, is essential Agee; costive, yes, but also perhaps the most darkly intimate of his books. No other work puts us in such close proximity to the divisiveness of the Agee persona, and the drama of what it might be like to live within the turmoil of that passionate nature. No other incarnation of himself involves us so thoroughly in his conflicted heart: his vanity and self-loathing, his tenderness and brutality, his spiritual vaunt and physical narcissism. Indeed, no other work plunges us so deeply to the core of his sadomasochism, or outlines so graphically his dazed discovery and guilty affirmation of himself, of the physical, sensual self breaking loose from the parental yoke and the church of his childhood, and finding residence in the violent, rank, and perplexed radiance of the sensuous world. In self-discovery, we see him by no means rejecting his faith, but actually attempting, however uncertainly, to broaden and deepen its base in human turbulence and profane transaction; pushing beyond doctrinal dispensation and in its place, compacting a raw, dark, semichoate, half-savage pattern of Christian myth founded upon a stormy dialogue between himself and the world's rough body.

The meagerness of incident, however, can barely support the extravagance of the intellectual superstructure, and as already indicated, the external action, much of which takes place only in the last third of the story, is relatively scant and attenuated. The tale is set in a small religious school for boys (modeled after Agee's own St. Andrews) in deep country Tennessee in 1923 during the last morning hours of Maundy Thursday, just before the dawn of Good Friday. Here it is customary, as part of the school's Easter service, for students to sign on voluntarily for hourly vigils or "watches" before the Blessed Sacrament where they fast and pray in memory of Christ's final hours at Gethsemene, and particularly of his admonishment to his disciples; "Could ye not watch with me one hour?" (4). Richard takes one of these watches; and the story begins in the cold, dark morning as he rises from his bed in the dormitory, his soul "ardent for release and celebration" (10), and, with two fellow students, Hobe and Jimmy, proceeds to Our Lady Chapel (part 1).

Part 2, the longest section, takes place inside the Chapel itself and consists mainly of Richard's attempt to pray and his failure to do so. The action is almost entirely internalized as Richard hopelessly tries to keep his mind from straying from the intended object of its devotions. The mental defections become more pronounced as the section proceeds, until it becomes clear that the defections themselves represent a legitimate need that cannot be satisfied by prayer. His immediate "watch" then becomes the one conferred over his own mental processes, the botched "vigil" that he attempts to keep "over thought and language" (45). In the short term, each of Richard's "distractions" ostensibly represent an unsuccessful operation to suppress the wayward self; but over the long haul, each also becomes a covert but successful stratagem for the self's confrontation and release.

"Lord," prays Richard, "make my mind not to wander" (72), for it is the wandering mind, committing one mental blasphemy after another, that incessantly undermines each of his prayers, that becomes the precise index not simply of his waning faith in the hallow rituals and meaningless rounds of submission and obedience, but of a starved sensuousness, and a defiant, irreverent, allusive intellect hungry for expression. Richard, for instance, cannot utter the words "Blood of Christ inebriate me" (32) without thinking of "good ole whiskey" (33); nor imagine the "wounds" of Christ (*"Within Thy Wounds hide me"* [34, italics Agee]) without associating them with Shakespeare's bawdy pun on "wounds" in *Venus and Adonis* and simultaneously concocting "the most insipid and effeminate" of vaginal Christs "with a huge torn bleeding gulf at the supine crotch" (35), etc. Nor, in a comic fit of vainglory, can he focus on Christ's crucifixion without substituting the logistics of his own; "he could undoubtedly nail his own feet (if someone else would steady nail)" (46); and conjuring a crowd of mourners composed of his sobbing mother, his adoring classmates ("Jesus, that kid's got guts," 50), and a newspaper photographer ("*Strange Rite at Mountain School*," 51). Throughout his watch, Richard is plagued by what is described as "the desire to suffer for religious advantage" (41), so that every time he manages a moment of true humility and attendance, he immediately surges with self-congratulatory pride, and thus realizes he has lapsed into sin all over again. This happens so often that his prayers are finally reduced to: "Let me not feel good when I am good. *If* I am good. Let me just try to be good, don't let me *feel* good. Don't let me even *know* if I'm good" (79–80).

When the first watch fails, Richard violates precedent by attempting a second vigil without official sanction; this too is a failure, but because independently initiated, it proves more fruitful than the first. Near its completion, he speculates, " . . . he was empty and idle, in some way he had failed. Yet he was also filled to overflowing with a reverent and marveling peace and thankfulness. My cup runneth over, something whispered within him, yet what he saw in his mind's eye was a dry chalice, an empty Grail" (87). In the midst of his official failure, that is, he has brought to the surface an irrepressible pool of personal desire and an overflowing sense of well-being that cannot find outlet in the iron confines of the chapel, *his* "cup runneth over" while the formally sanctified vessels remain "dry" and "empty." Throughout the episode, the chapel atmosphere has consistently been presented as dank and nullifying; the air "as numb and remote as the air of a cave" (17); the tabernacle "gawped like a dead jaw" (25); the nave "as secular as a boxcar" (26). Yet in the natural landscape beyond the chapel "the whole air and sky were one mild supernal breath" (13) and "the night smelled like new milk" (17). Thus, after completing his second watch, Richard once again defies authority and breaks ranks; and instead of returning to the dormitory, leads Hobe and Jimmy from the chapel into the woods. No sooner do their feet touch the ground than "a wave of energy swept upward through their bare feet and their three bodies into the sky that they were shaken as if a ghost had touched them" (92).

The soul "ardent for release and celebration" in part 1 realizes and exercises exactly those urges in part 3—but not in church. Once in the forest, the wandering mind translates and fulfills itself, quite literally fleshes itself out, in the wandering body, as Richard, following an unconscious urge, leads his two companions through the woods and then to his natural and "profane" destiny at the Sand Cut pond. All the impulses just barely suppressed throughout the first two sections—welling up now as if with a physical will of their own (the "cup" that "runneth over")—all the appetites of the sensual self, the hunger for independence, personal glory, violent physical assertion, and the adoration of proud flesh, all these find their expression and a tortured, ambiguous ratification in the last section of *The Morning Watch*.

The episode itself turns about two baptismal events, the second following almost immediately upon the first; specifically, the dive into the pond, which results in a gesture of self-discovery, and the stoning of the snake, which results in discovery of the other: or to reformulate this in terms of the intensely subjective perspective that governs the tale—indeed, the author seemed to think the story too subjective (and too religious)[7]— there is first a celebration of the self as a unique and autonomous entity (i.e., the subjective self, the unequivocal "I"); and then second, in psychic recoil, a chastisement of the self as reflected in, and incriminated by, its external twin (i.e., the objective self, the ambiguous "me").

At the water's edge, Richard strips off his clothes and performs the last of his hopeless attempts to identify with Christ in a sacrificial plunge to the bottom of the Sand Cut pond (the dark, freezing waters, an obvious reference to the time spent in the chapel) where he flirts with the notion of suicide. But the very psychic energy that rushes the mind toward darkness and suffocation simultaneously impels the awakening body in the opposite direction, toward exhalation and light. Once again Richard's wayward physical impulses "betray" his heavenly urges, affirm his egoistic ones; and the "ooze" at the bottom of the pond, "the deepest trench" (103), which might have served as his burial plot, becomes the point of primordial origin, the uterine chute for the amniotic infant's rebirth into the muddy world. "But even before he could command it or fully decide to command it, his body was working for him" (104); and leaping upward, lungs bursting, he breaks the surface of the water in a blaze of anatomical bliss that at once imitates the pattern of Christ's spiritual release from the cross, just as it turns His message upside down.

The dive that began with a dedication to the Lord (*"For Thee!,"* italics Agee) ends in a glory of self-affirmation: *"Here I am!"* (italics Agee).

> . . . he was thankfully sure now that he would never go down again. Yet except for his feet, which no longer seemed to belong to him, his body still blazed with pleasure in its existence, and it was no longer urgent and rigid but almost sleepy. He slid his slick hands along his ribs and his sides and found that in his sex he was as tightly shrunken as if he were a baby. I could have died, he realized almost casually. *Here I am!* his enchanted body sang. I could be dead right now, he reflected in sleepy awe. *Here I am!* (106)

Minutes later, however, Richard stumbles upon the shore, and there confronts "a snake more splendid than" he "had ever seen before":

> In every wheaten scale and in all his barbaric patterning he was new and clear as gems, so gallant and sporting against the dun, he dazzled, and seeing him, Richard was acutely aware how sensitive, proud and tired he must be in his whole body, for it was clear that he had just struggled out of his old skin and was with his first return of strength venturing his new one. His style and brightness, his princely elegance, the coldness of his eye and the knifelike coldness and sweetness of his continuously altering line, his cold pride in his new magnificence, were not at the first in the least dismayed, not even by Richard's shout; only the little tongue, to Richard's almost worshiping delight and awe, sped like a thready horn of smoke, the eye seemed to meet Richard's and become colder and still more haughty, and the vitality of his elegance advanced him still further along the stone: so that for a few seconds Richard saw perfected before him, royally dangerous and to be adored and to be feared, all that is alien in nature and in beauty: and stood becharmed. (107–8)

This is the climatic moment of Richard's morning watch, the covert end and purpose behind the distractions in the chapel, the secret destination of the wandering mind and the half-sentient flesh: the newly liberated boy stares in wonderment at the sensuous spectacle of his own unbridled self-adoration uncoiling in the morning sun. In contrast to his sporadic attentiveness before the Blessed Sacrament, Richard's engagement with the snake is virtually absolute; he cannot help but *watch* in "almost worshiping delight and awe." "Sensitive, proud, and tired," the snake in "his new magnificence" is the immediate embodiment of Richard's own recently discovered pride of flesh; the creature's newly acquired second skin (scales as "new and clear as gems") homologous with Richard's renewal from the bottom of the pond ("as if he were a baby") and his suddenly "enchanted body," the imagined fatigue of the snake ("how . . . tired he must be") rhyming with the "almost sleepy" limbs of the boy. But it is also very clear that Richard's "delight and awe" are fraught with anxiety and risk, his self-discovery has resulted in a confrontation that is to be both "adored" and "feared"; the snake is presented as vital in "his elegance," yet "royally dangerous"; as one of the pagan lords of creation ("in all his barbaric patterning"), as well as the Satanic intruder in the Garden (with "his cold pride" and "thready horn of smoke," the sulfurous dark one): the creature represents a deeply shaded moral pivot in which a healthy self-respect possibly curdles into "cold" narcissism, an independent self into an "alien" self, a defiant action into a "haughty" action, a brave figure into a cruel one. The morning watch chokes in an indecipherable cry that is at once a shout of triumph, "Watch me!" (*"Here I am!"*), and an ominous warning, "Watch Out!" (of the snake, Richard wonders *"is he poison? is he poison?"* [110]).

This double-edged attitude accounts for the strange feeling of un-settling reluctance that comes over Richard when Hobe and Jimmy are about to stone the snake; "he became aware that it was not only his habit of gentleness to animals which made him want to spare the snake, but something new in him which he could not understand, about which he was profoundly uneasy" (109). The "something new" is the pride taken in his own "new magnificence," which simultaneously renders him "profoundly uneasy" in his dark complicity with the forest creature, a sense of kinship with attitudes and powers that may prove "royally dangerous." Thus, after his companions have already wounded the body of the snake, Richard, in a gesture that is at once brave and desperate, self-protective and self-punishing, picks up a small rock, rushes to the lashing head, and violently pounds it to death: " . . . he cared only for one thing, to put as quick an end as he could to all this terrible ruined futile writhing, and unkillable defiance" (110). Richard's action isn't only a mercy killing: he certainly wants to put the snake out of its misery (the "ruined futile writhing"), but at the same time, he very much wishes to crush its "unkillable defiance." (He immediately indeed earns the respect of his companions "in killing so recklessly and with such brutality," 111, and from this moment on, he is regarded by them as "the hero of the occasion," 115). Of course, almost all of Richard's actions up to this point have been generated precisely by just this kind of "unkillable defiance" (e.g., the unsanctioned second watch, the many defections within, and finally from, the chapel, etc.). But now he is made unconsciously aware ("profoundly uneasy") of the overreaching danger of his position, and employs his newly acquired self-assertiveness, as it were, against itself; or more exactly, coming full circle, his "defiance" generates its own psychic backlash, by attacking a precise distillate of itself, a "royal" danger embodied in another.

It is equally important to recognize that this "defiance," however defied, is still "unkillable"; the power of the egotistic self once awakened may be punished, pounded again and again, but never obliterated. Perhaps this is the full implication of why Richard, as he delivers the death blow, finds "the one remaining eye" of the crushed head "entering his own like a needle" (110); that is, the snake both accuses Richard and brands him forever as one of its own (i.e., the demimythic origins of Agee's heightened powers of visual acuity?).

Richard now knows that "he has been brave in a way he has never been brave before" (111), and "is pleased with his own courage" (116), but he is also "sorry the snake had been killed, and unhappy and uneasy whenever he caught a glimpse of it" (116) (the boys carry it partway back to school). Thus, even as he is pounding the snake, his physical action recalls the nailing of the God to the cross; and in contemplating its Calvary-like slow "agony of death" (114), he attributes to it (and in part, to himself) much of the language and sentiment in which the expiring Christ had been described in his Chapel reveries. Finally (at the end of the narrative) the extinction of the creature is compared to the death of his beloved father six years earlier: " . . . he told himself that the snake was so far gone by now that he must be a way beyond really feeling anything, ever any more (the phrase jumped at him): (Who said that? His mother: 'Daddy was terribly hurt so God has taken him up to Heaven to be with Him and won't come back to us ever anymore')" (120). The paradoxical upshot of Richard's act then is that he feels he must participate in the snake's death, and at the same time, must suffer a deep and abiding burden of remorse for having done so; "he had never before known such heaviness or such cold, crushing sorrow" (118). He must be brave *and* guilty. And Richard's refusal to wash the snake's gore entirely from his hand—"his maculate hand" (118)—finally becomes a form of self-proclamation: his badge of courage and mark of Cain, his pride and his shame, his pride *in* his shame; for this is Agee, and the courage of one's "sins," one's "failures," may sometimes be the only marks of identity one can call one's own.

Neither "good" nor "evil," both sacred and profane, the snake represents that pattern of primal energy that infuses all the dying and reviving particulars of the earth, the consuming and regenerating fires at the core of all creatural striving (and that which finally manages to elude all the moral and religious constructs the author attempts to impinge upon it). It is also the force that Richard clearly hungers to realize in himself, but once realized, can only resume the arc of its cycle in a crucified, self-devouring form: a "rebel" passion that must defy all, including the citadel of its origins; a rage of self-assertion that, in a reflex of Anglo-Catholic conscience, finally atones for its insatiable needs in a torrent of pity and compassion for all that is lost, broken, and suffering. Richard's now chastened drive for self-empowerment peaks in a massive bout of bereavement for dethroned monarchs and all the fallen angels of the Self: a crushed forest god, a Man on a cross, a dead father, a bruised pride, a buoyant young manhood now made heavy and melancholic with self-flagellation.

In his final phases, the omniverous tenderness Richard seems to evince toward all thriving and expiring entities has been predicated upon first learning how to affirm and destroy them; and I suppose by this declension, we are led to believe that his "Fall" has been a "Fortunate" one. As he walks back to the chapel, indifferent to the punishment that he knows awaits him (after all, he now carries his own whip), Agee balances the killing of the snake against his hero's sudden, almost vestigial compassion for the locust shell that first attracted him upon entering the woods: "Richard hurried back to the tree on which he had left the locust shell, detached it gently and with great care, scarcely looking at it, settled it into the breast pocket of his shirt" (117). The shell is emblematic of both his newly chastened self, as well as the physical remnant of vanished powers; and in this respect readily suggests the "empty grail" and "dry chalice" that he left behind at the Blessed Sacrament, the husks of an old and abandoned childhood faith. In a gesture loving and nostalgic, he now attempts to consolidate this old dispensation into his new, highly complicated and conflicted sense of spiritual growth. And the author finishes his tale in full allegorical pomp, paying homage to the very uneasy truce effected between Richard's "Pagan" and "Christian" positions, his sensual/spiritual split, by focusing on the two hands, one swelling with snake blood, the other cherishing a fragile shell, the hand that destroys and the hand that preserves, the fist and the caress, selfish and selfless to the last: "When the boys turned from the sty he followed them towards the Main Building carrying, step by step with less difficulty, the diminishing weight in his soul and body, his right hand hanging with a feeling of subtle enlargement at his thigh, his left hand sustaining, in exquisite protectiveness, the bodiless shell which rested against his heart" (120).

I trust the reader will forgive me if it seems that in trying to make this tale come clear, I have intentionally, as it were, muddied the waters. The "snake" episode, and everything that follows from it, is indeed deeply problematic because the author can never quite make up his mind about the qualities—both the danger and the "magnificence"—represented by the snake; nor whether his young hero should feel "brave" or "crushed" after pounding this creature to its death (he feels both); nor whether Richard has "fallen" in order to "rise," or has missed his moment by tragically repudiating one of the lords of life. And all of this is simply a fancy figurative way of saying that Agee could never finally, definitively, make up his mind about similar surgings—both vital and "royally dangerous"—within himself. Just as no one can tell Richard whether or not the snake is poisonous ("*is he poison? is he poison?*"); so no one could set the seal on the author's self-worth—"not now, not ever"— and finally tell him who he was. "Poison" or "new milk"? Pure or addled? Craven or courageous? Strong and wise, or "softened and sophisticated"? Throughout the course of his writing, Agee manages to devise intriguing ways of affirming both sides of these conflicted questions. In *Famous Men*, for instance, the thrust of the author's intellectual idealism advocates the coronation of a free and radical mind, an "individual, anti-authoritative consciousness," yet one at the same time thoroughly chastened by its need for further "education." The recurring inquest throughout the film criticism again continues the hunt for the radical personage, here determined the "dangerous" artist, who at his most radical and most "dangerous," finds the brave grace to efface himself in service to the "selfless" film. Perhaps only the fused antinomies of the Rebel Saint could fully satisfy Agee such as he was, so riven within himself: a figure, impelled by a spiritual rather than a political agenda, at once scornful and "defiant" of all public endeavor, civic work, social ideology, and official ordinance, yet completely humbled by, and subservient to, the dictates of the divine imperatives of the earth, "the cruel radiance" implicit within the formal signatures of natural being.

But the young hero of *The Morning Watch* is no "Rebel Saint"; and the antinomies in his nature do not fuse, but rather glower at each other from their respective corners in the bloody prize ring that constitutes his moral and emotional makeup. And at least one reader can see Richard emerging, even at the close, as a thoroughly unsettled spirit, and imagine him oscillating endlessly between the pond and the chapel, forever the passenger en route and in between, never staying long enough to ever have fully arrived anywhere. The journey that this young boy makes from Our Lady Chapel to the serpent at the pond is of course a different version of the same journey that the young journalist makes from his home up north to the famished farm in Alabama;[8] and the same one that Rufus makes from his childhood home in the suburbs to the movies at the Majestic Theater. And this journey is the great moral, emotional, and finally archetypal stretch of motion inscribed forever at the center of this author's projective life—a motion between the two worlds that would not be described in their original terms, or called by their original names, until James Agee wrote the last book of his life: the book of his mother and his father.

2. INTESTATE

The assembled manuscript entitled *A Death in the Family,* the work that has done more than any other to establish the reputation and public legend of James Agee, was found in disarray among the author's papers shortly after his death. The largest part of this scattering, perhaps a full two-thirds, formed an obvious continuity: twenty chapters, dividing into three parts, concerning the death of a beloved family man in Knoxville, Tennessee, in 1916, and its profound effects on his surviving relations, particularly his wife and six-year-old son (see outline).[9] The events depicted in these chapters cover approximately four consecutive days; beginning with the father's last evening with his family, and the shopping expedition involving his son (with his great-aunt) on the following day (part 1, chapters 1–7); the vigil kept by his wife and his in-laws as they discover and recount the facts of his death in a car accident that night (part 2, chapters 8–13); the events of the next two days, concluding with a rendering of the hours immediately before and after his funeral (part 3, chapters 14–20). Taken as a unit of time, place, and action, this material more or less follows the formal and structural stipulations for a classical, tripartite tragedy, with most of the drama taking place inside the family home and in the connecting streets leading to and away from the home.

The transposition of much of this material into a reasonably efficient, not very disgraceful theater piece, Tad Mosel's prize-winning *All The Way Home* (1960), was already prompted, if not inspired, by the focused tableaus and limited structure of the chapters themselves. A flat-footed movie version, Alex Segal's *All The Way Home* (1963), aspired to recreate the modest virtues of the play rather than the major ones of the novel.[10] Both film and play, apart from the expected jettisoning of the novel's poetry, mysticism, interiority, and dense criss-crossing of family relationship, dismiss Agee's constellation of father-son-mother and generally place most of the dramatic stress on the character of Mary Follet; on the way she manages to survive her catastrophe by combining the austerity of her religious beliefs with a few of her husband's earthier and more liberal attitudes (e.g., toward death, pregnancy, etc.); and, through this new understanding, cements her relationship with her son. Both play and film, in other words, completely reverse and sugar-coat the more severe and complex implication of Agee's version in which the mother's fears and pieties stiffen into a liturgical crutch that begins to bar her from both everything that the father stood for, as well as the affiliations of her child.

In all likelihood, Agee had envisioned his novel as an even more capacious family study than the one just cited. For also found among his papers were materials, episodic and discontinuous, treating events that occur in the years prior to the father's death, mostly told from the perspective of the son at ages four and five.[11] These concern a child's growing knowledge of the world's ways, and his changing ties to parents, relatives, neighbors, and peers (e.g., night thoughts in the crib, a family visit to a great-great-grandmother, the petty cruelties of the kids in the street). All of this material remained unintegrated into the novel's relatively unified structure at the time of the author's death, and remains so today.

One can only speculate on how Agee might have treated these episodes, and specifically how he might have brought them in line with the twenty chapters he more or less completed (he was a tireless reviser). He may have wanted to shorten or lengthen some episodes (e.g., one seems to end in midsentence), delete some and/or add new ones. He may have wanted to compose transitional or bridging devices; and to clarify details (e.g., in the present text, we can't be certain if Aunt Amelia is Uncle Andrew's wife or sister). He may have wanted—as I believe he did—to intercut a few or all of these episodes in counterpoint with material now in the chapters. We just have no way of knowing what he would have done.

What we do know, however, is that the original editors at McDowell, Obolensky choose to present all the episodes in italics, and to place what purport to be the earliest ones at the end of part 1, between chapters 7 and 8, and the rest at the end of part 2, between chapters 13 and 14. They also chose to introduce the novel ("as a sort of prologue," *A Death in the Family*, note, vi) with the well-known prose poem "Knoxville: Summer 1915," even though this was composed in 1938 in a vastly more elaborate and strenuous style (i.e., closer in period and manner to the style of *Famous Men*) than anything that follows in the novel proper.

But then, in fact, this novel was never entirely "proper"; and what I want to know is, is the McDowell solution all round the best one possible? I raise this question with the full understanding that only a couple of commentators seem to have voiced serious objections to it;[12] that all subsequent editions have followed the McDowell arrangement; and that short of resurrecting the author and his explicit intentions, all "solutions" will be unsatisfactory. Still, we can safely assume that some "solutions" will be less unsatisfactory—less egregious, less presumptuous—than others. Aside from the relatively minor irritant of reading long uninterrupted dollops of italicized print, presenting half the episodes between some chapters and half between others hardly represents a neutral editorial decision, but rather aspires to an artistic decision, and one far more presumptuous in tampering with the author's intentions and effects than simply presenting all the episodes together before chapter one (and after, or even without, the Knoxville "prologue"), or at the end of the text as a "sort of" appendix. Since all the episodes occur in a time frame earlier than that of the chapters, I'm not at all sure that I wouldn't prefer a straight chronological arrangement, though either one (i.e., before or after all the chapters) would at least allow the reader a chance to experience the present time span, all twenty chapters, as an uninterrupted dramatic unit.

This solution—also unsatisfactory, I realize—mitigates against suggestions of temporal counterpoint or "flashback" effects, and thus also probably violates the author's intentions while the present arrangement does allow for some sense of temporal inflection. But I would argue that such allowance is made in so ungainly and imprecise a manner as to all but obliterate the dramatic and emotional advantages usually obtained through techniques of time-shifting (e.g., effects of memory, increased subjectivity and internality, etc.). Some of the specific episodes, indeed, fairly yearn to be juxtaposed against "echoing" materials *within* the chapters, but certainly not *between* them as they now appear in two huge, undifferentiated lumps. Rufus's early encounter with the older boys, for instance, which now appears after chapter 13 somewhere in the middle of the second lump, certainly contrasts with and illuminates his later meeting with them on the morning after his father's death in chapter 16: and perhaps belongs within chapter 16. But to exercise this or any other contrapuntal integration would demand application to an artistic license far more arrogant, and perhaps overtly damaging, than the relatively modest license the McDowell, Obolensky editors have already put to use—and, I believe, misuse.

I doubt if anyone would actually want to read, or even imagine, this book without these episodes; certainly the author would not have written this book without them. Many of them are of course superbly executed in themselves, and all add immeasurable range, depth, and vibrancy to the characters and atmosphere of the chapters; they are a necessary part of this work and must be included in it—somehow, someway. But I also seriously doubt if many readers (and especially the present one) can ever be entirely glad about the undigested and haphazard sprawl of their present appearance, particularly in contrast to the classical symmetries and continuities of the chapters themselves, like so many slabs of marble strewn about the base of a finished temple. Properly ingested, the episodes would not only add and enrich, as they do now, but also, I would argue, change the meaning of the text as we know it (see "Coda: All the Way Home, Sort of"). Because they have not been so ingested, however, we can never know for sure how *all* parts of the given structure are meant to work in relation to each other.

Thus: because the author did not live long enough to give a final form to his last book, he did not live long enough to give final shape—or arguably any shape at all—to the meaning and emotion governing the whole. So while the original editors insist that *A Death in the Family* represents "a near-perfect work of art" (vi)—that is, the "work" as they have chosen to arrange it for us—I persist in finding an enigmatic and equivocal work of art, one that presents problems that have never been— and may never be—finally resolved.

3. INVISIBLE AMERICA

Nevertheless: *A Death in the Family,* hobbles and all, episodes and chapters, was published in 1957, two years after Agee's death, and remains the one book of all the author's works that seems to have secured the devotion of what used to be called the "general" or "common" reader; that also seems to have found and held this reader almost immediately, quite apart from the promptings of critics and specialists. To this minute, this work endures as one of those novels that gets passed from friend to friend and sustains its reputation as much from word of mouth as from the continuing regard of so-called experts.

One may also ascribe such spontaneous and uncritical loyalty on the part of a general readership to plays such as *Our Town* and *The*

Glass Menagerie, novels such as *Look Homeward, Angel* and *East of Eden,* and films such as *It's a Wonderful Life* and *The Best Years of Our Lives.* True, these are all more showy and extroverted creations than *A Death in the Family;* some are also more overtly commercial; none I think even approaches the hushed, delicate, self-effacing intimacy of Agee's fictionalized memoir. Yet very much like these works and unlike any other of his major writings, this book has an indisputable common touch; that is, a direct pipeline to the common experience of its readership. The popular character of *A Death in the Family* guarantees its place among our short list of much loved and critic-proof pieces of domesticity and nostalgic Americana and cannot be ignored in assessing its uniqueness, as well as its reputation. On the contrary, the popular character and direct appeal of this novel take us very close to the kind of book Agee probably meant to make.

Of what does this popular character consist? What do we mean by a common touch? Unlike our best and most characteristic American novels, Agee has chosen to treat artistically those aspects of Middle American life, the being and doings of "ordinary" citizens, that have become familiar to the point of invisibility, unseen by virtue of their ubiquity and numbing repetition. Such invisible activity represents the daily business of a kind of living usually impervious to fiction because of its seeming exemption from every quality of the exceptional; that which doesn't get into made-up stories because it has been so deeply encoded into the unexamined folkways of its level of culture as to erase every trace of what may well have been its original character as artifact. Agee's project then becomes to resurrect to a level of poetic attentiveness what might be termed an anesthetized culture, and mesmerize his reader with the soft-sell of déjà vu, the cushioned shock of the already known. Thus we experience the anatomized minutia of watering lawns, of making beds, of getting dressed, of preparing breakfast, of taking strolls, of starting cars, of going to the movies, of watching stars, of listening to leaves, of following shadows across bedroom ceilings, of preparing the virtually endless gallons of coffee, tea, and milk that apparently give spring to the soft shoe of Knoxville's grave and tender suburban shuffle. For many Americans these activities simply represent the "way things are," but for Agee, they are all part of the buried but immortal archaeology of

Middle American habits of being circa 1916, the practical forms of daily ritual and craft as fascinating to him as Gudger's rooms or the motions of an Alabama sharecropper as he picks his cotton. Watering the lawn in Knoxville also represents a species of "classical" art, also the results of an instinctive combination of taste, moral grace, and the meticulous grading of fine discriminations:

> *The nozzles were variously set but usually so there was a long sweet stream of spray, the nozzle wet in the hand, the water trickling the right forearm and the peeled-back cuff, and the water whishing out a long loose and low-curved cone, and so gentle a sound. First an insane noise of violence in the nozzle, then the still irregular sound of adjustment, then the smoothing into steadiness and a pitch as accurately tuned to the size and style of stream as any violin. So many qualities of sound out of one hose: so many choral differences out of those several hoses that were in earshot. Out of any one hose, the almost dead silence of the release, and the short still arch of the separate big drops, silent as a held breath, and the only noise the flattering noise on leaves and the slapped grass at the fall of each big drop. That, and the intense hiss with the intense stream; that, and that same intensity not growing less but growing more quiet and delicate with the turn of the nozzle, up to that extreme tender whisper when the water was just a wide bell of film. (4–5)*

The widespread appeal of *A Death in the Family* is that of a series of indelible recognitions. In this work as in no other, Agee has striven to fix for the time capsules the "mean" (as in *"the mean goodness of their living"* [5]) or normative flavor of his Middle American heritage, and in this sense the experience of his text and that of his presumptive readership are virtually one and the same. Here is a book in which the manners and acts of a culture only two hundred years old—allegedly young, improvised, and ahistorical—acquire the stability, dignity, and slow-motion time sense of centuries upon centuries of Old World custom and tradition. No *"mean"* accomplishment for an American writer.

It's no secret that our great novelists have customarily shrunk from the commonplace aspects of middle-class life because, as our critics have recited by rote, the social texture in this country is thought to be too fluid and diaphanous for the commonplace ever to establish itself; common experience is just what we allegedly don't have here. In spite of the sobering example of William Dean Howells, most of our front-rank novelists have never been known to allow notions as porous or fluttering as social norms or an assumed commonality check the soaring expansiveness of singular and untrammeled literary dreaming, mental sky-writing invariably deemed more weighty than water from a nozzle dribbling on the forearm. For the "common reader," however, the bottom line has always been the same: what can one recognize in classic American fiction as one's own? How many regular consumers of such fiction have ever accomplished in their lives half of what has been regularly accomplished by characters in great American novels? It is a reasonable assumption, for instance, that most of us have never hunted for white whales or giant bears, battled Indians in the forests, stolen slaves from their masters, drowned sweethearts in the middle of lakes, committed suicide in Bowery flophouses, choked with the Okies in the dust bowl, fought the fascists in Spain, commandeered a movie studio, made fortunes in crime, raped debutantes, murdered spouses, lynched suspects, gone berserk in decaying southern mansions, lusted after nymphets, run howling in race riots, or unearthed conspiracies to subvert the postal system.

Even though our critics are here to tell us that there is little difference between ordinary America and invented America, between the private citizen and the collective fantasy, Agee is here to tell us something else: very quietly he speaks of and for a life that is lived every day and all around us, but has little or nothing to do with the giant cymbal clash of the classic American literary imagination. Rather, he takes pains to establish the Knoxvillians as an American social average, *"fairly solidly lower middle class with one or two juts apiece on either side of that"* (3); neither rich nor poor, the men neither young nor old, *"most of them between thirty and forty-five"* (4); the houses *"middle-sized"* (3).[13] The one act of violence in the novel, Jay Follet's smash-up, takes place off-stage, to be reconstructed and puzzled over by others; the only physical evidence of its fury, a tiny blue dent in the dead man's chin, a single, near extraneous, incision on an otherwise smooth and perfect body, the lone tracing of an eternal visitation upon a generally consonant continuity— as if such a death did not really oppose this continuity at all, but rather was an inflection of it in a different key. The death of a father is of course this book's signal happening, the one "event" in a relatively "uneventful" context; yet it is an *obvious* catastrophe, in its own way as commonplace as watering the lawn or going to the movies, another source of indelible recognition, and one for readers everywhere. Hunting the great white whale of classic American fiction can astonish the eye from its socket, but the passing of the flesh of one's flesh in Knoxville is a catechism in the blood, part of the shared failure of the race.

Now Agee treats the commonplace as neither datum, compromise, nor stratagem for deflation, but unabashedly as a repository of powerful, transpersonal forces swirling through local gesture. In its own way *A Death in the Family* musters a romanticism as intrepid and ecstatic as anything in Melville or Faulkner, but one flowering precisely and significantly from within the interstices of the humdrum. Agee's characteristic form of prestidigitation incessantly coaxes the ordinary into the extraordinary without sacrificing a scintilla of its flat, "boring," and redundant flavor. By sifting the prosaic through an entranced sensibility, he reinvents the normative in terms of his own affinity for the mysterious and the sacred. The visionary tug of "Knoxville: Summer 1915" strikes a sacramental chord that, intended or not, generally resonates throughout everything that follows; energy pools from the spirit world irrigate the language, rhythm, and imagery of chapters and episodes; characters superbly individualized—foibles, ambivalences, rigidities, etc., fully rendered—are yet seamlessly unified by a gossamer envelope of seraphic commiseration. This is a novel that not only fusses over making beds, boiling coffee, and the logistics of shaving, but equally (and more problematically: see *"Oceanic Roll: The Uses of Childhood"*) over a ghost returning to its home, the transfigured soul in the form of a butterfly, a peach tree that oversees a lover's farewell like "a celestial sentinel" (38), "the forehead" of a blacksmith's anvil that gives off "the stunning shadow of every blow it had ever received" (197), fathers watering their lawns like gardeners in Eden just before the Fall, " . . . *gentle happy and peaceful, tasting the mean goodness of their living like the last of their suppers in their mouths*" (5).

In centering the sacred powers of the commonplace within the commoners themselves, the author aligns his spiritual focus with his social focus, and in so doing garners instant precedent among the familiar tenets of American intellectual history. The watering fathers—blessed by neither affluence, breeding, nor privilege, but by the divinely appointed miracle of their ordinariness, the relish of integral being—represent the sanctified heroes of a Democratic idyll, custodians of the American Garden, and in this sense embody one of the cherished myths of early-nineteenth-century majoritarian politics: the individual commoner as vessel of the moral force and righteousness of a divine collective. The Ageean texture of transcendence, nostalgia, and simple egalitarian pre-disposal all combine to recall some of the visionary freshness found in the writing of the morning days of the Republic, and especially in the doxologies of Emerson, Thoreau, and Whitman, those first expounders and promulgators of the supernal aura casting about the shape of the American mean, of "the Democratic wisdom underneath, like solid ground for all."[14] Agee may thus have entirely circumvented the tradition of the classic American novel of melodrama and sensation, only to resurrect our very early, and perhaps only original, tradition of poetry and metaphysics. But who ever heard of a transcendental *novel*? *A Death in the Family* may be the primary, lone, most worrisome and bewitching example of its kind.

4. OCEANIC ROLL: THE USES OF CHILDHOOD

At the heart of things, then, the paradoxes of an immemorial romance: the ordinary investments of the extraordinary, the extraordinary emanations of the ordinary. At the heart of things, then, a puzzle, an "energy" storming at the core of quiet living without direction or purpose, never to be organized, parsed, or conciliated, never to be understood except as that which reverberates beyond understanding.

To live, then, in a spirit of ardent and unappeasable befuddlement is to coincide—to synchronize as near as humanly possible, like sign and countersign—with the racking miracle, "the cruel radiance" that is all we may sense of existence at the quick. To persist in such a manner is one way, Agee's way, as he apothesizes in his 23rd sonnet, of going "mindless into truth."[15]

Not-knowing is the proper condition for the proper reception of riddles and tracings of the cosmic daze; and all of this—this blizzard of ultimate reality—apprehended without preconception or cognitive alibi. This condition adheres to, and in large part defines, the provenance of Childhood as this author conceives it. If the mysteries of being and doing present themselves in a blaze of paradox and contradiction, the most capable and authentic response appears not in the form of an interpretation or an explanation, but in that of a wide-eyed beginner, a child asking questions; that is to say, a human daze to correspond with its supernal counterpart. Accordingly, the child in Agee is characterized not so much by his pristine morality as by his not-yet-fallen mode of perception, his never-to-be-satisfied spirit of inquiry, the archetypal posture of mental and emotional questing.

Rufus Follet officially enters *A Death in the Family* as his father's silent intimate, his little crony in the acquisition of forbidden knowledge, the passive sharer in his father's secrets, and, symbolically, even as the parthenogenetic offshoot of his body. At no point in the narrative, however, does Agee allow a comparable sequence of intimacy between Rufus and his mother, nor does he ever permit Mary and her son an extended scene without a third party present. Accordingly, Rufus's second appearance, his first with his mother, also includes his younger sister, Catherine. Here for the first time he actually opens his mouth and speaks for himself, and in a manner that characterizes him throughout the rest of the novel: that of an unstoppable curiosity with an underlying hint of contrariness, of innocently yet forthrightly plundering the shibboleths of his elders. If he is almost the soulmate of his loving father, he is halfway toward becoming the adversary of his loving but exasperated mother. Rufus is also a loving child, guileless and trusting. But relentless:

> "Daddy had to go up to see Grandfather Follet," their mother explained. "He says to kiss both of you for him and he'll probably see you before you're asleep tonight."
>
> "When?" Rufus asked.
>
> "Way, early this morning, before it was light."
>
> "Why?"
>
> "Grampa Follett is very sick. Uncle Ralph phoned up very late last night, when all of us were asleep. Grampa has had one of his attacks."

"What's attack?"

"Eat your cereal, Catherine. Rufus, eat yours. His heart. Like the one he had that time last fall. Only worse, Uncle Ralph says. He wanted very much to see Daddy, just as quick as Daddy could come."

"Why?"

"Because he loves Daddy and if . . . *Eat,* wicker, or it'll all be nasty and cold, and *then* you know how you hate to eat it. Because if Daddy didn't see him soon, Grampa might not get to see Daddy again."

"Why not?" (55–56)

Rufus's questions become progressively more serious, as the conversation proceeds. He wants to know what happens to people after they die? Where do they go? And do animals go there too? Did the rabbits, for instance, go there after the dogs attacked and killed them? And finally his questions become not just serious, but ultimate:

"Why does God let us do bad things?"

"Because He wants us to make up our own minds."

"Even to do bad things, right under His nose?"

"He doesn't *want* us to do bad things, but to know good from bad and be good of our own free choice."

"Why?"

"Because He loves us and wants us to love Him, but if He just *made* us be good, we couldn't really love Him enough. You can't love to do what you are *made* to do, and you couldn't love God if He *made* you."

"But if God can do *anything,* why can't He do that?"

"Because He doesn't *want* to," their mother said, rather impatiently. "Why *doesn't* He want to?" Rufus said. "It would be so much easier for Him." (57)

While this first sequence between Mary, Rufus, and Catherine at the breakfast table never quite loses its tone of humorous innocence, it's clear that the colloquy is presented less in the spirit of question and answer than that of parry and thrust—Mary's responses tending not so much to resolve Rufus's problems, or even to reveal her deepest beliefs (though that is what they are), as to fend off the discussion itself and make an end to the nag and shove of her son's inquiry. Rufus's questions are in fact an implicit foreshadowing of the kinds of questions—fundamental, aggressive, benighted—that the adults themselves will have to ask in stunned recoil from Jay's death and the preternatural conditions created by it. On the night of the accident, for example, the family gathers in Mary's living room, and in the course of much conjecture and consolation, is suddenly made aware of an invisible presence entering the home. But Joel Lynch, Mary's father, isn't exactly sure what, if anything, has happened; and the persistence of his querulousness takes on some of the adversarial bewilderment of his grandson:

> "I don't like to interrupt," Joel said, "but would you mind telling me, please, what's going on here?"
> "You felt it too, Papa?" Mary asked eagerly.
> "Felt what?"
> "You remember when Aunt Hannah said there was something around, someone or something in the house?"
> "Yes, and she told me to shut up, so I did."
> "I simply asked you please to be quiet, Joel, because we were trying to hear."
> "Well, what did you hear?"
> "I don't know's I *heard* anything, Joel. I'm not a bit sure. I don't think I did. But I *felt* something, very distinctly. So did Andrew."
> "Yes I did, Papa."
> "And Mary."
> "Oh, very much so."
> "What do you mean you *felt* something?" (187)

The perspective of children and that of adults intersect at that point where reality drops its pretense of familiarity and reveals itself as mystery and paradox, at that point where the consensual charade conducted by grown-ups and kids also sheds its mask. It is here too that one must make a distinction between the role of the child as Agee sometimes presents it and what we have been describing as his notion of Childhood itself. In the famous opening sentence of the prologue, we listen to the words of a mysterious and indefinite "I" that *"lived . . . so successfully disguised to myself as a child"* (3). Here when we speak of a *"child,"* we also in a sense speak of a sham, a contrivance of the flesh, a partly illusory conjunction of size, shape, and years, a transitory condition replaced by other conditions just as fleeting ("youth," "age," etc.). But when we speak of Childhood, we speak of nothing so ephemeral: a *"child"* may be time-bound, but Childhood is eternal. It is the abiding residence of the archetypal *"I,"* the primary and transpersonal self (*"We* are talking now . . . in the time that *I* lived there . . . ,*"* italics mine) still blinking in the wake of its prenatal origins, the spellbound stranger wandering forever amid oceans of energy as mysterious to him as he is to himself (*"but will not ever tell me who I am"*). This condition has little or nothing in common with all those well-known romantic paradigms traditionally attributed to the world of small people. It is not a magic isle, a lost splendor, a sequestered and perishing innocence; rather, it is a quasi-mystical condition of being both human and meta-human, available to young and old, to both Rufus and Joel, whenever one surrenders the false redoubts of clarity and intellect and stands in helpless humility before the infinite tangle of things as enigmatic and imponderable.

The onset of death itself—the second of life's most painful miracles of ordinariness—restores for a time the major characters to the status of the puzzled, incantory, and ghostly *"I"* of the prologue. The whole, long "waiting" section (part 2)—the greatest single stretch of domestic drama in all of Agee—with Hannah and Mary, then Joel and (wife) Catherine, patiently desperate for news of whether Jay is alive or dead, and then finally with Andrew, bundling together in their pain and confusion—becomes one grandly sustained, near operatic metaphor (as in a vocal quintet) for the boundless Not-Knowing, the stumbling, "mindless" ruminations of the childlike position itself.[16] Naturally, the adults, unlike children, attempt to fall back on their intellectual dispensations, the accrued understanding of a lifetime of transaction with the world, to shield them from the stunning web of turmoil that has suddenly descended upon them: Joel has his pessimistic fatalism; Andrew his pugnacious and ambiguous agnosticism; both Hannah and Mary have their different levels of religious conviction, the former, a rocklike and deeply tried stoicism, the latter, a somewhat shrill and overwrought righteousness; and undoubtedly each gleans a modicum of solace from beliefs that reaffirm the self in its losing struggle to contain truths that are by definition ineffable. But the pluralistic strategy of the book denies privilege to any single personal philosophy and all are finally reduced to blown chaff, a chattering of "views," a casting about of "notions," remedies, and bromidic cross-talk wielded like a kid's lucky but finally futile charm to ward off a maelstrom of uncertainty:

> "None of us know what we're doing, any given moment."
>   How you manage not to have religious faith, Hannah wanted to tell him, is beyond me. She held her tongue.
>   "A tale told by an idiot . . . signifying nothing."
>   "Signifying something," Andrew said, "but we don't know what."
>   "Just as likely. Choice between rattlesnake and skunk."
>   "Jay knows what; now," Mary said.
>   "I certainly won't swear he doesn't," her father said.
>   "He does, Mary," her aunt said.
>   "Of course he does," Mary said.
>   Child, you'd better believe it, her aunt thought, disturbed by the "of course." (176)

Perhaps the most brilliantly conceived instance of failed consolation philosophy in the face of Childhood's abiding anomalies emerges within Mary Follet's wretched moment of religious affectation. Early during the "waiting" period, before she has received any concrete report of Jay's condition, that is, before she has received any actual cause for suffering at all, Mary forces Hannah to kneel on the kitchen floor and join her in prayer. Hannah senses at once that there is a kind of "pride or poetry" (134) in her niece's conduct at this time; that she is perhaps all too eager to mount her cross even in advance of her crucifixion, like an actress trying out for a part; and that such a parade of religious faith "was very mistaken and dangerous" (134). (Compare Mary's behavior with the "hidden vainglory" of Richard in *The Morning Watch* and his "desire to suffer for religious advantage.")

But then Agee follows this scene of false readiness with one of spontaneous and childlike authenticity. Shortly after saying her prayers, Mary realizes that she has to go to the bathroom and feels thoroughly "humbled" in having to obey the awkward timing of her physical needs:

> Mary, whispering, "Excuse me," retired to the bathroom, affronted and humbled that one should have to obey such a call at such a

time; she felt for a few moments as stupid and enslaved as a baby
on its potty, and far more ungainly and vulgar; then, with her wet
hands planted in the basin of cold water she stared incredulously
into her numb, reflected face, which seemed hardly real to her, until,
with shame, she realized that at this of all moments she was mirror
gazing. Hannah, left alone, was grateful that we are animals; it was
this silly, strenuous, good, humble cluttering of animal needs which
saw us through sane, fully as much as prayer . . . (136)

As Hannah's reflections indicate, it is *this* "lowering" of Mary, not
kneeling on the kitchen floor, that proves to be as behovely as formal
rite. Agee structures the sequence of events to show us how one of
Mary's simplest and strongest moments of character can follow from
one of her shakiest, and how real spiritual fortitude can pivot about
the sobering realization of one's infantile bodily functions and innocent
"animal" narcissism. Mary emerges from the bathroom and sits silently
with Hannah for ten minutes waiting for the kettle to boil, and then says
very simply, " 'I only wish we'd hear now, because I am ready.' Hannah
nodded, and felt: you really are" (136).

Agee's double-edged presentation of Mary Follet as both imposing
but insecure adult and chastened but resolute little girl (like "a baby on
its potty") is thoroughly typical of the bifocal lens sustained throughout
the narrative on Knoxville and its citizens. The major characters are
consistently seen as simultaneously tall and small, the author employing
both ends of his telescope on Childhood alternately and at once; thus,
sometimes the adult characters are perceived as if a child might perceive
them, and then sometimes as if they themselves were children. For
roughly half the narrative, for example, the authorial voice subordinates
itself to the tone and sensibility of six-year-old Rufus, who generally views
the older figures about him from a kind of low-angled moral and physical
crouch (*"All my people are larger bodies than mine . . . ,"* [7])—from his
looming mother and father (*"My king and my queen"*), or his fragrant
and majestic nursemaid, Victoria (*"the biggest woman he had ever seen"*
[105]), to the odious Father Jackson (almost "as tall as Daddy") with
his "long" chin and "glaring" collar (290), whose voice behind the door
on the second-floor landing, as heard from below, overpowers all. (The
"Rufus" tone is maintained through all of chapter 1, part of chapter 7,

most of the episodes, and most of part 3.) For the rest, when Rufus isn't present (and occasionally when he is) the narrative voice shifts freely from character to character, any given adult depending on the circumstance, taking on the role or attitudes of a child in relation to one or more of the other characters: as Mary often does in relation to Hannah or Andrew (e.g., to Andrew: "there she stood waiting, her eyes, her face like that of an astounded child which might be pleading" [146]); as Jay sometimes does to Mary (e.g., in taking leave of her, she studies him earnestly "as if he were her son" [37]); as Ralph, Jay's alcoholic brother, does to practically everyone (e.g., "But I'm not a man," he worries, "I'm a baby. Ralph is the baby. Ralph is the baby" [70]); as Rufus's great-great-grandmother does to Rufus, grinning for joy and urinating on the floor in the excitement of recognizing her kin; as the gardening fathers of the "prologue" do to that archetypal *"I"* who suddenly (reversing the telescope) envisions the row of men with hoses *"as the urination of huge children stood loosely military against an invisible wall"* (5). In such a context, it is no surprise at all that paramount among this book's eidolons shines Charlie the Tramp, ultimate man-child of the Western dawn; more than personal homage and far more than period detail, "the little fellow" becomes a kind of icon for the whole, a symbolic touchstone of a late-morning world, a summer-in-decline, viewed partly through the wide eye of an imagined little boy and partly through the golden eye of an enveloping parental nostalgia that consistently perceives all its holdings, huge and little, smooth and withered, as precious and unsullied as creatures newly born.

AQUATICS

> They walked to the edge of the porch. The moistures of May drowned all save the most ardent stars, and gave back to the earth the sublimated light of the prostrate city. Deep in the end of the back yard, the blossoming peach tree shone like a celestial sentinel. The fecund air lavished upon their faces the tenderness of lovers' adoring hands, the dissolving fragrance of the opened world, which slept against the sky.
>
> "What a heavenly night, Jay," she said in the voice which was dearest to him. "I almost wish I could come with you"—she remembered more clearly "—in whatever happens." (38)

Mary and Jay about to take leave of each other for what proves to be the last time—it is an evocative, provocative, and in most ways characteristic passage. "The moistures of May" saturate the landscape, the odors of earth ("the dissolving fragrance") infiltrate the night (". . . slept against the sky"): elements interpenetrate. And just as there is a familial embrace that hovers about Rufus, the passage indicates another embrace, just as palpable, equally loving and watchful, that also hovers about his parents—in the "peach tree" that watches "like a celestial sentinel," in the "fecund air" that caresses with "the tenderness of lovers' adoring hands," etc. This embrace results from the deep spreading flush of the author's love and regret for the offspring of his art, the lost family of his childhood, the found children of memory and desire. This enveloping emotion allows him to play both a child to his parents in the form of Rufus Follet, and, in the general narrative voice, a parent to his parents—a kind of guardian or watchman (as on Gudger's porch)—the authorial source of, and virtual participant in, their regenerated beings. But I say "regret," as well as "love," for in resurrecting these figures, he must relive the period—indeed, the very summer night—when he will lose them all over again, and discover both his long-lost and newly found family bereft and riven once more. Surely the peach tree that watches and the drenched air that caresses do so in commiserating foreknowledge that Mary and Jay are parting forever.

But what does one make of the quality of the sentiment itself—half lullaby, half threnody, protective of its characters almost to the point of covetousness? In its milder accents, this sentiment is not uncharacteristic of the whole narrative, and in the passage above comes perilously close to the tone and affect of the high-level mash note cum condolence card (not to belabor the obvious collapse into pathetic fallacy). "Nostalgic," of course—but such an overworked appellation (which I perforce must use) in no way does justice to the saturated, near wounded quality of Agee's moist tenderness. In its personal intensity, this sentiment is reminiscent of that gush of the heart that the young journalist experiences on that special night in Alabama when he abandons his stalled car and stands in the dark before Gudger's home. Yet even Gudger represented only a surrogate family, a tiny clearing in the wilderness of deracinated wandering; and Agee's emotion there was deeply focused, exclusive, directly affixed to its unique discovery. Where his need in Alabama was to segregate his relation to one family, and particularly to one domestic space, from the alien darkness surrounding them, his need in Knoxville is to remain in intimate connection with the *totality* of the familial universe he has recreated. Here in Knoxville nothing is alien, every particular softened and blurred, familiarized and finally *fused* in a great centrifugal flow—circle upon widening circle—of personal identification. Of course the "tenderness of the lovers' adoring hands" allude to Mary and Jay as well as the "fecund air" as well as the ardor of the author who also virtually caresses this moment of communion; and of course the various reflections and interminglings of earth and sky gather up both the affections of the young couple and those of the "celestial sentinel"— that authorial stand-in—as all three reluctantly bid farewell to each other. Here and throughout, great arcs of feeling consistently flood the traditional thresholds of distinction between figure and ground, cosmos and leaf, the projections of the characters and the introjections of the author.

In all the great range of modern American fiction, one would be pressed to find many more sustained images of what Freud once famously described as "primary ego feeling" than the one conjured up by the language and rhythm of Agee's last novel. Freud's formulation represented the essential shape of the earliest and mostly hypothetical stage of self-development, one referred to by the (borrowed) designation "oceanic": the mode of the preconscious, semimythical infant, rapturous in its "feeling of indissoluble connection, of belonging inseparably to the external world as a whole."[17] Later this ego would learn to see itself as a unitary thing, separate and distinct from its enveloping ambiance. But deep in its "oceanic" phase, still resonant with sensations of amniotic warmth and umbilical tie, the self enjoins its universe, and subject and object, near and far, now and then, swim together in one boundless dilution of indivisible feeling.

Much of Agee's emotional lavishments throughout his book may be at least understood—if not always justified—as a semiconscious effort to find lyrical forms for the expression of his own soft-fingered version of oceanic rapture. And when he deliberately chooses to focus on the first six years of childhood, this author may well be something of a pioneer among our major novelists. It's still worth remembering even at this late date that what most of our best authors have meant by "childhood" and "innocence" has resulted in actual practice in many portrayals of late boyhood and girlhood, adolescence, and/or young manhood and womanhood: Huck and Tom, Daisy Miller, Jo and Meg Marsh, Penrod and Sam, Nick Adams, Ike McCaslin, Studs Lonnigan, Holden Caulfield, Lolita, Tex and D.J., Billy Bathgate. (The initiatory experience of Agee's twelve-year-old Richard in *The Morning Watch* springs of course right out of the Native American mold; c.f., "Art Novel: The Maculate Hand.") In *A Death in the Family,* however, Agee's version of the national fetish stakes out a mood and time zone as close to late infancy as it is to very early boyhood, and in fact concludes his book at exactly that point where the classic American treatment would characteristically begin; that is, at childhood's end technically on the threshold of an American boyhood, and significantly at that very moment when Rufus has begun to think of himself in the traditional manner as a cub-sized specimen of our national archetype, the Lone Wolf (after his father's death, he insists on defining himself as a "norphan," 288). In this manner, most of this book's incident and atmosphere shun the characteristic rites and practices of standard American child-worship, drawing primary inspiration from the earliest wells of postnatal memory and sensation. Accordingly, we learn of— and remember—Rufus carried to his bed, or holding a grown-up's hand in walking the street, or "lifted, high, and seated on the bar" (166), or conversing to the siren song of the shadows surrounding his crib.

What the adult sees as fixed, the child sees as fluid, and Agee does not hesitate to evoke watery textures everywhere—from hosing the lawn, or the "moistures of May," "dissolving" odors, and "drowned" solids, to the blood and sea imagery, and rivers of assonance streaming throughout; to all forms of liquid libation—from the ubiquity of the kettle (i.e., the aforementioned reservoirs of coffee, tea, and milk) to the dreaded whiskey, Jay's nemesis and Ralph's succubus (the latter goes for the mouth of his bottle "as ravenously as a famished baby takes the nipple" [67]). Especially striking is the inordinate stress on urine and urination: Mary, Jay, Rufus, his sister Catherine, and his great-great-grandmother are all presented at one time or another in either acts of incontinence or contexts of allusion to such acts. Even the book's genus loci, Charlie the Tramp, soaks his seat and reminds Rufus of his own urine-stained sock.

The image of this waterworld constitutes the verbal poetics for a sea of saturated emotion. Agee's stress on all manner of fluid, flux, and flotation becomes a function of his overwhelming need to dissolve self and subject in a uniform stream of self-generated feeling, to fuse himself with his created offspring (families, settings) and together spin slowly in a soft, sad rapture of accord. Thus in his aqueous reverie of early Knoxville, objects shirk their integral spaces, cut loose, as it were, from their moorings, and swim off on dark, torpid tides of wistfulness. Windows and porchfronts, for example, literally sail past, buoyed along slow currents of yawn and melancholy, rooms submerging in the thick "honey" of the spectator's grogginess (i.e., here Andrew):

> Yes, and between the treetops; the pale scrolls and porches and dark windows of the homes drifting past their slow walking, and not a light in any home, and so for miles, in every street of home and of business; above thy deep and dreamless sleep, the silent stars go by. . . . Little houses, bigger ones, scrolled and capacious porches, dark windows, leaves of trees already rich with May, homes of rooms which chambered sleep as honey is cherished, drifted past their slow walking and were left behind, and not a light in any home. (206–7)

Or sometimes people and places, voices and lights simply hang suspended in a filtered glut of murmur and haze, fed, fatted, basking in a "dream" of postamniotic contentment and the rack-focus of baby's bliss:

> *They were so full up and sleepy they hardly even tried to talk, and he was so full up and sleepy that he could hardly see or hear, but half dozing between his father's knees in the thin shade, trying to keep his eyes open, he could just hear the mild, lazy rumbling of their voices, and the more talkative voices of the women back in the kitchen, talking more easily, but keeping their voices low, not to wake the children, and the rattling of the dishes they were doing, and now and then their walking here or there along the floor; and mused with half-closed eyes which went in and out of focus with sleepiness, upon the slow twinkling of the millions of heavy leaves on the trees and the slow flashing of the blades of the corn, and nearer at hand, the hens dabbing in the pocked dirt yard and the ragged edge of the porch floor, and everything hung dreaming in a shining silver haze, and a long, low hill of blue silver shut off everything against a blue-white sky . . . (227–28)*

It was once said disparagingly of the conductor Bruno Walter (reputedly by Toscanini) that "when Walter comes to something beautiful he melts"; and the running butter of Agee's late music will probably never remain entirely immune to similar charges. For years, admirers of this book have been defending it against accusations of "sentimentality" by pointing out, and with justice, too, Agee's ironic, complex, and subsequently sharp-edged treatment of character.[18] But these accounts, as resourceful as they may be, will probably always fall beside the main point as long as they continue to side-step (as they have) all discussions of style and the affective life of this author's late manner of expression. One of the two main problems of *A Death in the Family*—the other is structural (those unintegrated episodes)—apparent on virtually every page, is the way alluring diffusions of image, diction, tone, and rhythm manage to drop lush scrims of silky sound between reader and situation, shoving deep into the background those very effects of irony, complexity, and reserve that defenders insist on urging into the foreground.

In this context, it's instructive to recall the author's reassurances to his sister that in writing this memoir, "he would never do anything to hurt mother and father." (In fact we know that an earlier draft of his text was more abrasive in its presentation of the relations between Mary and Jay than the one we now have.)[19] And it's hard not to understand the lingering caress of the prose—the diffusions of sound, the Rufus tone itself (e.g., the young journalist in *Famous Men* alludes to "my poor bitched family," Rufus to *"my king and my queen"*), the demure, almost maidenly rapture of it all—as also the most effective means of buffering the characters from both the author's personal demons as well as his natural bent toward a fully critical assessment of his lost past.

The truth is that *A Death in the Family* is not just a "sentimental" novel, but a fairly intoxicated one; that is to say, one profoundly *swollen* with sentiment, so much so that for the prose to suddenly turn brittle, gelid, and detached, as it never does, rather than soft, melting, and engaged, as it almost always is, would not just constitute an inconsistency, but an outright disfigurement of manner far more disturbing than any problem of "sentimentality" we now entertain. This means that while Agee's book may be deeply sentimental (if not that, not anything), it is so in an unusual sense, and with results not necessarily deleterious, but provocative and ambiguous. On the one hand, the mellifluous manner provides this book with a cohesiveness of tone and texture that acts as an aural bridge that, without effacing them, actually smooths us across the structural fissures. Consistent and diffused throughout, the sentiment forms the basis of a unified prospect, an entire world suspended in dilutions of tenderness that never quite become "sentimental" in the conventional manner; that is to say, the uniform dispersal of sentiment is never "in excess of its object," for such dispersal magnifies the object to a size where it always is, as it were, in excess of itself. On the other hand, one may question the character—the nature and quality—of this unity. As a distinct by-product of the author's aqueous ardor, I cannot help but note (and reluctantly so) a palpable diminishment of sharpness and particularity throughout virtually every scene of this late novel, and especially so in comparison with the almost holographic clarity in passage after passage of the earlier work. There persists a relative blurring of detail, a blandness of unqualified common nouns, a generality of setting and placement, and, most prickling, even when the prose is at its best, an all too genial, almost facile convergence with all things pertaining to Energy and Aura, to realms of psychic and spiritual force.

Of course I make this judgment with Agee's earlier and (to me) greater creation in mind; and perhaps only those unswerving admirers of *Famous Men* and *Agee on Film* would bother to carp at all about the assumptions and generalities in a work so obviously comfortable within its own level of power and effectiveness. Yet if the early writing matters at all, then the gradational differences between it and what came after also matter; for these late dimmings cast those earlier brilliancies into even more startling relief. The discursive manner of the younger Agee was above all an original construct of unprecedented adventure, in effect, a fluid, ever-changing organism of journey and discovery. Once a typical, long, long (too long, for some) Agee sentence began one would never know where it was going, or how or where it would end, or for that matter what surprises would turn up along the way. The sentence would be full of rare and startling diction and locution, thrilling pop-up images, rhythmic commas, mystical colons, precipitous, often devastating veerings and switch-backs, perilous pauses in obscure verbal thickets; and then usually—(for me) always in fact—sudden bursts into the clearing: and treasures of raw oxygen and paralyzing sunlight. It would be an arduously inductive sentence deeply bound up with the concrete particulars of the immediate moment; and would bear down, even fetishize, those particulars (say, the stitching in Gudger's overalls), culling their level of energy from an almost lustful penetration and exploration of fractions and joins, pushing language to that (sometimes impossible) acme where whatever continuum of the human spirit riveted word to thing would finally flush free.

In such a manner, Agee contrived to *work for* and *earn* his ecstasy, those auguries of vision and luminance. In *A Death in the Family*, the immediacy of the concrete loses its edge as it sifts through the soft-focus rubbings and erasures of memory; and details of the ordinary and familiar are deduced almost entirely from the vantage of some great Unknown—call it Divinity or Demiurge, Mystery or Childhood or the Oceanic, or simply the lèse majesté of the author himself. Whatever we call it, these deductions are neither entirely earned nor fully legitimated, but assumed a priori: the struggle ended, the search uninitiated, the journey stranded in dry dock. In summoning up the lost world of his childhood benefactors, Agee has placed himself as deep into the haunts of his heavenly hosts as his secular faith can allow; and so slips from the material to the sacred and back again as routinely as a practiced swimmer doing flip-turns. Deep in his oceanic roll (and role), drenched in the viscosity of lost time, all sentimental journeys now become contradictions in terms. With nostalgia as his rudder the novelist can lay claim to his past without ever acknowledging the prior need to discover it.

5. HOME AND THE WORLD: THE STRUCTURE OF NOSTALGIA

It was Agee's sister who gave us what remains to date the sanest clue on how to read her brother's book: "It is, after all," said Ms. Emma Agee Ling, "only a novel."[20] Amid the spoilt honeycombs of the Agee cult, however, where the hero must be portrayed as forever chasing life over art, robust men and women in actual situations as against slippery words and effete literary forms, and so on—only here could a stance as commonsensical as Ms. Ling's actually smack of heresy. Is the accuracy of her statement so self-evident that cultists chose to ignore it for fear of belaboring the blatant? Or does embracing her position and all its implications also mean thinking the unthinkable and permanently closing one door on Agee the personality and the hot fascinations of "his true story," and opening another on Agee the artist and the paler, cooler orderings of the intellectual imagination?

Will these old bones never lie still? This once let us agree to slip past the by-now obligatory and over-rehearsed tussle between life and art by arguing what is much more accurate in the matter of this author; that our two "doors" are more properly attended to as one; that in treating Agee's fiction as before all else fiction, we are not only so far from ignoring his "real life," but are in fact focusing upon the most lucid and intelligible life this author may be said to have had; and that any artist in taking the mire of himself as the measure of his art isn't of course just making his art, but making his life as well.

It is the figures and oppositions, stresses and transformations of what is, after all, "only a novel" that constitutes the living legend Agee made for himself out of the welter of his lived moments—moments that in themselves might mean anything to anyone. One thing, say, to a member of his family, another to one of his wives, another to a friend like Father Flye, another to a very different friend like Dwight Macdonald, and still another to one of his biographers. And these different constructions only mean that Agee's lived moments, like anyone's, were and will continue to be subject to the dispositions of those who have interlaced their moments with his. But if we wish to know what his moments meant to him—and if we don't, what do we think we're doing here?—let's begin to talk about those truth-making fabrications through which he organized them for himself.

This means talking about a good bit more than simply recognizing the things he invented in conjuring up characters and events from his past life. It means more, for instance, than simply enumerating the changes wrought upon his original models—such as the figures he coarsened and exaggerated, like "Ralph," or hardened and darkened, like "Andrew" and "Father Jackson," or simply softened, like "Mary." It means more, too, than simply citing persons and situations wholly imaginary, such as the family visit to the great-great-grandmother, as well as "Gran'ma" herself. Above all, talking about one's life as primarily a product of one's imagination means taking a very different tack toward everything Agee was known to have reproduced from the so-called family ledger. It means that if he attempted to reproduce something that was known or believed, or at least agreed upon, to have actually happened—say, the sequence of events in the "waiting" section leading up to and including the entrance of the "ghost"—he did so not because that was "the way it was," but because "the way it was" made some kind of artistic intelligence in terms of the expressive design by which he explained this happening as part of an invented teleology. The fact that something happened the way it did wasn't the reason why it became part of the design, but rather the prospect of the design itself insisted that that was the way it should have happened—even if it did not.

Now what is the nature of this design, how does it operate, and why?

THE TWO ORBITS

I think it is reasonably clear that in his final years Agee's interests in the plenitude and contingencies of the great world about him had shrunk considerably from those of the young northern journalist who had gone to live with sharecroppers in Alabama. He had in essence decamped from the public arena, and in the process, mellowed. His fiery commitments to the moment-by-moment exigencies of the social and historical crisis receded in tandem with his abdication from his critic's watch. The nameless, vaguely politicized struggle and defeat depicted in the final columns of the *Nation* seemed to have left him weary, but becalmed. An increased dependency on alcohol and an ever-worsening heart condition could only have further debilitated the animus generating his activist zeal. Still the "good artist," but now "dangerous" only in a vestigial sense, he was free to view his middle-class origins with a marked diminishment of that radical fury that determined much of his "pre-"—and immediate "post-"—Gudger moral and political posture. And with this relatively muted and quiescent stance went a notable winnowing of concerns. By the time he came to write the book of his childhood, the boundaries of his imagination—indeed, his whole sense of a child's being and the world in which he developed—were focused more or less exclusively by the terms and coordinates of a permanent and seemingly ubiquitous family triangle: for the most part his general intuition of the spectacle of his early development was confined to three interlocking human constellations: a mother, a father, and a child.

According to this design, the chief concerns of the child center upon and are entirely gathered up by his parents, presiding monarchs of his growth and being in the world. In turn, the chief concerns of the mother and father revolve about the child and often about each other in terms of the child's development, urging him to enter the world under the tutelage of one or the other or the combined influence of both. The concern of the parents apart from the child—say, Jay's relations to his work (or even the nature of this work), or Mary's to her activities outside the home, or their interests in each other that cannot be eventually related back to their interests in Rufus (say, their sexual identities)—are never really explored, at most merely intimated, and possess an altogether minor status within the world of the triangle. This means that the "outside" world, a world of plenitude and contingency, may enter this child's world but only in terms apposite to one side or the other of his position in the triangle. From Rufus's vantage, for instance, most of the characters, not just his parents but aunts, uncles, grandparents, friends, neighbors, and strangers, as well as most of the specific contexts enveloping these characters—everything from dwellings to commercial occupancies (home, theater, bar, farm, department store), to suburban and country landscapes (lawn, street, lot, field, road, mountains) to associated objects (bed, stove, bottle, kettle, chair, pipe, ash, car, cap, etc.)—present themselves as projections, metonyms, surrogates, or simply near relations, of either a maternal or paternal orbit.[21]

Now while Agee envisioned these two orbits as magnetically drawn to, and even intersecting, each other through a commonality of love and family aspiration, he also dramatized them as ontologically distinct realms, sharply divided, even antagonistic, through contrasting habits of living and being that determine each as virtually the polar opposite of the other. The tale that he tells then became essentially that of the two contrary orbits, a child's ceaseless oscillation between them, and the isolation, perplexity, and disarray that devolve upon the child when the most vivid and powerful representative of one of these orbits is permanently withdrawn. Certainly there can be little doubt that the author viewed these contraries as more than merely rhetorical, more, say, than simply the technical aperçù that enabled him to keep his diverse materials in focus. In fact there can be little doubt that he imagined this particular child, product of these particular contraries, as the father of the volatile, excessive, deeply divided figure central to the legend of himself he had already forged; or that about this figure, grounded in this child, there circulated a body of critical and imaginative writing which in its structural gesture bore the legacy and the burden of those particular childhood oppositions—as if the intellectual terrain itself were merely the racked impress of a ceaseless shuttle between armed encampments. Tensions between parental orbits can be seen to provide the secret charge behind most of Agee's feuding dualisms: between, for example, that of Our Lady Chapel and the Sand Cut pond, a struggle between a sanctified harness and an explosion of self-interest (in *The Morning Watch*); or between that of a northern radical's logic of political activism and a southern conservative's quasi-mystical genuflection before the crippled heirs of a "royal" patrimony (in *Famous Men*); or between that of the high church of art and the garage sale of the movies, in which a culture of elite self-consciousness attempts to equilibrate one of populist spontaneity (in *Agee on Film*). Now in *A Death in the Family* Agee creates the distinct impression of having distilled all the issues of his earlier writing, of having stalked all his far-ranging antinomies back to a single, prototypical root, "parental" in every sense—and found even this, as we might have foreseen, cloven as well.

What are the dimensions and holdings of this duality? In terms of the novel's topography, the orbit of the mother centers itself in the home, or technically in a series of domestic enclosures (e.g., rooms, porch settings, etc.). The "prologue" fixes the key signature of mothers-on-the-porch and fathers-on-the-lawn, and from this point forward, throughout all the subsequent chapters and episodes, no significant female character may be observed leaving the home unaccompanied by a male. Mary Follet, the leading exponent of this orbit, stations herself in her home throughout most of the four days covered in the chapters (kitchen, yard, and bedroom, part 1; kitchen, living room, and bedroom, part 2; bedroom, part 3), and does not leave it until the concluding sections, where leaning "very heavily" (307) on Father Jackson, she exits from the bedroom, eventually making her way to the burial service. Both the phone call that snatches Jay from the maternal nest and the call reporting his accident, as well as the retrieval of his body from the blacksmith shop, are strictly all-male affairs. During this period, Mary functions as the anxious and involuntary holding center for centripetal waves of family convergence, the stationary host for the company of first Hannah, then Catherine and Joel, then Andrew (with briefly, the neighbor Walter Starr), then, climactically, Jay's "ghost"; then on the following day, Hannah and the children, and finally Hannah and Father Jackson. Her last appearance is in the bedroom once again, but this time in her father's house, where with Aunt Amelia, she consoles her tearful daughter Catherine who has just wet herself—a final female triptych thoroughly emblematic of the maternal ambit. For the space of the mother is the bastion of domestic intimacy (bedroom) and the cradle of early childhood (wet panties); of family love, groupings, and support systems (Mary to Catherine: "Heavens and earth, have you been all *alone?*" [332, italics Agee]); of sheltering confines, nutritional comforts (food, drinks), and the healing embrace (Mary to Catherine: "Why, bless your little heart, come to mother" [332]).

But the embrace of the mother may also be a function of maternal rule—literally, home rule—part of the politics of her loving grasp inseparable from all forms of obedience and control. This means that the realm of the mother is also the center of order and orthodox authority, both social and religious; of doctrinal lessons (Mary to her children: *"God-doesn't-believe-in-the-ease-way"* [57]) harsh stricture (Hannah to Rufus: *"Take off that cap!"* [250]), and the methodology of the well-intentional martinet (Mary: *"Now you listen very carefully to me, do you hear? Say yes, if you hear?"* Rufus: *"Yes"* [106]). Of protection and overprotectedness: Mary for instance is furious with "Uncle" Ted when he fools Rufus by telling him the cheese will jump into his lap if he whistles for it; and her spirited defense of her son is, of course, that of a loving guardian, but her overemphatic delivery is also that of the humorless schoolmarm whose reactive displays of righteous indignation in even the most niggling of instances often betray the operations of a worried will made rigid with imaginary threat: *"But he's been brought up to trust older people when they tell him something. Not be suspicious of everybody. And so he trusted you. Because he likes you, Ted. Doesn't that make you ashamed?"* (246). By contrast, Jay's laconic response is tougher on Rufus, softer on Ted, and more tolerant of the whole matter: *"It was just a joke"* (246).

Here and elsewhere, the irreverence of the joke actually represents a vacation from home rule, and reveals the structures of the home—the adjudicating mother, the acquiescent child, the submission to authority, etc.—as the dour and repressive agency it can sometimes be. And the making and appreciation of the joke belongs to the orbit of the father, as do all forms of laughter; such as, the tonic and liberating roar of the crowd at the Majestic Theater; or the warm and friendly banter of the men in the bar; or even the abrasive and humiliating jibes of the older boys who corral Rufus on the block where he watches his father off to work; or the best laughter of all, shared and binding, like that which opens the first chapter and quite literally takes the child out of the home and the influence of his mother and into the streets and the arena of his father: "Well, spose we go to the picture show" (11) says Jay to his wife and son, knowing that only the latter will accompany him. This particular tease has to do with sparking Mary's repugnance for Charlie Chaplin ("that horrid little man"), another fellow who, like "Uncle" Ted, like Jay, makes jokes. Even though this one joke has become stale through repetition, Rufus feels that the laughter "cheered him" and "enclosed him with his father" (11); and most often that is where he wants to be.

The orbit of the father is the world you enter when you leave the regimen of the home and the child's enclosure in a network of family dependencies. In opposition to the domestic cluster, the paternal orbit is the realm of the independent self and of the great, seemingly limitless vistas available to the self beyond the confines of the front porch, where one can walk the streets, or go to the movies or the department store, or drive off in a car at any hour of the night. The wandering streets of the paternal world are the natural habitat of the private and discreet individual either alone or in company with other singles—say, in order to share secrets, as Jay and Andrew respectively share them with Rufus— just as the home becomes the court of the interlocking group. As against the edicts and directives of the bedroom and the kitchen table, the streets introduce you to a very different kind of education, an endless, unprocessed, disinterested torrent of knowledge and raw experience, including the scandalous image and data flow at the movies with its cascade of motion, ruckus, and geography, laughter and sexual peeping, gunsmoke and ritual death. Beyond the home is indeed the world of the undifferentiated matrix—from which social units such as the family ordering may emerge and against which they may finally define themselves—of liberation and lawlessness, the anarchic swarmlife and the natural panorama from the vacant lot to the far-away mountains, from "the pavement streaked with horse urine" (15) to the "trembling lanterns of the universe."

But there are limits to the sallies of the father, just as there are limits to the acquisitions of an independent self. These limits represent a braiding of basic human needs—urgings and longings for shelter and security, the comforts of love, warmth, and order, that act as a check upon the vagrant aspirations of the outward bound, an emotional leash extending from hearth to heart that is periodically drawn tight and pulled back as one approaches the outer edges of self-sufficiency. For the orbit of the father, so stirring with adventure, incident, information, and nature's fecundity, is also a sphere of physical hardship (death on the road), human cruelty (street bullies, spiteful jokes), shattering passions (the furor of Uncle Andrew). Above all, it is a realm of loneliness, of solitary strangers, of isolated country women staring from under the awnings of covered wagons, of an odd, even scary, dark-faced man gnawing on a turnip against a white brick wall who "looked sorrowfully, somehow dangerously, after them [Jay and Rufus]" (15).

Solitude is the dark side of the independent self, just as repression is the price exacted by a loving home. In the home you can be protected and watched over by different hands (mothers, aunts, uncles, grandparents) with the same interchangeable adult authority; pampered, caressed, and punished all at once; maybe make a rumpus and get hushed up quick; maybe cry and wet your pants; get cuddled and consoled and maybe suffocate a little in infant fealty to a collective embrace. In the streets, by contrast, you can roam wide and free; laugh and learn and stare at strangers; go anywhere; maybe make, and then lose, a pal; then find yourself alone and hungry in the dark, perishing of a homesickness so nameless, deep, and unquenchable that even the actual family ordering one has made for oneself cannot stem the tidal pull of one's longing.

"[Jay] was more lonely than the contentment of his family love could help" (19): Rufus senses that his father, in some remote but real corner of his being, is a "homesick man" (19), and that his stop at the local bar results from a thirst deeper than his need for whiskey. Searching in vain among the men for a face from his childhood home in the Powell River country, Jay eventually seeks out the vacant lot, plants his feet on "undomesticated clay," and stares off into the night "toward the deeply folded small mountains and the Powell River Valley" (20). That is why when the call comes to tend his ailing father, reluctant as he is to leave his wife and family, Jay is ready, even looking forward to make his drive north, "to give himself over entirely to the pleasures of the journey and its still undetermined but essentially grave significance" (44); ready to meet the Charon-like ferryman from the hill country, "an agent at once so near his sympathies" (46), ready to rush into the fast-fading night toward "the real, old, deep country now. Home country . . . and quite unconsciously he drove a little faster than before" (48).

Jay "unconsciously" seeks a deeper, more "ancient" and consuming matrix than the one represented by either his home, or perhaps even his father's farm (about which he hardly reflects at all). Rather, it is a mystique of primary roots and rootedness that transfixes him, and his true "pleasures of the journey" fulfill themselves in an unconscious rush toward a collective fount, a kind of universal Ur-Parent, the source and bottomless gathering pool of origination. In this manner, the drama of the contrary orbits, essentially a social and moral drama, is played out against an all-pervasive backdrop of archetype, an interpenetrating ground-bass of preconscious and transpersonal psychic energy that attempts (successfully or not) both to unify and resolve the conflicting categories of mother and father, parent and child, home and world. This Deep Home, timeless and changeless, genderless Parent-in-Nature and correspondent of the heart's solitude, takes dramatic and imagistic form in different aspects of the natural landscape, in, for instance, the mountains north of Knoxville, "the real, old, deep . . . Home country"; in certain human figures, such as the great-great-grandmother ("—*why she's almost as old as the country"* [232], exclaims Mary); and above all, in the enveloping night sky that, starting with the prologue and dominating the first two-thirds of all the chapters, not only blesses the union of father and son in the vacant lot, and caresses the faces of the parting lovers, but terrifies Rufus in his crib and enshrouds his father on the road to his death. A force both creative and destructive, nurturing and consuming, the sweeping cape of night represents both the apotheosis of Jay's independent orbit—for he characteristically dies alone, "maybe more alive than ever before" (133), imagines Andrew—as well as the ultimate collapse of this orbit, for in dying, a "homesick man" and just as characteristically homeward bound, Jay returns to the engulfing source indeed, goes all the way home at last, back to that dark mouth (as in the *"huge, ragged mouth"* of the *"darkness"*), the irrevocable kiss of the Shadow-Parent from which one fled as a child. It is of course that same black kiss from which Rufus flees when the Spirit of *"darkness,"* described as both soulmate and succubus, a kind of Knoxville Earl King, embraces him in his crib and transforms him accordingly into *"two creatures"* (85), one with an affinity for the night—*"you don't even want to get away"* (85), croons the *"darkness"*—and one, victimized and repulsed by it, who cries for his father to save him from its suffocating caress. Both Rufus and Jay are claimed by the power of the Shadows, but each according to his respective stage in life moves in a different direction in relation to it: the father, lonely in his independence, rushes home to the arms of the Dark Parent; the child, eager for selfhood, attempts to break free of this Parent's ambiguous embrace and struggles toward the equally ambiguous freedom of the world.[22]

LOVE AND BRAVERY

The characters themselves are of course richer, more complicated and resilient than the foregoing scheme, and my own structural persistence, might imply (a scheme, after all, is a scheme: a way of clarifying through omission). They are certainly larger, and, I trust, more rambunctious than the orbits in which they generally, but not exclusively, may be found. While most of the adult female characters, for example, are by and large legitimately associated with the maternal orbit and most of the comparable male characters with the opposing sphere, gender, I hasten to specify, is *not* the primary determinant in fixing character to orbit. While Mary and her mother, Catherine, and Andrew and his father, Joel, all more or less remain in their respective circles, a figure such as Aunt Hannah can travel freely between spheres. Her shopping expedition with Rufus, brilliantly conceived and navigated of course by Hannah herself, climaxes with the dramatic entry of this admirable "spinster" (i.e., another independent self), child in tow, into Harbison's "which sold clothing exclusively for men and boys . . . indeed a world most alien to women" (77). Rufus throughout is appropriately awed by the grace and efficiency of his great-aunt, and in terms of the parental dialectic, Hannah—in most instances, a champion of home rule—has every right to leave the maternal base because she can handle the streets with as much authority—albeit with greater self-consciousness (she plans the expedition like a battle campaign)—as Jay himself. In this respect, she can serve Rufus as much of an example of the paternal mode as his father.

By contrast, Father Jackson, bearing his deeply loaded and ironic designation, appears deceptively on the Follet doorstep as the characteristic solitary male, an intruder in a world of women. But regardless of his gender, Jackson immediately makes himself at home (in every sense), enthroning himself in Jay's favorite chair, and shortly after subjugates both Mary and Hannah to his overweening will, not so much because he is male (though his sexual dominion is also suggested), but primarily because in the eyes of his chastened acolytes, he incarnates almost completely the power and majesty of officialdom. In short order, Jackson becomes the grande dame of home rule and institutional sanction; and Andrew's instinctive chauvinism inverts his gender by referring to this ambiguous Father in his "stinking, swishing petticoats" (337).

It is self-reliance as against commitment to received dispensation, not male vs. female, that in most instances determines the ultimate distinction between the world of the father and that of the mother. "All his life," Agee wrote of himself (through the mask of Rufus) in his notes for this novel, "he had fiercely loathed authority and he had fiercely loved courage and mastery": and that is the crux of the domestic schism.[23] Transposing this distinction in terms of the categories we have been developing, "courage and mastery" would refer to the self-determination and sufficiency of the individual in thought and deed—as in Jay's walk with Rufus, Hannah at Harbison's, Andrew informing Jay's parents of his death and navigating Ralph's incoherence and self-pity. Similarly, "authority" would refer to the subordination of the individual to the determinations and sufficiencies of an external and shared system of value and belief; that is, orthodoxy, as in the lessons of the kitchen table, Mary and Hannah humbled before Father Jackson, the family unit as an agent of home rule in relation to Rufus and Catherine.

Agee's insistence on "courage and mastery," for instance, helps us to understand why his collateral insistence on bravery, as the most esteemed form of personal conduct, runs like a ballad refrain throughout his text (and virtually his life's work; see "Art and Bravery"). "There was never a braver man than your father" (303), neighbor Walter Starr tells the children. "What he wished was not to be reckless, but brave" (69), reflects Ralph in his alcoholic desperation. And "you don't brag about smartness if your son is brave," Rufus anxiously tells himself, qualifying his father's praise of his intelligence in deference to his own sense of timidity. It is also the lack of this privileged distinction that, in the period following Jay's death, finally determines Rufus's pained and disillusioned view of his mother's dependency on Father Jackson and church ritual (i.e., " . . . that it was something evil, to which she was submitting almost without a struggle, and by which she was deceived" [296]). When the children overhear their mother and great-aunt at their prayers, they are immediately aware of a diminished "humanity" in their elders; "their voices [Mary's and Hannah's] were more tender, more alive, and more inhuman, than they [Rufus and Catherine] had ever had them before; and this remoteness from humanity troubled them" (298). They also feel personally slighted, " . . . that this [prayer] meant more to their mother and great-aunt than they did" (298). And finally they sense a specific moral and emotional submissiveness to alien enforcement in their mother, and by inference, one adds, a falling away from those very qualities of "courage and mastery" that anyone (and Mary above all) who knew their father would unhesitatingly attribute to him: "But now she [Mary] was wholly defeated and entranced, and the transition to prayer was the moment and mark of her surrender" (298).

Agee's professed loathing of "authority" should also help provide us with the means necessary to effectively dispose of one of the reigning canards about this book, that major male figures such as Jay and Andrew are deep-dyed nonbelievers, and in this respect completely immune to religious impulse.[24] Actually, Jay's and Andrew's alleged isolation from faith can be measured almost entirely by their distance from church orthodoxy, not from any insensitivity to spiritual vibration. Though each may consciously define himself as agnostic—Andrew aggressively so, Jay actually defined as such by others—neither is without his intimations of transcendence, of ordinary life as fraught with mystery and miracle. It is Andrew, for instance, who is keenly aware of the strange "energy" circulating about Jay's corpse in the blacksmith shop; and it is to Andrew, not Mary or Hannah, that Agee allows the pivotal vision of the butterfly and the equally vital awareness of its supernal significance. "That butterfly has got more of God in him," says this self-confessed agnostic to an entranced Rufus, "than Jackson will ever see for the rest of eternity" (337). We further learn in the italicized passages that Jay too has his own brand of faith, very different from Mary's but thoroughly typical of the paternal orbit's epical and highly unorthodox reach, and in all likelihood not far removed from what Agee once described as his "own shapeless personal religious sense,"[25] a subrational, half-visionary intuition of the self as part of a swarming family declension, that *"maybe"* (Jay's word) originates in Deity, a mystique of generational continuity linking parent to child in a vast "chain of flesh" regressing infinitely back through human time and culminating at the dawn of Myth and a tentative glimpse of the God of Origins and his offspring. All this comes to Jay deep in the night as he watches over Rufus in his crib, his hand resting on his son's forehead:

> *A great cedar, and the colors of limestone and of clay; the smell of wood smoke and, in the deep orange light of the lamp, the silent logs of the walls, his mother's face, her ridged hand mild on his forehead:* Don't you fret, Jay, don't you fret. *And before his time, before even he was dreamed of in this world, she must have lain under the hand of her mother or her father and they in their childhood under other hands, away on back through the mountains, away on back through the years, it took you right on back as far as you could ever imagine, right on back to Adam, only no one did it for him; or maybe did God?* (94)

Jay's faith in the family chain incorporates his mother and the entire Follet lineage as part of his living present. His union with Rufus—in the laying on of hands (a homespun version of apostolic succession)—resurrects a lost past, another variant of the "real, old, deep . . . Home country" (the log cabin, etc.), and the mother young once more. The logic of the passage is such that we realize that what Jay does for his mother, Rufus may someday do for him. Further, Jay's devotion to his family combined with his authority in the streets, his matchless example of both love *and* bravery, provide Rufus with a sense of seamless continuity between the contrary orbits, between home and world, the sufficient self and the family regimen. Such continuity exists at least as long as Jay himself exists to ratify it. With his father as guide, Rufus can leave the home against the doubts of his mother, engage in a little boy's version of grown-up and even seditious activity—as observer of, and pupil to, William S. Hart's violence, Chaplin's sexuality, the secrets of the father, etc.—and sleep soundly in the home once more without tint of guilt or shame: the entire journey, both the going away and the coming back, the ceaseless pendulum of desire from merger to separation and back again, and forever throughout the lifetime of the heart, sanctioned by one man and his immediate rapport with his son. In spite of Rufus's awareness of minor strains of tension and slippage in the home, he also feels "that there was really no division, no estrangement, or none so strong, anyhow, that it could mean much, by comparison with the unity that was so firm and assured, here" (19).

THE THREE WALKS

All this while Jay lives. But after his initial walk with his father, Rufus goes on three subsequent walks—with his Great-Aunt Hannah, by himself, and finally with Uncle Andrew—each designed to show his growing sense of independence and maturity. The first indicates an advancement of personal taste (i.e., aesthetic choice) when he picks out a cap for himself on the shopping trip with Hannah; the second, an effort in self-reliance when he sneaks out of the house alone the morning after his father's death to tell the boys on the block about the accident; and the third, a sophistication of moral judgment, when on his concluding walk with Uncle Andrew, he makes a critical assessment of Andrew himself, an adult he both fears and admires. Each walk also, and on a scale of increasing significance, represents a defiance of the maternal principle and an attempt to move closer to the sufficiency of the father. The cap he selects from Harbison's—"a thunderous fleecy check in jade green," his face "all but lost" beneath "the great scoop visor" is a comic emblem of goofy self-importance and overreaching machismo. ("Mary would have conniption fits" [78], Hannah reflects.) And when he joins the boys on the block, he does so in specific disobedience of Hannah's directive not to leave the home. In the final walk with Andrew, rebellion against maternal orthodoxy tears into the open, the domestic fabric irrevocably shredded, as in shocked disbelief, Rufus listens to Andrew fulminate bitterly against Father Jackson, Hannah, and "Mama."

But Jay of course is absent from all three of these significant journeys (for the last two, he is already dead); and without the sanction of his presence his son's movements to and from the home become increasingly fretted with pain and doubt. As Rufus's sense of independence and defiance evolve, so too does his sense of guilt, confusion, and isolation. His acquisition of the new cap, for instance, results in failure—i.e., essentially a rejection of his choice—when he runs to his parents' bedroom hoping to show his selection to Jay, only to be greeted by the coauthor of its purchase (Hannah) and the command, *"Take off that cap!"* Rufus removes the cap and that ends the matter. Angered and incensed by this adult turn-about—Jay's absence, his mother's inaccessibility, Hannah's "betrayal"—he sneaks out of the house hoping to recoup his losses and exploit his novel family situation among his (almost) peers. But this new enterprise only ends in shame and contrition, as the older boys respond by attempting to tarnish Jay's image (saying he was "drunk" [271], "crazy as a loon" [273], etc.). Rufus returns home filled with remorse, and imagines his father's "soul" sitting in judgment of him, "and that was the worst of anything because there was no way to hide from a soul, and no way to talk to it, either" (280). He particularly remembers telling a stranger in the streets the news of Jay's accident and receiving a friendly but firm admonishment, "How would your Daddy like it, you out here telling strangers how he's dead?" (267). As Rufus views it, he's been caught out bragging again ("Don't you brag"), and once more chastises himself for his lack of true bravery—"Showing off because he's dead, that's all you can show off about" (280)—and ends by performing an act of penitence and licking the ash from his father's pipe tobacco: "His tongue tasted of darkness" (281).

Rufus's guilty befuddlement here is mirrored by the deracination of virtually all the major characters throughout part 3, a vision of a family in disheveled transition. By the end of part 1, we had the sense of a child's world as a fusion of opposites, that is, self-development and individuation founded upon a cushion of domestic bonding; by the end of part 3, that fusion has been replaced by a sense of unappeasable fractures and schisms, such as a child's self-development curdled by a reflex of self-abasement, or the principle of unity reduced to an important but fleeting secondhand glimpse of a giant butterfly flashing from the shadowed grave into the glare of the sun, the last remnant of paternal dazzle, a god in absentia. In four short days, most of the familiar character couplings and alliances have either reshuffled or come irrevocably apart. Resentments flare from every quarter; Rufus and Catherine against Father Jackson; later both children against Mary; Andrew against the whole orthodox wing of the family.

As against the lyricism of part 1 and the intense drama of part 2, the mood and texture of the final section is relatively flat, blunt, and benumbed, the prose tending toward reportage, enumerations, and lists. As the cast of characters bulges and spreads, relatives, neighbors, strangers, and interlopers from the "outside" enter the now stunned and shattered family triangle, awkwardly, sometimes wretchedly, attempting to simulate the missing side. Comfort and sustenance now must be garnered from relative "outsiders," as the kindly neighbor Walter Starr becomes in the eyes of the children their father's most heartfelt eulogist, while upstairs Father Jackson denies the unbaptized dead man the right to a full Christian burial service. When Mary embraces Rufus and Catherine after the funeral and a nearly two-day absence, the children are keenly aware that "everything had changed. They put their hands against her, still knowing that nothing would ever be the same again, and she caught them so close they could smell her, and they loved her, but it made no difference" (325). Rufus explicitly rejects Mary's orthodox interpretation of his father's death, knows "the cotter pin" and not God took him away, recites his prayers mechanically and indifferently, stiffens at Father Jackson's proffered consolations, etc. But out of love and commiseration for his mother, he feigns a piety and sympathy for her own view of her situation that he does not feel. Ignorant of the deception, Mary sees only her son's "understanding" of her plight, and in this "absolute moment" (236) offers him the preference of her gratitude—and in so doing, deeply offends his sister Catherine: "There they stayed quiet, the deceived mother, the false son, the fatally wounded daughter" (326). In the wake of Jay's death and family realignments, this is the new triangle that has formed, not a union, but an anomaly of hurt, misunderstanding, and bad faith. It is exactly at this point that Uncle Andrew appears and invites Rufus to join him in a walk ("Come for a walk with me" [326]).

This fourth and final walk is of course meant to be compared with the first, just as Andrew is meant to be compared with Jay, and in general we are right to read the comparison as a way of measuring the losses Rufus must sustain in respect to the paternal orbit. Strictly speaking, what Rufus feels for Andrew is incomparable to what he felt for his father; the advantage in almost every respect of course resides with Jay. Yet at the same time no reader should disvalue the importance, the sheer formidability, of Andrew himself, or the significance of his central role in this final walk. Surrounded by decent, well-intentioned, and generally "soft" figures, Uncle Andrew glows with a special ferocity of will denied the others. Even more than Jay, he is the most fearless and independent of the paternal figures ("*God, if you exist, come here and let me spit in Your face*" [166, italics Agee]). If "courage and mastery," both the example and the acquisition of them, matter to Rufus—and of course, they do—then Andrew matters too. And coming upon his recent sense of estrangement from his only living parent, Rufus is especially pleased to accept his uncle's invitation; "He felt honored, and worked hard to keep up with him" (333). For on this last and decisive stroll into the world, Andrew offers Rufus the only real consolation philosophy for his father's death that (inasmuch as we learn of it) actually seems to strike home. This of course resides in his recounting of the butterfly incident that in the light of everything Agee came to believe, a well as by its significant position in the narrative, will be for Rufus the germ of a new "shapeless

personal" dispensation, the seed of a secular faith, to replace the received
and "heavenly" one that he has only just begun to doubt:[26]

> "There were a lot of clouds," his uncle said, and continued to
> look straight before him, "but they were blowing fast, so there was
> a lot of sunshine too. Right when they began to lower your father
> into the ground, into his grave, a cloud came over and there was a
> shadow just like iron, and a perfectly magnificent butterfly settled
> on the—coffin, just rested there, right over the breast, and stayed
> there, just barely making his wings breathe, like a heart."
> Andrew stopped and for the first time looked at Rufus. His eyes
> were desperate. "He stayed there all the way down, Rufus," he said.
> "He never stirred, except just to move his wings that way, until it
> grated against the bottom like a—rowboat. And just when it did
> the sun came out just dazzling bright and he flew up out of that—
> hole in the ground, straight up into the sky, so high I couldn't even
> see him any more." He began to climb the hill again, and Rufus
> worked hard again to stay abreast of him. "Don't you think that's
> wonderful, Rufus?" he said, again looking straight and despairingly
> before him.
> "Yes," Rufus said, now that his uncle really was asking him. "Yes,"
> he was sure was not enough, but it was all he could say. (334–35)

Here Andrew speaks to Rufus not just from a post of "courage and
mastery" and adult vantage, but equally in his formal capacity as an
artist (he is a painter, a poet in his youth, etc.)—indeed, the only such
figure in the text—and his vision of the butterfly connotes not just a
metaphorical version of the spirit's resurrection, nor simply a notion of
renewal in nature (though both concepts are entailed in his account),
but more precisely, a sense of the power and the grace, the aesthetic
perfection, still available in the living world outside the home even after
so much power and grace have been taken from it when Jay himself
was taken from it. Of all the characters it is given only to Andrew to
comment upon the personal beauty of Jay's physical presence; "He had,"
he tells Mary, "the most magnificent physique I've ever seen in a human
being" (174). And here in the vision of the butterfly, Andrew evinces, if
nothing else, the qualities of an artist in the Ageean mold, not primarily
either a maker or a self-confessor, or perhaps least of all a prophet—
though the effects of his vision on Rufus's potential evolution, spiritual,

vocational, and otherwise, can hardly be ignored—but before all else, a man who sees, an ardent and independent eye, a point of focus and attentiveness (e.g., the coffin "grated on the bottom like a rowboat"), and who now, like Jay himself, provides Rufus with a sense of the natural visual field as an occasion for wonder and possibility. Even in the midst of his sorrow, Rufus finds this vision "magnificent" and "miraculous" (half guessing at the meaning of these words), and even though he must now live in the world without his father, his uncle's recounting of the incident seems to make the world itself "all right"—for him, for Andrew, and even for Jay; "it was almost as if he [Rufus] had been there and seen it with his own eyes, and seen the butterfly, which showed that even for his father, it was all right. It was all right and he felt as his uncle did" (336).

But while Rufus is ready and glad to accept his uncle's vision of the world—almost literally a vision of Jay in animistic survival—he cannot, much to his own dismay, accept Andrew himself—just as conversely at home, he is eager to accept his mother, but not her professions of faith. No sooner does Andrew finish the account of the butterfly, than he launches into a violent attack upon Father Jackson and those members of his family obedient to religious practice (i.e., "prayers"). While Andrew can make the world "all right" to be in, he cannot make being itself "all right" if being means being someone like Andrew—a man whose vision is inseparable from intolerance and contempt for those whose way of being in the world is different from his own. Andrew, like Jay, has found a way of taking pleasure in the beauty and freedom of ordinary existence outside the home, but unlike Jay, cannot find his way back into the home, as the independence of his position isolates him in hate from people that he also obviously loves. "He doesn't hate them," Rufus thinks, "he loves them, just as much as they love him. But he hates them too" (338). He hates "all of them," not just Father Jackson, but "mother" and "Aunt Hannah too" for all their "bowing and scraping and hocus-pocus and things like that" (338); "because he hates prayers. And them too for saying them" (339). And while Rufus has already begun to share some of Andrew's disdain for orthodox "authority"—"He did not like Father Jackson and he wished his mother did not like him either" (337–38)—

he does not share Andrew's contempt for the people who embrace it; ". . . but I don't hate them, I love them . . ." Rufus wants to accept Andrew's secret, but "not if he hates" his mother and his great-aunt. So Rufus balks, hesitates to accept the world as it is now presented to him by his uncle.

Andrew has exposed Rufus to the full blast of his ambivalence ("like opening a furnace door") and so underscored some of Rufus's own ambivalence, and shown him what being in the world can really mean now that his real father is no longer around to make being in it seem "all right." In so doing, he has also exposed Rufus to the dangerous deficiencies in the paternal orbit itself by pushing the principle of independence to its bitter extremity, that point where "courage and mastery" shades off into a vainglory that views every version of self-abnegation as weakness ("all that bowing and scraping and hocus-pocus"), as a betrayal of the integral self. In this extremity, Andrew also represents the antitype of Rufus's other uncle, Jay's weak and alcoholic brother, Ralph. Just as the one uncle reveals the perils of a total repudiation of the maternal orbit, a vengeful pride that reveals one frozen in a kind of rictus of self-regard, so too does the other uncle reveal the dangers of total dependency upon the domestic nest. Ralph knows, if anyone does, what it means to live one's adult life without bravery as the "baby" of the family: "And he [Ralph] lived so near at hand [to his family] because he had no courage, no intelligence, no energy, no independence. That was really it: no independence. He always needed to be near. He always needed to feel their support, their company, very near him" (68).

These then are the outer edges of Rufus's quandary: the two uncles, a storm of aggression against a swamp of self-pity, the two sides of a sadomasochistic coin and each side bearing the head of the mother-in-her-circle-of-control, the Scylla and Charybdis through which Rufus must sail the skiff of his child's identity. And who will show him how to navigate? The streets are now walked by a brave man, deficient in love; the home now ruled by a loving woman, deficient in bravery. In the former there is a faith to be embraced (i.e., the vision of the butterfly), but not a priest worthy of embracing it; in the latter, there is a loving priestess bedazzled by false idols. He cannot enter the world he admires without guilt if such entry means isolating the self in hatred from the people he loves; nor can he enter the home of the people he loves without shame if such entry means humiliating the self in its journey toward sufficiency. Both orbits then are equally alluring, equally troubled; the great world offering power and beauty, the home, a moral order founded on love. Without morality, however, power and beauty turn cruel and vain (recall the serpent of *The Morning Watch*); without power and beauty, morality withers and simpers (recall Our Lady Chapel of *The Morning Watch*). Until the home and the world fuse once more the energies of the street will be devoid of warmth and generosity, the virtues of the home barren of grace and vitality. In unifying them, Jay was able to complete each orbit with qualities of the other. But without Jay, Rufus's position is precisely that of a "norphan" suspended between alternatives, fully comfortable in neither home nor world; heir to a doctrine of contraries, self-consciousness, and isolation; an expert in subterfuge (he must now keep his real feelings about Uncle Andrew and "Mama" to himself); alternately strong and weak, man and boy, fiercely ambitious yet cringing in self-abuse, both the child who never really got away and the man who never really came back (i.e., came all the way home); a representative modernist coming of age in a representative instance of crisis and duress.

6. CODA: ALL THE WAY HOME, SORT OF

This then, for me, is the ending as we now have it, neither resolved nor uplifting, and surely leaving many readers, like Rufus, mournful and perplexed. But not, I must add, devastated. The nostalgic tone and the murmurous fluency of the prose, etc., make even the ending seem less anxious than it really may be. It is indeed sad and wistful, but not dire, not even tragic; the new family situation is unsettled and fretted, but not obliterated; the new role models, flawed, more conflicted than the old ones, but not malevolent. We all grow up a bit crooked—duality and paradox, internal strife and mirages of otherworldly perfection, criticism and self-doubt at the midnight hour; our common lot as contemporaries in a post-nuclear moment. Who would have thought it otherwise? Perhaps only an American.

And if by pushing our sanguinary impulse a bit harder we wish to read the material in the chapters in light of the material in the italicized passages—and perform the act of integration that Agee may have wanted, but never lived to accomplish—we may emerge with another perspective entirely and even mitigate some of the sorrow and the wistfulness.[27] Throughout these sumptuous vignettes, the grief of the individual (the loss of childhood, death itself) is generally subsumed by a vision of family continuity and generational recognition. This latter occurs through an act of consciousness, actually a leap of memory and imagination, in which the individual realizes himself as part of a vast and possibly endless lifeline that persists as long as the generations themselves persist; that is, as long as one has children to release that burst of memory and imagination, and restore one to the lost child and childhood in oneself: *"You have a boy or a girl of your own,"* reflects Jay over the sleeping Rufus, *"and now and then you remember, and you know how they feel, and it's almost the same as if you were your own self again, as young as you could remember"* (94). A flash of understanding between the generations ignites the link and charges the continuity that blurs the distinction between parent and child, youth and age, the dead past and the living present. Rufus, for instance, cannot make contact with his "one hundred and three or one hundred and four years old" great-great-grandmother merely by reciting his name, but when, at his father's urging, he redefines himself in terms of the family declension—*"I'm Jay's boy Rufus"* (240)— and kisses the ancient crone as silent as the grave, the connection is made; "Gran'ma" comes back to life, the withered witch reborn as a gurgling infant (*"as young as you could remember"*), grinning, and wetting herself with excitement. She *"smiled and smiled, and cocked her head to one side, and with sudden love he kissed her again"* (240). Generational recognition represents a vision wherein the singular personality with his singular turmoil (e.g., the conflict between "authority" and "courage and mastery") is subsumed entirely in the transcendent and inexorable dance of genetics, a mystique of biochemical typing in which one's transpersonal destiny as part of a potentially infinite "chain of flesh" supersedes one's individual fate as merely mortal.

But the visit to the great-great-grandmother, along with Jay's night-time meditation over Rufus, as well as everything else in italics, have not been expressively calibrated with the chapters (see "Intestate"). In the present arrangement, we are most likely to understand the italicized material as representing a vision of family unity that exists *before* Jay's death, not one that persists after it. Agee may very well have imagined a structure in which individual loss would be compensated by generational survival, but of course he did not live long enough to give his book that form or any other that could be called fully realized or entirely satisfactory.

And why not? Not a superfluous query, after all. Commentators have speculated that Agee had time enough to finish his novel had he wanted to, that he may have allowed a plethora of other interests to intervene between himself and his book: screenwriting, alcohol, masochistic indulgence, etc.[28] Perhaps there are other reasons as well. Certainly finishing for any professional writer would also mean publication, and publication for this one professional would just as certainly mean airing his family business in public; and Agee would certainly be self-reflexive enough, and above all writers hard enough on himself, not to be deceived about how easily homage could devolve into a covert form of exploitation. Wouldn't all those thousands upon thousands of words represent to the child's heart in him just another version—a consummate and epical version, to be sure—of a little boy's boast ("What was bragging? It was bad," 15)? "How would your Daddy like it," a stranger chastises Rufus, "you out here telling strangers how he's dead?" And how would this family-obsessed writer really like it, sharing his parents with strangers? Perhaps he would want to keep them to himself a bit longer—and longer still. Wouldn't keeping his work unfinished and "in progress" also mean keeping the subject alive, keeping the links in the family "chain" between past and present, fact and memory, warm, flowing, and current, and finally give him more time to remember, and more to remember? Having finally near the close of life resurrected the sources of his childhood—the home, the parental nexus, the hands of the father, the voice of the mother, the rapturous oblivion of the evening shadows—it is not so unnatural to assume that he might have wanted to *hesitate* just one more time, to linger about and wander amid "the texture of time" (Nabokov's phrase) as long as humanly possible.[29] So James Rufus Agee hung on. Not to his life, of course—that badly abused, vastly overscrutinized, finally piddling, and very mere mortality. But to a different fate altogether—a continuation of the "chain of flesh" but in unprecedented form—to the open, unfinished, quickening, thriving, everafter life of his book. Perhaps only the example of his father—or at least the legend of his father as he had fashioned it—could have necessarily countenanced this final retention: there was a kind bravery in it after all.

NOTES

CHAPTER ONE. **INTRODUCTION**

1. The publisher's blurb for the Morrow Paperback edition of Geneviéve Moreau's *The Restless Journey of James Agee,* a popular distortion of this artist and his work that twists even further as it continues: "In a very real sense, Agee's life was his most successful artistic creation, for although he had recognized very early his vocation as a writer and perused that vocation vigorously and with great devotion, in the end he left many unfinished projects and only a few works of any note." A more accurate and intelligent assessment of the situation is the following: "Some writers, among them James Agee, most certainly, make of their lives compelling dramatic presentations—companion pieces to what they have written. We readers end up contemplating not only essays, poems, stories, but the way a particular writer chose to spend his or her time on earth. Sometimes, as in Agee's case, the life becomes a legend, shadowing or even thoroughly overshadowing even a significant body of literary work." Robert Coles in Ross Spears and Jude Cassidy, eds., *Agee: His Life Remembered,* 3.

2. "By the year's end [*Let Us Now Praise Famous Men*] sold only 600 copies." Lawrence Bergreen, *James Agee: A Life,* 260.

3. Quoted in Spears and Cassidy, eds., *Agee: His Life Remembered,* 178.

4. Much of the early published reminiscence is gathered in David Madden, ed., *Remembering James Agee.* Many of the first Ageeans (Father Flye, Robert Saudek, Dwight Macdonald, Robert Fitzgerald, Walker Evans, John Huston, David McDowell, et al.) are interviewed in *Agee: His Life Remembered;* some of this material also appears in the documentary film *Agee* (1979) by Ross Spears and Jude Cassidy, along with other interviews (e.g., former President Jimmy Carter). See also F. W. Dupee's "Memories of James Agee" in *The King of the Cats and Other Remarks on Writers and Writing,* 74–78; Alfred Kazin's *New York Jew* (New York, 1978), 53–59; John Huston's *An Open Book,* 187–90. The most recent published recollection appears to be John Hersey's "Agee," *New Yorker* (July 18, 1988): 72–82.

5. Fitzgerald and MacDonald are both collected in Madden, ed., *Remembering James Agee,* 35–94, 119–44 respectively; Fitzgerald's "A Memoir" also appears in

The Collected Short Prose of James Agee, and Macdonald's "Jim Agee, A Memoir" in *Against the American Grain: Essays on the Effects of Mass Culture,* 143–62; see also "Agee and the Movies" in *Dwight Macdonald on Movies,* 4–14. Coles's "narrative" appears in Spears and Cassidy, eds., *Agee: His Life Remembered,* 3–13, 79–102, 122–33, 181–84; and writing on *A Death in the Family* in *Irony in the Mind's Life: Essays on Novels by James Agee, Elisabeth Bowen, and George Eliot,* 56–106.

    6. Dwight Macdonald quoted in Bergreen, *James Agee: A Life,* 255.

    7. John Huston, "Foreword," *Agee on Film: Five Film Scripts by James Agee,* ix–x; also in Madden, ed., *Remembering Agee,* 145–47. Subsequent references to this edition of *Agee on Film* will appear in the text.

    8. His comments on the collaboration in *An Open Book* (188–90) remain essentially anecdotal, misty-eyed ("James Agee was a Poet of Truth," etc.), and noncritical.

    9. James Dickey, quoted on dust jacket of Bergreen, *James Agee: A Life.*

    10. Blurb for the Bantam paperback edition of *Letters of James Agee to Father Flye* (New York, 1963); see also blurb for Bantam paperback edition of *A Death in the Family* (New York, 1980).

    11. Dwight Macdonald, in Madden, ed., *Remembering James Agee,* 138.

    12. The four books with sustained critical treatments are Peter Ohlin, *Agee;* Kenneth Seib, *James Agee: Promise and Fulfillment;* Alfred T. Barson, *A Way of Seeing: A Critical Study of James Agee;* Victor A. Kramer, *James Agee.* Of these, I find Peter Ohlin's treatment to be the most lucid and sensible. There is also a good forty-seven-page monograph by Erling Larsen, *James Agee* (Minneapolis, 1971). Better still, however, I recommend the following special studies of individual books: On *Let Us Now Praise Famous Men,* William Stott, *Documentary Expression and Thirties America,* 261–314; Richard King, *A Southern Renaissance: The Cultural Awakening of the American South, 1930–55,* 204–31, the best single study of this book. On *A Death in the Family,* Coles's *Irony in the Mind's Life,* a loving and ruminative appreciation. On *Agee on Film,* Manny Farber, *Movies,* 84–88; William S. Pechter, *Twenty-Four Times a Second: Films and Filmmakers,* 261–75, an often negative assessment more stimulating than most positive ones.

    Recently, another critical study has appeared, the first in almost two decades; fortunately, it is a useful one. James Lowe's *The Creative Process of James Agee* treats his subject as artist, not as cultural phenomenon, and successfully pursues a pattern of "disparateness" and "unity" through the early prose and poetry, and then at much greater and more revealing length in *Famous Men.* Oddly, much shorter shrift is given to *The Morning Watch* and *A Death in the Family;* more oddly, the film criticism gets only a single reference.

The remaining six books are Moreau's *The Restless Journey of James Agee;* Bergreen's *James Agee: A Life;* Madden, ed., *Remembering James Agee;* Spears and Cassidy, eds., *Agee: His Life Remembered;* Joel Agee, *Twelve Years: An American Boyhood in East Germany;* and Mark F. Doty, *Tell Me Who I Am: James Agee's Search for Selfhood.*

13. To date, my own research has uncovered only *The Harper American Literature,* vol. 2 (New York, 1987), 1784–95, which excerpts from *Let Us Now Praise Famous Men.*

14. This aptly chosen adjective belongs to Robert Coles: "This is a modest novel, not a family saga, not a book of social criticism made to fit the demands of fiction." *Irony in the Mind's Life,* 67.

15. "A Mother's Tale," mostly faux-naif fakery. Some critics admire the fact that all those talking cows don't exhibit any cow traits (Ohlin, *Agee,* 176). I'm bothered by that, and also by the fact that they don't exhibit any persuasively human ones either; throughout I'm equally bothered by the lack of local and concrete detail, which drains the allegory of body and vigor. For a successful welding of animal fact and human symbol see Tolstoy's "Strider: The Story of a Horse." My objections to the screenplays as a group appear in chapter 5.

16. This bias includes a reluctance to pursue my subject in terms of what is promiscuously and inaccurately referred to nowadays as "Theory." It is one of the many dispiriting features of the current climate in the academic community that when one speaks of "Theory" one often means only one kind of "Theory," and that is of course "French theory" (more periphrasis) and not abstract speculation in general. And while this book contains a good deal of the latter—particularly in chapters 2 and 3, much of it home-brewed, some of it inspired by popular models established by such non-Gallic practitioners as Freud, Jung, Klein, etc.— there is little or nothing here that makes use of the writings or Anglo-derivatives of Lacan, Foucault, Derrida, et al. This has been done deliberately because I find it impossible to appropriate this sort of discourse without also drawing upon the language—the terms, methodology, etc.—of such discourse, and that means drawing upon the language of a cabal, hermetically sealed, jargon-ridden, and opaque. More important, I find most French and French-derived maneuvering deeply impractical for my purposes, virtually useless in analyzing and evaluating a writer's writing. Such discourse, in spite of its frequent intent, usually ends up summoning a writer's writing only to illuminate and elaborate, and finally confirm, the discourse itself. Since my own approach to Agee reverses these priorities (i.e., employing the discourse only to elucidate the writing), and rather than spend many pages defending this approach as well as questioning the tenets of the opposition party—which would have resulted in another and very different kind of book—I have decided, save for these remarks, to circumvent

the matter of "French theory" altogether. Perhaps what I find most depressing, however, is the fact that the hegemony of the "Theory" Establishment in the American university has become so seemingly absolute that one feels politically compelled to squander one's energy by composing tedious, and what ought to be superfluous, declarations such as this one in order to navigate around it.

17. On *Famous Men*, for instance: "Agee is not writing fiction but fact; his emphasis is on the mystery, not the evocation of what is" (Barson, *A Way of Seeing*, 100); or on Agee in general: "The following pages will focus on the works themselves, with particular attention given to the aesthetic problems confronting Agee in his absolute commitment to the holiness of human reality" (Ohlin, *Agee*, 11).

CHAPTER TWO. **TALES OF THE SELF**

1. Walt Whitman, "Song of Myself," from *Leaves of Grass* in *Walt Whitman, Complete Poetry and Selected Prose,* edited by James E. Miller (Boston, 1959), 41. Henry Adams, *The Education of Henry Adams: An Autobiography* (Boston, 1961), 109. Ernest Hemingway, "Soldier's Home," from *In Our Time* (New York, 1958), 98.

2. James Agee, *A Death in the Family,* 271–72. Subsequent references to this edition will appear in the text.

3. The foregoing three paragraphs present a rough scheme of Rufus's relations with his parents in *A Death in the Family.* Much of it, however, is also confirmed by the Agee biography. Here, for instance, is Bergreen: "Of course he learned to ally himself with both his parents, but the impossibility of reconciling their divergent temperaments left him in a continual state of unease and hypersensitivity to every undercurrent of tension in the household." *James Agee: A Life,* 11.

4. Richard King also cites this retrieval as a main reason for Agee's journey south in *Let Us Now Praise Famous Men*: "The process of recalling his Alabama experience was a way to return to his own childhood . . . What he sought, then, was a recovery of that period before the death of his father, before the fall into time, awareness, and estrangement." *A Southern Renaissance,* 212–13.

5. James Agee, *Let Us Now Praise Famous Men,* 415. Subsequent references to this edition will appear in the text. James Joyce, *Ulysses* (New York, 1961), 213. Recently, film historians have questioned Agee's "biographical-psychological" interpretation of the Sturges persona: "What Agee took as the Sturges facts were at least partly a self-made myth [by Sturges himself] . . . [Agee's interpretation] has become that most insidious of critical phenomena—an interpretation that is later taken as fact." Brian Henderson, "Introduction" to *Five Screenplays by*

Preston Sturges (Berkeley, 1985), 24. James Agee, *Agee on Film: Reviews and Comments,* 116–17. Subsequent references to this edition will appear in the text.

6. "His father was the nurturing one," says Bergreen, "his mother the disciplinarian . . . Other little boys cried for their mothers; James cried for his father." *James Agee: A Life,* 11.

7. *The Apocrypha,* Ecclesiasticus, chap. 44. James Agee, *The Morning Watch,* 108; subsequent references to this edition will appear in the text. Agee's "Plans for work: October, 1937" include the following: "Conjectures of how to get 'art' back on the plane of organic human necessity, parallel to religious art or the art of primitive hunters." In *The Collected Short Prose of James Agee,* 132.

8. "The artist's task is not to alter the world as the eye sees it into a world of aesthetic reality, but to perceive the aesthetic reality within the actual, and to make a faithful and undisturbed record of the instant in which this moment of creativeness achieves its most expressive crystallization." James Agee, *A Way of Seeing,* introduction to photographs by Helen Levitt (New York, 1965), vi.

9. Quoted in "Memories of James Agee" from Dupee, *The King of the Cats,* 75.

10. As I write this, I'm reminded of how Agee's first wife, Olivia Saunders Wood, once described their life together: "He'd bang his head on the wall and say 'I'm no good' and that sort of thing. He talked a little about suicide, enough so that I thought, well, he won't ever do that . . . I learned how to make scenes from Jim, because I was brought up not to cry and not to get angry and all that. So I thought, if Jim's going to do it, I'll do it, too. So we'd have scenes and we'd both feel a great deal better." Quoted by Spears and Cassidy in *Agee: His Life Remembered,* 53.

11. "My trouble is, such a subject cannot be seriously looked at without intensifying itself toward a centre which is beyond what I, or anyone else, is capable of writing of: the whole problem of existence . . . If I could make it what it ought to be made I would not be human." Agee to Father James Flye (August 12, 1938), *Letters of James Agee to Father Flye,* 104–5.

12. "Following the unfathomable death of her husband, James's mother sank into the arms of the church . . . For James it was a lonely, empty period. He resented his mother's piety and remoteness, especially at Christmas time." Bergreen, *James Agee: A Life,* 20–21.

13. Agee's work notes on *A Death in the Family,* quoted by Doty in *Tell Me Who I Am,* 105. Rufus thinks, "You don't brag about smartness if your son is brave." *Death in the Family,* 24.

14. From "Fellow-Traveler" in *The Collected Poems of James Agee,* 144.

15. Bergreen, *James Agee: A Life,* 21–23.

16. Sometimes, particularly when the severance is not enforced, but seems to be self-willed, the grieving child may envision an equally grieving parent; that is, for every abandoned child seeking strength, protection, and tutelage from the past, there also exists the possibility of an abandoned parent seeking regeneration and futurity in the recognition and memorials of the departed child (e.g., Rufus kissing his ancient and immobile great-great-grandmother enacts an acknowledgment of kinship that stirs her to life and reciprocation).

17. Letter to Father Flye (May 4, 1949), in *The Letters of James Agee to Father Flye*, 178.

CHAPTER THREE. **A FANTASIA OF THE ACTUAL**

1. Lionel Trilling, "Greatness with One Fault in It," *Kenyon Review* 4 (winter 1942): 99–102. Alfred Kazin, "A Wounded Life, A Father Perfect in Death," *New York Times Book Review* (June 29, 1986), 3.

2. I should remind the reader that the capitalization of "Actual" and its variants "Actuality" and (even) "Actualism"—all of which appear regularly in the subsequent argument—represent my own devices and not Agee's usage: the author always presents the first two terms in lower case and the third not at all. "Actualism" is entirely my own invention employed to summarize Agee's aesthetic attitudes and homemade recipes for language and reality (most of which appear in "On the Porch: 2").

3. Fitzgerald is quoted by Spears and Cassidy in *Agee: His Life Remembered*, 56. Agee to Father James Flye (June 18, 1936), *Letters*, 92.

4. Such books might include proposals for the care and feeding of babies, or flushing fermentable carbohydrates from the body, or deploying the limbs in the "art" of love, or sly puss schemes for equilibrating wealth and virtue, or even instructions for setting up at Walden Pond, fishing the Michigan rivers, or picking cotton with sharecroppers in Hale County. Whatever the project, American writers from Franklin and Thoreau to Hemingway, Spock, Pritikin, and Agee will show you how-to, and maybe, sometimes, also provide step-by-step procedurals for an apprenticeship in personal salvation.

5. I have made little effort in the subsequent discussion to follow the *sequence* of Agee's thoughts and feelings. These roam freely, digressing, returning repeatedly to some notions, dropping others altogether, introjecting, interrupting, etc. In the interests of clarity, order, and emphasis, however, I may have presented his views in the form of what looks suspiciously like a progressive argument. If so, permit me to insist that this is false both to the spirit and the letter of the author's highly personal manner of rumination. So, too, is any hint of systematization or dogmatism, both of which may inadvertently creep into my thoughts about his thoughts. The above-mentioned interests of clarity, order, and emphasis will

have to account for these sins, and perhaps others, and I apologize here for all of them.

6. The full statement reads, "Failure, indeed, is almost as strongly an obligation as an inevitability, in such work: and therein sits the deadliest trap of the exhausted conscience," 238.

7. Most modern linguists would probably find it close to impossible to ratify any elemental union between word and thing. Still, Agee's intuition may not be so far-fetched. The late novelist Walker Percy, for example, quotes Ernst Robert Curtius to the effect that "despite all change a conservative instinct is discernible in language. All the peoples of our family from the Ganges to the Atlantic designate the notion of standing by the *phonetic group sta-;* in all of them the notion of flowing is linked with the group *plu,* with only slight modifications. This cannot be an accident. Assuredly the same notion has remained associated with the same sounds through all the millennia, because the peoples felt a certain *inner connection* between the two, i.e., because of an instinct to express this notion by these particular sounds. The assertion that the oldest words presuppose some relation between sounds and the representations they designate has often been ridiculed. It is difficult, however, to explain the origin of language without such assumptions." *The Message in the Bottle* (New York, 1975), 75.

8. Now taking our cue from the direction in which the Ageean spirit seems to move, let us conclude that our designation "chair" becomes a shared Anglo-American fantasy of one concrete object amid an ocean of such objects, our recognition of, attentiveness to, and finally separation from the object so designated. It is (common sense insists) a collectivized designation in that we understand one another in its usage even though the object itself remains opaque and indifferent to all our exertions, to the whole commonality of peoples established by such mutual understanding. Still, our designation remains the most capable and enduring of the cultural ties that bind, fusing all speakers, all writers, both to a shared fantasy of the Actual, as well as to each other in shared service to the brotherhood of the word.

9. "It seems very possibly true that art's superiority over science and over all other forms of human activity, and its inferiority to them, reside in the identical fact that art accepts the most dangerous and impossible of bargains and makes the best of it, becoming, as a result, both nearer the truth and farther from it than those things which, like science and scientific art, merely describe, and those things which, like human beings and their creations and the entire state of nature, merely are, the truth." *Famous Men,* 238.

10. Whitman, "Song of Myself," *Complete Poetry and Selected Prose,* 26. Henry Miller, *The Tropic of Cancer* (New York, 1961), 1–2. William Burroughs, *Naked Lunch* (New York, 1966), 229.

11. Presumably Lincoln is "mistaken" to believe that the South can be restored to its antebellum pride and stability, for his death only unleashes the horrors of Reconstruction, sixty years (and more) of irreparable confusion and humiliation crystallizing in the current crisis of the small farmer (i.e., "those reins left loose whose raving runs six decades nor shall ever cure," 391).

12. Agee may be much aware of this "shifted focus" when in composing the final pages of his book ("On the Porch: 3") he compares, in the penultimate paragraph, the antiphonal cries of a pair of foxes—symbols of the ineffable and uncapturable Actuality that has eluded him throughout the narrative—to "two masked characters" who enter from the periphery of "a stage" and push the principal actors to the side: "It was thoroughly as if principals had been set up, enchanted, and left like dim sacks at one side of a stage as enormous as the steadfast tilted deck of the earth, and as if onto this stage, accompanied by the drizzling confabulation of nocturnal-pastoral music, two masked characters, unforetold and perfectly irrelevant to the action, had with catlike aplomb and noiselessness stept and had sung, with sinister casualness, what at length turned out to have been the most significant, but most unfathomable, number in the show; and had then in perfect irony and silence withdrawn" (470). From this perspective, the "principals" would of course refer to the farmers, the "two masked" intruders to Agee and Evans themselves, who throughout the text have frequently been referred to as "spies."

13. Consider, for example, the following: "the guards pacing, meeting, pacing, the odors of southern winter, and all centered upon these captives that slow, keen, special, almost weeping yearning of terror toward brutality, in the eyes, the speech, which is peculiar to the men of the south and is in their speech" (391); the phrase "men of the south" must refer to "the guards," yet because of its unmoored and floating position toward the end of the sentence, attaches just as comfortably to "these captives."

14. Frost, "Directive," from *The Selected Poems of Robert Frost* (New York, 1963), 253.

15. Paraphrasing Thomas Pynchon's infectious quip " . . . there was high magic to low puns," in *The Crying of Lot 49* (New York, 1986), 129.

16. Boris Pasternak, *Doctor Zhivago*, translated by Max Hayward and Manya Harari (New York, 1958), 165.

17. The above list of writings, like many such groupings, tends to shave distinctions to the bone. Tolstoy's early masterpiece, *The Cossacks: A Tale of 1852*, in particular seems to suffer most from this treatment. On the face of it, the attempts of the Muscovite Olenin to enter into the communal life of the Cossacks seems to end in a shambles (e.g., he meddles clumsily in the affairs of the village beauty Maryanka, who finally, and definitively, rejects his proposals

of marriage, etc.). Still, I would argue that Olenin's life in his new habitat has made of him a wiser, healthier, more meditative spirit; his growth has been in the area of moral and intellectual interiority. The young officer-gentleman who decamps from Moscow to the Caucasus is a well-intentioned sentimentalist; the disillusioned and alienated loner who leaves the Circassian village is a budding Tolstoyan philosopher.

18. Agee's description of fallen innocence in *A Way of Seeing*, xiv.

19. The phrase attributed to young Isaac McCaslin in Faulkner's "The Bear" who cannot find his way into the spirit-life of the Big Woods until he first rids himself of his technological impurities: gun (power), watch (time), and compass (space), in *Go Down, Moses* (New York, 1973), 208.

20. Agee imagines sharing Emma with Evans and George Gudger, and all four participants having a grand time (especially Emma, 62). As a gesture of conciliation, and even affection, between father figures and sons, and among potential sibling rivals, shared love becomes a vagrant but palpable minor motif in Agee's life and writings. Compare the fantasy in *Famous Men* with the ménage à trois dramatized in "Noa, Noa" where a happy truce is achieved by Gauguin ("I outgrew jealousy"), Tehura, the mother of his child, and their young friend and Tehura's probable lover, Jotefa (in *Agee on Film: Five Film Scripts*, 81–92). Compare both of these "fictions" with their factual counterpart in Agee's life, the very brief liaison established between Evans, Agee, and Agee's second wife, Alma Mailman, culminating in a single sexual encounter in which the reluctant Evans performed with the dutiful but uneager Alma while Agee instigated, watched—and wept. Apparently nobody emerged happily from that one. See Bergreen, *James Agee*, 238–39. Belinda Rathbone, in a recent biography of Walker Evans, offers the following assessment: "For Evans, connecting with Agee through his women was a way of expressing his love for him; it was also a way of exploring Agee's tremendous appeal to women, which he admired. For Agee, the connection had another meaning. He subtly encouraged these affairs as part of his impossible campaign to break down all barriers, both physical and emotional, between the people he loved, between those people and his own powers to empathize." *Walker Evans* (Boston and New York, 1995), 169. On Agee's childhood home see Bergreen, *James Agee*, 8–9.

21. Up to this point I have resisted pointing out what must be obvious to the student of Melanie Klein's work; and that is the fact that much of the shape of Agee's psychosexual profile finds its operative psychoanalytic referents in the models of childhood behavior found in her writings; particularly in that whole inchoate complex of loneliness, guilt, rage, and frustration that engulfs the child when denied access to the nourishment and protections of the parental source (i.e., the results of separation anxiety). It was this immense saturation

of feeling and conflict that became the special provenance of Ms. Klein, and it isn't hard to discover—if one is so inclined (no pun)—Ageean patterns of emotion and response especially in Klein's version of the child's reaction to the withdrawal of the mother's breast (the traumatic turn usually occurring in the first four months of infancy with the onset of the weaning process). Upon withdrawal of the nourishing source, Klein argues, the child may often fantasize a tension between himself and the world in terms of an excessive idealization of the lost love object (i.e., breast, parent, or, in Agee's case, both parents and the constituents of the early world associated with them) as the repository of all potency, joy, and well-being; and at the same time, an excessive denigration of the self as greedy, brutal, and insatiable beyond all toleration, as the primary cause for the loss of the love object. In other words, the child cannot conceive of his separation from the ideal source as independent from something that he may have done to it, or from the offensiveness of simply being who he is (c.f., Agee's self-immolation before the idealized black couple; or his imagination of himself as an ugly little beast before the "gentling hand" of Mrs. Ricketts; or his quest for an idealized dream lover resolving itself in a suicidal rush). Nor can the intolerable self attempt union with the idealized source without a sense of intrusion upon sacred ground, or fear that he might in some way harm or destroy his paradise all over again (c.f., Agee's whole posture of apologetics and self-disgust in relation to the southern poor, black and white, merely for daring to enter into their presences). Further, unlike many other psychologists of children (say, the followers of Freud), Ms. Klein would argue that the child's primary urges are not libidinous in nature, but rather represent urges toward nourishment, protection, care, and tending (c.f., "Food, Clothing, and Shelter"), the satisfaction of which are necessary to identity and ego-formation.

Etc., etc. You see what has already begun to happen to the cast of my thought. As is frequently the case in literary studies of this kind, one begins by annexing the model in order to illuminate one's subject, but ends by reducing one's subject in order to illuminate the model. Models—particularly one as brilliant, original, and persuasive as Ms. Klein's—have a way of colonizing the internal resources of not only true believers, but even of pinch-hitters like myself, of employing employers, of moreover streamlining the necessary indeterminacy, contradiction, and grayness, the sheer largesse of lifelike entities—like authors or characters in books—into the shiny coils and tiny wheels of well-behaved clockworks. Since I must confess that my own true belief resides in the at-bottom mystery of personality, I will thus—having already underscored the legitimacy of its presence—leave the full-scale pursuit and employment of Ms. Klein's remarkably suggestive tool to others. In the meantime, see Melanie Klein's *The Psychoanalysis of Children,* translated by A. Strachy (London, 1932).

22. Agee refers to the "On the Porch . . ." materials as the "center of action" (245), the unchanging ground base, that gives the illusion of a continuous single night's meditation split into three separate units and placed at the beginning, middle, and end of the book respectively; thus, absorbing all the different temporal and spatial levels of the different sections within a single, fixed "frame" (245), and enhancing the effect that wherever the central character may be within the many changing phases of the narrative action—whether riding the road in a hunt for sharecroppers (as in "July 1936") or back in New York, the Alabama summer behind him (as in "Intermission")—he is still, and forever, on the porch. Further: the centrality of the "Porch" material envelopes the entire southern enterprise in a kind of subjective enclosure, as if the contents of the whole book have been fully imagined on one magical night in the head, or "globe"—brain of a restless writer before he goes to sleep. It is this spherical shape, in fact, that becomes one of the organizing metaphors and dominant symbols of Agee's meditation. We are told in "Colon" that the structure of the individual self is to be thought of as "globular" (101), and that this self is also to be thought of as a world or "planet" (101) which in turn may remind us of that other globe, "The Great Ball on Which We Live" (xx, from the Epigraph). Agee still seems to have a mingling of big and little globes in mind when he analyses the lamp above his writing table (in "A Country Letter") in which the flame is of "such holiness and peace that all on earth and within extreme remembrance seem suspended upon it in perfection as upon reflected water" (51). All earth-within-lamp, world-within-self, all perspectives-within-one, an entire epic within a single night's reverie: just as this fusion and interchangability of spheres, private and cosmic, is central to all mystical and visionary enterprise, so too is it central to the structural sleight-of-hand that attempts to unify this book.

23. "In essence, the book should be as cheap and ephemeral as the share-cropper's meager possessions were," Bergreen, *James Agee*, 236.

24. The phrase "rightborn energy" derives from the "three crazyeyed boys of eighteen" observed in "Gaffney's Lunch," "sick and desperate with nothing to do and with the rotting which the rightborn energy of their souls could by no chance have escaped": an episode from "Inductions."

25. "But it is not so much his empirical observation of their lives that disturb as his refusal to grant them any space of freedom. In comparison with Faulkner's *As I Lay Dying* or even Erskine Caldwell's fiction, Agee's depiction of 'poor whites' fails to begin to do justice to the complexity of their lives." Richard King, *A Southern Renaissance*, 222.

26. Agee renders his farmers as static and monumental, more like eternal, cherished, and never-to-be-dissected memories than highly individual charac-ters, and throughout his text, festoons their separateness with strange demurrals,

fancy feints, and embarrassed retreats. Even in the famous scene in which the author identifies with the sleeping members of the three families (in "A Country Letter"), the night-thoughts of the sleepers tend to be tenuous and elliptical when related to single persons (e.g., a fragment of Annie Mae's dream in which George points a triggerless shotgun at her), and for the most part don't even relate to individuals at all. Rather, Agee evokes the restlessness of a collective, a nexus of nocturnal anxiety (including the group's internalization of the larger community's contempt for it) in the form of a single communal outcry: "In what way were we trapped? where, our mistake?" (78). But even the lyrical anonymity of this cadenza is far too intimate and dangerously novelistic to sustain for more than a few pages, and Agee abruptly concludes his night-time ramble by breaking off in midsentence and beginning the next section ("Colon") with: "But there must be an end to this . . . Herein I must screen off all mysteries of our comminglings—all these, all such, must be deferred" (99). Needless to say they are deferred indefinitely, never to be resumed.

27. In many passages Agee seems to have attributed to Gudger's world the full force of his own idealized memory of childhood, and indeed perhaps the most egregious assumption of this book is that the early youth of these families and their circumstances must have been as full of radiance and hope as he imagines his own to have been. Agee, for example, cannot even view the underside of Gudger's house without also rhapsodizing that "once this house was all fresh and bridal, four hollowed rooms brimmed with a light of honey"; or examine Anne Mae's hat without dreaming her back to her younger self of 1911, turning before the mirror in her wedding dress ("she was such a poem as no human being shall touch," 286); or work his way into the night worries of the sleeping farmers without reiterating yet another variant of a seemingly endless refrain, "Where lost that bright health of love that knew so surely it would stay; how, how did it sink away, beyond help, beyond hope, beyond desire, beyond remembrance?" (78).

28. Never a student of the obvious, Agee will stress the "beauty" of the farmers' homes "in favor of their shortcomings as shelters; and in part because their esthetic success seems to me even more important than their functional failure; and finally out of the uncontrollable effort to be faithful to my personal predilections, I have neglected function in favor of esthetics" (202). These "personal predilections" apply to almost every aspect of the farmer's life.

29. The influence of the farmer upon Agee's personal habits would continue to be felt for some years after the Alabama sojourn. "I'm sure that in changing his life he was moved by feelings that the Alabama experience had brought up in him. That is, I think, that bourgeois accoutrements and bourgeois routines were less acceptable to him, if anything, after he'd been to Alabama than they

had been before . . . only in the mid-forties, I think, did he again feel that kind of thing was okay [i.e. life as lived before the Alabama experience]." Robert Fitzgerald in *Agee: His Life Remembered,* 110–12.

CHAPTER FOUR. **THE MILK OF PARADISE**

1. My remarks on American film theory and practice before Agee have been greatly aided by Myron Osborn Lounsbury's critical study, *The Origins of American Film Criticism 1909–1939* (New York, 1973), and the invaluable review anthology *American Film Criticism: From the Beginnings to Citizen Kane,* edited by Stanley Kauffmann and Bruce Henstell (New York, 1972).

2. This list cites only names of those who worked in the United States, and even within this narrow frame, means to be suggestive rather than inclusive. Missing, for instance, are those writers whose film work was perhaps more "occasional," less prolific, but no less perceptive than that of those listed—among them, Lincoln Kirstein, Hilda Doolittle, Louise Bogan, and Edmund Wilson.

3. Of the year in which *Agee on Film* was published, Stanley Kauffmann writes, " . . . a year that marks the beginning of change in general attitudes toward serious film criticism. Few posthumous recognitions have been better deserved than Agee's, but a widespread inference from his book was: 'oh, so *that's* when serious American film criticism began—'way back in 1943.' Before Agee, a presumable desert." "Introduction," *American Film Criticism,* ix. "Before James Agee no American film critic was respected *as a film critic,*" writes Edward Murray in *Nine American Film Critics: A Study of Theory and Practice.* "The reason for this is simple: film was not, until the late fifties, widely respected as one of the arts in America" (1).

Specialists in the visual arts have of course always been aware of Farber, Warshow, and Tyler. Wider recognition, however, in Warshow's case began in the 1960s with the publication of *The Immediate Experience* (New York, 1962), and even later for Farber with *Negative Space* (a.k.a. *Movies*). Parker Tyler's first three landmark film studies were actually published in the forties—*The Hollywood Hallucination* (New York, 1944), *The Magic and Myth of the Movies* (New York, 1947), and *Chaplin* (New York, 1948)—but to a generally apathetic audience of nonspecialists. All three were republished in the early seventies (the first two in 1970; the third in 1972), by which time Tyler was better known for three more film books that had appeared in the 1960s (i.e., *Classics of the Foreign Film* [New York, 1960], *The Three Faces of Film* [New York, 1960], and *Sex Psyche Etcetera in the Film* [New York, 1969]), and the widely publicized reference in Gore Vidal's novel *Myra Breckenridge* ("Parker Tyler's vision . . . is perhaps the only important critical insight this century has produced"). Of his first two publications, Richard Schickel wrote, " . . . they are the more remarkable in that they were published in 1944 and 1947. For at that time a man attempting to seriously comprehend the phenomenon of film was really working on his own," with, "as the indifferent commercial reception of these books proved, no genuine audience to address—just a handful of fellow buffs, nuts, fans . . . you pick the patronizing word." "Introduction," *The Hollywood Hallucination* (New York, 1972), vi.

4. See Harry Alan Potamkin, *The Compound Cinema* (New York, 1977).

5. Ferguson died in 1943 at age thirty-six. His film work for the *New Republic* (and elsewhere) finally appeared in book form in the early seventies as *The Film Criticism of Otis Ferguson* (Philadelphia, 1971).

6. The phrase "film generation" was I believe invented and first used by the perceptive Stanley Kauffmann in the final section of *A World on Film* (New York, 1966): " . . . there exists a Film Generation: the first generation that has matured in a culture in which the film has been of accepted serious relevance, however that seriousness is defined" (415).

7. Agee began reviewing films for *Time* in October 1941; for the *Nation* in December 1942. He left the *Nation* in September 1948, and later that year left *Time;* he then published sporadically on film (for *Life, Sight and Sound*) through September 1950. I have not made a systematic study of the phenomenon of compiling a film reviewer's columns into books, nor do I care enough to undertake such a study. Agee may well have been the first film journalist to be so "booked." One year before *Agee on Film* appeared, Arthur Knight published his popular critical film history, *The Liveliest Art* (New York, 1957) in which the author lists and describes the "100 Best Books on Film": no collection of any single critic/reviewer's work appears. Rather, practical criticism (as opposed to history, aesthetics, biography, etc.) is represented by two anthologies, *Garbo and the Night Watchmen* (1937), edited by Alistair Cooke, a sampling of reviews and reviewers from the thirties; and *The Best Moving Pictures of 1922–23,* edited by Robert E. Sherwood. Auden is quoted from "A Letter to the Editors of 'The Nation,' " reprinted in Agee on *Film Reviews and Comments*, iii. Lawrence Bergreen describes the intelligent readership and Agee's impact upon it in the following manner: "Agee's *Nation* column quickly attracted a cult following. For the first time in his career he found an appreciative audience that greeted his ruminations with respect and glee. *The Nation's* 60,000 readers consisted largely of intellectuals, it was true, and he was reviewing movies rather than writing poetry, it was also true, but he made these limitations into strengths and emerged as a writer's reviewer . . . Everywhere he went, people had read what he had written, and nothing is more intoxicating to a writer than having an appreciative readership near at hand . . . As his circle of admirers grew,

an Agee legend sprang up. Younger journalists at *Time*, in particular, looked up to him as a shining example of what they wished to be" (*James Agee: A Life*, 273).

8. "Although Agee threw himself into his new assignment [reviewing films for *Time*] with vigor and enthusiasm, he was, as always, beholden to [T. H.] Matthews' [his editor] savage blue pencil. To complicate matters further, some anonymous hand sprinkled Agee's copy with Timestyle's annoying neologisms, staccato sentences, and bizarre word order" (Bergreen, *James Agee*, 264).

9. Manny Farber, for instance, insists that the editors of *Agee on Film* slight "Agee's rashness" by presenting "no evidence of his conflicting reviews on the same picture for the power (*Time*) and the glory (*The Nation*)," *Movies*, 87. If there is indeed no evidence of outright conflict, there are still sufficient differences between the two performances, in tone, emphasis, and degree of enthusiasm and advocacy, to warrant further comment. Farber also feels that the selection in *Agee on Film* shortchanges his work at *Time* and is too "conscious of the art-minded and carriage trade" (i.e., his work for the *Nation* appears in toto). "His journalistic manner in the smaller *Time* reviews is flawless," says Farber, "but, unfortunately, Agee's reputation is based on heavier writing which has a sensitively tinctured glibness" (*Movies*, 88).

10. See, for instance, Edward Murray's attempt: "For the most part, Agee's approach can be described as *impressionistic . . . moral . . . and evaluative*" (italics Murray), *Nine American Film Critics*, 7. But so can, to some extent, the "approach" of any critic who has ever chosen to rank one work or artist over and above another.

11. A sample of his response to *The Human Comedy*, for instance, is typical of his "special" focus on many of these films. "The picture is mainly a mess, but as a mixture of typical with atypical failure, and in its rare successes, it interests me more than any other film I have seen for a good while" (30).

12. "Chain of Flesh" from Agee's Sonnet IV, "I have been fashioned on a chain of flesh" (*The Collected Poems of James Agee*, 38).

13. For example, Dwight Macdonald: "Jim could always fill out the botched, meager, banal outlines of what was actually projected on the screen with his own vision of what, to his sympathetic, imaginative eye, the director had clearly intended to be there—and what would, had he been the director, undoubtedly have been there" (*Dwight Macdonald On Movies*, 7). To assert, as I have, that Agee's suggestions for the improvement of most films were often impractical, however, does not mean that he did not wish to direct films. We know that he did, and Macdonald is on firmer ground when he says "of some of" the film scripts that they "are so needlessly specific in their visual and technical instructions as to suggest that they are those of a frustrated director," 10.

14. See, for instance, the chapter on Agee entitled "James Agee: The Man Who Loved the Movies," in Tom Dardis, *Some Time in the Sun* (New York, 1981).

15. Pauline Kael, "That Clean Old Peasant Again," *Going Steady* (Boston, 1970), 49. Although Ms. Kael has technically retired from the field, the impress of her tastes and attitudes on current conditions in American film reviewing remain essentially undimished.

16. Kael, "Trash, Art and the Movies"; "Movies—a tawdry corrupt art for a tawdry corrupt world—fit the way we feel," *Going Steady*, 87.

17. Kael, "That Clean Old Peasant Again," 49–50.

18. Marcel Proust, *The Captive*, translated by C. K. Scott Moncrieff, vol. 2 (New York, 1934), 509–10.

CHAPTER FIVE.   **CHAINS OF FLESH**

1. See, for instance, particularly thorough treatments in Tom Dardis's *Some Time in the Sun*, 218–51, and throughout Alfred T. Barson's *A Way of Seeing: A Critical Study of James Agee*.

2. This somewhat overdrawn estimate conspicuously avoids reference to the more specialized and obviously valuable employment of the screenplay as a tool for scholars: for the film scholar, say, to traverse the evolution of a filmmaker's intentions through the stages of a script to the finished product; or, as in Agee's case, for the literary scholar to explore the personal focus of the screenwriter himself. My concern here, however, has been with the aesthetic value of the screenplay as it affects critics and general readers.

3. Many critics have examined the influence of Joyce's work upon Agee's life and art. Barson's *A Way of Seeing,* for example, places special stress on this relationship, particularly as it influenced the creation of *Famous Men;* see 74–76, 110–12. Agee himself once referred disparagingly to the young protagonist of *The Morning Watch* as a "backward, scrub-team version of Stephen Dedalus" (quoted by Bergreen, *James Agee,* 331).

4. James Joyce, *A Portrait of the Artist as a Young Man* (New York, 1964), 168.

5. Joyce, *A Portrait,* 142.

6. Here for comparative purposes is Stephen Dedalus drawing allegory and myth from a reading of the clouds:

"Disheartened, he raised his eyes towards the slowdrifting clouds, dappled and seaborne. They were voyaging across the deserts of the sky, a host of nomads on the march, voyaging high over Ireland, westward bound. The Europe they had come from lay out there beyond the Irish Sea, Europe of strange tongues and valleyed and woodbegirt and citadelled and of entrenched and marshalled races. He heard a confused music within him as of memories and names which he was almost conscious of but could not capture even for an instant; then the music seemed to recede, to recede, to recede: and from each receding trail of nebulous music there fell always one longdrawn calling note, piercing like a star the dusk of silence. Again! Again! Again! A voice from beyond the world was calling," *A Portrait,* 167.

7. Bergreen, *James Agee,* 306.

8. Compare, for instance, Richard's "royally dangerous" fate at the pond with the young journalist's lost legacy from the farmer as a "royalty purloined."

9. A relatively plotless work, *A Death in the Family* is heavy with feeling and internal analysis and light on incident. The major events, however, included in the chapters are as follows: After taking his son Rufus to a movie, Jay Follet receives a phone call from his brother Ralph informing him that his father may be dying. Deep in the shank of the night, Jay eats the early breakfast that his wife Mary prepares for him and then begins the drive to his father's farm in the Powell River Valley. Before leaving Knoxville and entering the Tennessee farm country, he is ferried across the river as dawn begins to break.

The next day Rufus is taken shopping by Mary's aunt, Hannah Lynch, and selects a loud and "vulgar" cap that he is eager to show to his father. Mary learns that the danger of Grandpa Follett's condition had been greatly exaggerated, and that Jay is going to drive back that night. Later that evening, however, while Rufus and Catherine are sleeping, she receives a phone call informing her that Jay has been in a car accident and requesting someone from the family to bring him home. Not knowing whether he is alive or dead, Mary sends her brother Andrew, along with a friend of the family, Walter Starr, to meet this request, and asks Hannah to wait with her until the men return. (Each senses that Jay may already be dead, but without official confirmation, neither will fully admit this to the other or herself.)

Later, Andrew returns with the official account of Jay's death; and then joined by Mary's parents, Joel and Catherine Lynch, the immediate family discuss the accident, mourn and console each other, deep into the night. At one point toward the end of the vigil, some members of the group (most emphatically, Mary and Hannah) are aware of an invisible presence entering the home and making its way through the rooms. Mary is certain that this presence is Jay come to take his final leave of the family.

The next morning the children are informed of their father's death. Hannah tells Rufus not to go to school and to stay inside the house. Puzzled and annoyed, Rufus disobeys, sneaks out, boasts of his father's accident to the neighborhood boys, and returns to the house feeling guilty and ashamed.

On the following morning, the day of the funeral, Father Jackson appears at the home, and offends Rufus and his sister Catherine by sitting in Jay's favorite chair. This dislike intensifies when outside his mother's door, Rufus hears Father Jackson's voice rising to dominate the protesting voices of Mary and Hannah. Later that day, he learns from Andrew that Father Jackson had refused to give Jay, who was never baptized, the full Christian burial service.

After viewing their father's body for the last time, the children are placed in the care of Walter Starr, who, in his parked car, allows them to watch part of the funeral procession at a distance.

After the burial, Andrew invites Rufus for a walk in which he delights his young nephew by recounting the incident of the giant butterfly that flew from the grave as Jay's coffin was being lowered; and then frightens him as he rages violently against Mary and Hannah for their obsequious devotion to religious ritual and observance. Then "all the way home they walked in silence."

10. Mosel's stage adaptation of *A Death in the Family* had its Broadway opening on November 30, 1960; it won both the Pulitzer Prize and the Drama Critics Award. Major credits the film *All the Way Home* are as follows: producer, David Susskind for Paramount/Talent associates; director, Alex Segal; photography, Boris Kaufman; music, Bernard Green; screenplay, Philip Reisman, Jr. (from the Mosel play and the Agee novel); major players, Robert Preston (Jay), Jean Simmons (Mary), Michael Kearney (Rufus), Aline MacMahon (Hannah), Pat Hingle (Ralph); Running Time, 107 minutes.

11. The major incidents depicted in italics include the following: (a) four-year-old Rufus is frightened by the dark, and cries for his father who sings him to sleep; Jay reflects on his life and his parents; (b) Rufus lies on the lawn between his mother and father who harmonize folk songs and Afro-American spirituals; (c) Mary is pregnant (with Catherine) and puts Rufus in the care of a black nursemaid, Victoria, who answers the child's inquiries about the color of her skin; (d) the older boys tease Rufus about his name (i.e., "nigger's name"); later they gull him into singing and dancing for them; (e) the families (Jay's and Ralph's) visit Rufus's great-great-grandmother, who is more than one hundred years old, at her farm in the backcountry; (f) friends of the family, "Uncle" Ted and "Aunt" Kate, play a joke on Rufus, which infuriates Mary, who defends her son.

12. Alfred T. Barson observes that "[Victor A.] Kramer and others have pointed out that, in addition to the incomplete state of the manuscript the published version is in need of reediting"; and concludes that "what remains and has been published is perhaps little more than half the novel Agee intended to write" (*A Way of Seeing*, 146). Kramer himself states that "the composite working draft for a *Death in the Family* consists of 194 handwritten manuscript pages, and an additional 114 pages of variants," and finally suggests that "all of the variants written for *A Death [in the Family]* should eventually be made

available." He also contends (along with the present writer) that "Agee's methods for uniting different episodes which have no place in the primary time sequence remains unclear," but that still "the italicized sections are as essential to the final effect as the main narrative" (*James Agee*, 143–44).

13. I would imagine that most critics would probably want to associate *A Death in the Family* most readily with the "regional" traditions of the post-Faulknerian southern novel (Wolf, Warren, O'Connor, McCullers, Capote, Welty, et al.) with its awareness of a preserved historical past and social ambiance of stable communal values. But just as germane to this tradition is the southern penchant for gothic extravagance, grotesque eccentricity, and local *bizarrerie* of every variety (e.g., names, characters, customs, speech patterns, etc.). Little of *this* penchant emerges in Agee's novel: the stress on shared commonplaces, on the generally recognizable aspects of his private experience, obviously renders the author reluctant to cultivate down-home exotica.

14. Whitman, "The Commonplace," *Complete Poetry and Selected Prose*, 381.

15. Agee, *The Collected Poems of James Agee*, 48.

16. The first miracle of ordinariness, of course, is birth itself. The conjunction between the two miracles is noted by Andrew, who actually compares Mary's torment to childbearing " . . . it's as if she were in labor. *And she is*" (148, italics in original). Such pain is shared and enlarged by all the mourners in Mary's living room. One may further conjecture that it is this aggregate of intense "labor" that finally gives birth to Jay's ghost.

The analogy between the lyrical form of the conversation in the home and operatic form is not gratuitous: William Mayer's opera, *A Death in the Family* (based largely on Tad Mosel's stage adaptation *All the Way Home*) premiered in Minneapolis in 1983.

17. Sigmund Freud, *Civilization and its Discontents*, translated by Joan Riviere (New York, 1958), 6, 2.

18. The point about Walter is quoted by B. H. Haggin in *The New Listener's Companion and Record Guide* (New York, 1967), 222. The best of these admirations of *A Death in the Family*, and very persuasive it is too, remains Robert Cole's *Irony in the Minds' Life*.

19. Agee's reassurance to his sister is quoted by Doty, *Tell Me Who I Am*, 92. Doty also notes the more abrasive earlier version: "The sharpest and most clearly revealing interchanges between Rufus' parents occur in Agee's working drafts for the novel. In an eight-page manuscript, most of which was deleted from the book, the two frequently quarrel bitterly" (*Tell Me Who I Am*, 90).

20. Quoted by Doty, *Tell Me Who I Am*, 98.

21. The term "orbit" is taken directly from Agee's notes for *A Death in the Family*: "He [Rufus] is drawn always more deeply into his mother's orbit,

always the more wishing he could be in his father's" (quoted in Doty, *Tell Me Who I Am*, 105). This may have been Agee's plan, but not, I would argue, his accomplishment. In the novel, as we now have it, Rufus effectively remains suspended between the two orbits.

22. This whole paragraph with its reference to Ur-Parents, Shadow figures, and archetypes draws freely from terms, symbols, and attitudes popularly associated with the working vocabulary of the depth psychologist C. G. Jung. The rich Jungian amalgam of psychic fact, mythic image, and religious aura would—and did—fascinate an artist such as Agee, who by 1935 found himself entranced (albeit reluctantly) by Frances Wicke's Jungian study, *The Inner World of Childhood. A Study in Analytical Psychology* (New York, 1927), and by 1945 began what Bergreen describes as "an on-again, off-again" three-year therapy session with Ms. Wickes herself (*James Agee*, 152–53, 298).

23. Quoted by Doty, *Tell Me Who I Am*, 114.

24. See, for instance, Kenneth Seib's categories: "agnosticism (Andrew)," "atheism (Jay)," *James Agee*, 76.

25. Letter to Father Flye, September 20, 1950, *The Letters of James Agee to Father Flye*, 184. In this respect, Dwight Macdonald wrote of his friend: "Although he was deeply religious, he had his own kind of religion, one that included irreverence, blasphemy, obscenity, and even Communism (of his own kind). By the late forties, a religio-conservative revival was underway, but Agee felt as out of place as ever. 'If my shapeless comments can be of any interest or use,' he characteristically began his contribution to a *Partisan Review* symposium on Religion and the Intellectuals, 'it will be because the amateur and amphibian should be represented in such a discussion. By amphibian I mean that I have a religious background and am "pro-religious"—though not on the whole delighted by this so called revival—but doubt that I will return to religion?'" (*Against the American Grain*, 156).

26. The choice of the "butterfly" incident as the climax of the image patterns associated with the father is neither glowing nor original—another incident drawn from the family record, a selection perhaps less judicious than others (e.g., Jay's "ghost" is more successfully dramatized and integrated into the narrative structure). Yet the relative aesthetic failure of the "butterfly" passage should in no way diminish its intellectual and thematic significance in relation to the whole.

27. Geneviéve Moreau, for example, implies that an optimistic reading would by no means be unjustified in terms of the book Agee meant to write: "The manuscript contains two projects that were distinct from the beginning. One consists of a family saga, with highlights from a period of five years or more, showing the differences that separate the generations and the love that unites

them. The second, chronologically organized, is a story describing the few days preceding the father's death. These two narratives were to be integrated into a single work, ending on the day of the funeral. Love and life, which are celebrated in the first narrative, are confronted with death in the second, only to emerge altered but victorious" (*The Restless Journey of James Agee*, 262).

28. Barson worries that "in May, 1950 Agee wrote to Father Flye that he thought he could finish the book that summer . . . That he repeated the same estimate five years later in his last letter to Father Flye and also nights before his death to his friend and publisher David McDowell, suggests that he got little further in the writing" (*A Way of Seeing*, 146). Bergreen at one point implies the intervention of Agee's movie-making ambitions: "Agee . . . was not interested in being consistent, only in making the most of the opportunities that came his way. For example, once he had mastered the art of the screenplay, he would move on to directing, exactly as his hero [John] Huston had. How he would find the time to complete *A Death in the Family* while directing he did not know. In his attempt to excel at a variety of forms—poetry, journalism, fiction, film—Agee was truly a maverick among writers of his generation" (*James Agee*, 363).

29. Specifically, the title of a projected philosophical study by Nabokov's hero Van Veen in *ADA* (New York, 1969).

SELECTED
BIBLIOGRAPHY

PRIMARY BOOKS

Agee on Film: Reviews and Comments. Vol. 1. New York: Mcdowell,
  Obolensky, 1958. Reprint, New York: Perigree Books, 1983.
Agee on Film: Five Film Scripts by James Agee. Vol. 2. New York: Mcdowell,
  Obolensky, 1960. Reprint, New York: Perigree Books, 1983.
The Collected Poems of James Agee. Edited by Robert Fitzgerald. Boston:
  Houghton Mifflin, 1968.
The Collected Short Prose of James Agee. Edited by Robert Fitzgerald.
  Boston: Houghton Mifflin, 1968.
A Death in the Family. New York: Mcdowell, Obolensky, 1957. Reprint,
  New York: Bantam Books, 1969.
James Agee: Selected Journalism. Edited by Paul Ashdown. Knoxville:
  University of Tennessee Press, 1985.
Let Us Now Praise Famous Men. Boston: Houghton Mifflin, 1941. Reprint,
  Boston: Houghton Mifflin, 1960.
The Letters of James Agee to Father Flye. Edited by James Harold Flye.
  Boston: Houghton Mifflin, 1971.
The Morning Watch. Boston: Houghton Mifflin, 1950.
Permit Me Voyage. New Haven: Yale University Press, 1934.

SECONDARY BOOKS

Agee, Joel. *Twelve Years: An American Boyhood in East Germany.* New
  York: Farrar Straus Giroux, 1981.
Barson, Alfred T. *A Way of Seeing: A Critical Study of James Agee.* Amherst:
  University of Massachusetts Press, 1972.

Bergreen, Lawrence. *James Agee: A Life*. New York: E. P. Dulton, 1984.

Coles, Robert. *Irony in the Mind's Life: Essays on Novels by James Agee, Elisabeth Bowen, and George Eliot*. Charlottesville: University Press of Virginia, 1974.

Doty, Mark A. *Tell Me Who I Am: James Agee's Search for Selfhood*. Baton Rouge: Louisiana State University Press, 1981.

Dupee, F. W. *The King of the Cats and Other Remarks on Writers and Writing*. Chicago: University Press of Chicago, 1965.

Farber, Manny. *Movies* (Original title: *Negative Space*). New York: Hill-stone, 1971.

Frohock, W. M. *The Novel of Violence in America*. Dallas: Southern Methodist University Press, 1957.

Huston, John. *An Open Book*. New York: Alfred A. Knopf, 1980.

King, Richard. *A Southern Renaissance: The Cultural Awakening of the American South 1930–55*. New York: Oxford University Press, 1980.

Kramer, Victor A. *James Agee*. Boston: Twayne Publishers, 1975.

Larsen, Erling. *James Agee*. Minneapolis: University of Minnesota Press, 1971.

Lowe, James. *The Creative Process of James Agee*. Baton Rouge: Louisiana State University Press, 1994.

Macdonald, Dwight. *Against the American Grain: Essays on the Effects of Mass Culture*. New York: Random House, 1962.

———. *Dwight Macdonald On Movies*. Englewood Cliffs, N.J.: Prentice Hall, Inc., 1969.

Madden, David, ed. *Remembering James Agee*. Baton Rouge: Louisiana State University Press, 1974.

Moreau, Geneviéve. *The Restless Journey of James Agee*. New York: William Morrow, 1977.

Murray, Edward. *Nine American Film Critics: A Study of Theory and Practice*. New York, Ungar Publishing Co., 1975.

Ohlin, Peter. *Agee*. New York: Obolensky, 1966.

Pechter, William S. *Twenty-Four Times a Second: Films and Filmmakers*. New York: Harper and Row, 1971.

Rathbone, Belinda. *Walker Evans*. Boston and New York: Houghton Mifflin, 1995.

Seib, Kenneth. *James Agee: Promise and Fulfillment.* Pittsburgh: University of Pittsburgh Press, 1968.

Spears, Ross, and Jude Cassidy, eds. *Agee: His Life Remembered.* New York: Holt, Rinehart and Winston, 1985.

Stott, William. *Documentary Expression and Thirties America.* New York: Oxford University Press, 1973.

INDEX